BEYOND FREEDOM

Beyond Freedom

Disrupting the History of Emancipation

EDITED BY DAVID W. BLIGHT
AND JIM DOWNS

The University of Georgia Press   *Athens*

© 2017 by the University of Georgia Press
Athens, Georgia 30602
www.ugapress.org
All rights reserved
Set in ITC New Baskerville Std by
Graphic Composition, Inc., Bogart, Georgia

Most University of Georgia Press titles are
available from popular e-book vendors.

Printed digitally

Library of Congress Cataloging-in-Publication Data

Names: Blight, David W., editor, author. | Downs, Jim, 1973– editor, author.
Title: Beyond freedom : disrupting the history of emancipation / edited by David W.
    Blight and Jim Downs.
Description: Athens : The University of Georgia Press, 2017. | Series: Uncivil wars
Identifiers: LCCN 2017013381 | ISBN 9780820351483 (hardback : alk. paper) |
    ISBN 9780820351490 (pbk. : alk. paper) | ISBN 9780820351476 (ebook)
Subjects: LCSH: Reconstruction (U.S. history, 1865–1877) | Reconstruction (U.S. history,
    1865–1877)—Historiography. | African Americans—Civil rights—History—19th
    century. | Liberty—History—19th century.
Classification: LCC E668 .D58 2017 | DDC 323.1196/07309034—dc23
    LC record available at https://lccn.loc.gov/2017013381

For all the past and present editors of the
Freedmen and Southern Society Project

Contents

Acknowledgments

This book would not be possible without the groundbreaking scholarship of the editors at the Freedmen and Southern Society Project, who heroically excavated, organized, and preserved the Freedmen's Bureau Records at the National Archives. Their work, which formally began in 1976, not only exposed the richness of these vast and often neglected records that detailed emancipation; their work also revolutionized how historians, scholars, teachers, students, and the public conceived of the Civil War and Reconstruction. All of the contributors in this volume owe an enormous debt to their scholarship, which continues to inspire, inform, and challenge our research more than forty years later. Dedicating the volume to them is our collective way of expressing our gratitude.

This volume grew out of a conference organized at the Gilder Lehrman Center for the Study of Slavery, Resistance, and Abolition. We would like to thank all of the members of the staff—Dana Schaffer, Melissa McGrath, and Thomas Thurston—who helped make the conference an enormous success and who have assisted us with the publication of this book. David Spatz and Michelle Zacks deserve special recognition for their help in getting the book ready for its final stages of production.

Historian Catherine Clinton attended the conference and enthusiastically supported the idea of transforming the papers into a volume. She has been the book's fairy godmother, offering advice on how to shape it, suggesting ways to broaden its coverage, and working her magic in the publishing world. She put us in touch with Mick Gusinde-Duffy, the editor-in-chief at the University of Georgia Press, who eagerly supported our proposal. Mick has been a dynamic, supportive, and impressive editor. He understood the vision for the book and has offered incisive ways to make it stronger. Thomas Roche has been a most astute production editor and has skillfully and quite generously handled many of the unique challenges that develop with edited volumes. Lori Rider has done a tremendous job of editing more than a dozen authors in a single volume, which is an accomplishment in its own right, but she has achieved this work with an impressive balance of cheer and precision. We would also like to thank the anonymous peer reviewers, who carefully read each of the essays and offered constructive and important feedback.

Finally, we hope the book contributes to an important conversation on the meaning of freedom. Our motivation is not fueled by a scholarly desire to advance an argument or to upset a particular way of thinking but rather to better understand the emancipation of four million people during the Civil War and Reconstruction.

Prologue

ERIC FONER

When one reaches a certain age, as a historian, an odd phenomenon sets in. The scholar realizes that he has made the transition from young turk to elder statesman. Approaches once considered cutting edge are now viewed by one's students as old hat. Some readers will be old enough to remember the excitement, the liberating power, produced by the first appearance of the works of E. P. Thompson, Eric Hobsbawm, Herbert Gutman, and other pioneers of the "new social history." Today, my graduate students consider this the "old" history, which scholars need to move beyond. In writing about emancipation and Reconstruction, I suppose I now represent the old school. But this is altogether natural. As I wrote in 1988 at the beginning of *Reconstruction: America's Unfinished Revolution*, nothing is more essential to the study of history than reinterpretation.[1] Or, to paraphrase Oscar Wilde, the only thing we owe to history is to rewrite it.

Reconstruction: America's Unfinished Revolution appeared at the end of an incredibly creative thirty-year period of scholarship on emancipation and Reconstruction. Although the critique of the Dunning school, which saw Reconstruction as a sordid era of corruption, the lowest point in the saga of American democracy, can be traced back to W. E. B. Du Bois's *Black Reconstruction in America* in the 1930s, and even earlier to the works of John R. Lynch and others, the modern revisionist wave began with the civil rights revolution. By the time my book appeared, the traditional interpretation of Reconstruction had been laid to rest, and in dozens of monographs the building blocks had been created for a new overall account of the era.

Of course, the rewriting of Reconstruction's history did not stop in 1988. The essays in this volume demonstrate that the reinterpretation of the transition from slavery to freedom is continuing apace. What impresses me about recent scholarship is how it reflects an expansion of historians' approaches, or to put it more precisely, a series of expansions that hold out the promise of redefining the study of emancipation, Reconstruction, and the problem of freedom.

One can begin with the expansion of the source base available to scholars brought about by the digital revolution. When I began work on Reconstruction, the Internet did not exist (nor did email, so that scholars wasted a lot less of their time than nowadays). I was used to writing on an electric typewriter (those who have never heard of this device can probably see one at the Smithsonian Institution). High tech meant consulting documents on microfilm or microfiche. When I wrote *Freedom's Lawmakers* in the early 1990s, I searched the manuscript census for weeks for black officials. Today, that research could be done at home in an afternoon. Numerous other sources for the Reconstruction era are also now available and searchable online, including congressional debates and documents (among them the indispensable Ku Klux Klan hearings), plantation records, and nineteenth-century newspapers.

Of course, historical sources are only as useful as the questions historians ask of them. And like our source base, historians' approaches have expanded significantly in recent years. First, there is the expansion of Reconstruction's cast of characters itself. Some of the best recent work has introduced gender as a key category of analysis, examining changes in gender roles and relations resulting from the Civil War and emancipation among both white and black women.[2] These scholars see the family and kinship ties as central to the early emergence and long persistence of black political activism. In the eyes of emancipators, freedom carried with it specific definitions of gender roles, with women remaining at home to look after their families, something denied them in slavery, while men entered the wage-labor force. Everywhere, a gendered division of social space was to be part of the legacy of emancipation. In the United States too, it is now clear, women experienced emancipation differently from men in significant ways, and patriarchal assumptions were built into black men's understanding of freedom.

Recent work also embodies an expansion of the chronological definition of emancipation as a social process. My book considered Reconstruction as beginning in 1863 and ending in 1877, although it noted that the process of adjustment to the end of slavery continued well beyond the latter date. Since then, the chronological boundaries of Reconstruction have continued to expand. Steven Hahn's *A Nation under Our Feet* begins with black political ideas under slavery as the seedbed of Reconstruction politics and takes the story of rural black politics down to the twentieth century.[3] The implication of this chronological redefinition is significant. Historians now recognize Reconstruction as part of the long trajectory of southern and national history, not a bizarre aberration, as the Dunning school saw it. We now have what might be called a long Reconstruction, just as scholars have begun to speak of the long civil rights movement (which begins in the 1930s or 1940s) or the long nineteenth century (1789–1914). Of course, this expansion was anticipated by Du Bois, who used the dates 1860–1880 for *Black Reconstruction in America* and began his book with a chapter on slavery.

Taking the story into the 1890s also allows for comparison with developments in other parts of the country. Indeed, another expansion has been to embed the southern story more fully in a national narrative, with more attention to the North and West. The retreat from universal suffrage was not confined to the South in these years. Nor were debates over the definition of freedom, or the relationship between political and economic freedom, fought out in the streets of Homestead and Chicago, in the courts and voting booths.

To understand history, E. H. Carr observed in *What Is History*, study the historian. Reconstruction historiography has always reflected the preoccupations of the era in which it was written. In the aftermath of the terrorist attacks of September 11, 2001, historians turned renewed attention to home-grown American terrorism. Recent books on Reconstruction aimed at an audience outside the academy have tended to infuse their subjects with drama by focusing on violent confrontations (rather than, for example, the operations and accomplishments of biracial governments). One thinks of works such as Nicholas Lemann's *Redemption* on the violent overthrow of Reconstruction in Mississippi, Stephen Budiansky's *Bloody Shirt*, a survey of violence during the entire period, and two recent books on the Colfax Massacre, the single bloodiest incident in an era steeped in terrorism by the Klan and kindred white supremacist groups.[4]

As I have noted, Reconstruction historiography has always spoken directly to current concerns. The Dunning school, with its emphasis on the alleged horrors of Republican Reconstruction, provided scholarly legitimation for Jim Crow, black disenfranchisement, and the now long-departed solid Democratic South. The revisionist school arose in tandem with the civil rights movement. What I once termed the "post-revisionist" writing of the 1970s reflected disappointment with what seemed to be the limits of civil rights activism, especially in terms of the economic status of black Americans. Today, issues central to Reconstruction are still part of our lives—terrorism, the rights of citizens, the relationship between the national government and the states, the limits of presidential power, and American empire.

A recent book by Jeremy Suri, *Liberty's Surest Guardian*, uses the postwar "occupation" of the American South to remind us, however, that the newly empowered national state created by the Civil War and Reconstruction could be used for all kinds of purposes, not all of them benevolent. Shortly before the end of the war, Francis E. Spinner, the treasurer of the United States (whose signature appeared on every greenback issued by the federal government, itself a key expression of the expansion of national power), made this point in a different way: "What a school we have kept, and what a lesson we have taught the Secesh in particular and mankind in general. The thing to be feared now is, that we will be running around the world with a chip on our shoulder. If we can avoid this, a glorious future is ours."[5]

The warning reverberates in our own time. To be sure, the national state was simply too weak during Reconstruction to impose its will effectively in the South. But even during Reconstruction the reborn Union began to project its power abroad. As the struggle between President Andrew Johnson and the Congress reached its climax, the United States acquired Alaska as one aspect of an imperial agenda long advocated by Secretary of State William H. Seward. Under President Grant, the government attempted to annex the Dominican Republic. But the question is more complex than simply territorial acquisition. The emancipation of the slaves greatly strengthened the emerging American empire's ideological underpinning. In his excellent study of the British movement to abolish the slave trade, Christopher Brown shows how abolition created for Britain a stash of "moral capital" that it expended throughout the nineteenth century.[6] The very act of abolition demonstrated irrefutably Britain's noble motives as it expanded its imperial holdings in Africa and elsewhere. So, too, emancipation in the United States gave new meaning to Jefferson's description of the United States as an "empire of liberty," a notion somewhat tarnished before the Civil War by the powerful presence of slavery. With emancipation, it could no longer be denied that American expansionism meant the expansion of freedom.

One additional focus of recent scholarship is the historical "memory" of Reconstruction. Bruce Baker has recently examined this subject in *What Reconstruction Meant*, which shows how in South Carolina, politicians used a particular understanding of Reconstruction as a weapon in the construction of the Jim Crow South.[7] In this white supremacist narrative, the Redeemers and Red Shirts took on heroic status. A counternarrative, Baker shows, survived in black communities, to be rediscovered in the 1930s by southern radicals who found in Reconstruction a model for the interracial cooperation they hoped to bring to the twentieth-century South.

On the uses and abuses of history, American historians can learn a great deal from a recent book by two Australian scholars, Marilyn Lake and Henry Reynolds, *Drawing the Global Colour Line.*[8] Lake and Reynolds point out that the late nineteenth and early twentieth centuries were a time of global concern about nonwhite immigration, a global assumption of the white man's burden, and a global sense of fraternity among "Anglo-Saxon" nations, including Australia, New Zealand, Canada, the United States, and South Africa. Political leaders in these countries studied and copied each other's racial policies. South Africa was influenced by American segregation in implementing segregation. Australia, the United States, and Canada borrowed from each other in implementing Chinese exclusion.

The "bible" of those who implemented such measures, Lake and Reynolds write, was James Bryce's *American Commonwealth*, which depicted Reconstruction as a time of corruption and misgovernment caused by the enfranchisement of the former slaves. Bryce's account allegedly proved that blacks, coolies, aborigines, and others were unfit to be citizens. It was frequently invoked by the founders of Australia's federal nation in support of their vision of a white Australia, and by white South Africans. Around the world, the "key history lesson" (as Lake and Reynolds put it) of Reconstruction was taken to be the impossibility of multiracial democracy. Like other recent historical writing, *Drawing the Global Colour Line* suggests the need to breach the boundary of the nation-state that has defined so much of American historical writing, including the history of emancipation and Reconstruction. This is, to be sure, a difficult task. But it holds out the promise of a truly new account, one fully embedded in the long processes of American and global history. I do think, however, that in such a narrative, the question of freedom—its contested meanings, its social relations, and who is entitled to enjoy it and why—will remain central to our understanding of the complex historical process known as emancipation.

NOTES

1. Eric Foner, *Reconstruction: America's Unfinished Revolution* (New York: Harper & Row, 1988), xvi.

2. See, for example, Thavolia Glymph, *Out of the House of Bondage: The Transformation of the Plantation Household* (Cambridge: Cambridge University Press, 2003); Kidada E. Williams, *They Left Great Marks on Me: African American Testi-*

monies of Racial Violence from Emancipation to World War I (New York: New York University Press, 2012).

3. Steven Hahn, *A Nation under Our Feet: Black Political Struggles in the Rural South, from Slavery to the Great Migration* (Cambridge, Mass.: Belknap Press of Harvard University Press, 2003).

4. Nicholas Lemann, *Redemption: The Last Battle of the Civil War* (New York: Farrar, Straus & Giroux, 2006); Stephen Budiansky, *The Bloody Shirt: Terror after Appomattox* (New York: Viking, 2008); LeeAnna Keith, *The Colfax Massacre: The Untold Story of Black Power, White Terror, and the Death of Reconstruction* (New York: Oxford University Press, 2008); Charles Lane, *The Day Freedom Died: The Colfax Massacre, the Supreme Court, and the Betrayal of Reconstruction* (New York: Henry Holt, 2008).

5. Letter from Francis Spinner to Timothy Day dated February 23, 1865, quoted in Sarah J. Day, *The Man on a Hill Top* (Philadelphia: Ware Bros., 1931), 300.

6. Christopher Brown, *Moral Capital: Foundations of British Abolitionism* (Chapel Hill: University of North Carolina Press, 2012).

7. Bruce Baker, *What Reconstruction Meant: Historical Memory in the American South* (Charlottesville: University of Virginia Press, 2007).

8. Marilyn Lake and Henry Reynolds, *Drawing the Global Colour Line: White Men's Countries and the International Challenge of Racial Equality* (Cambridge: Cambridge University Press, 2008).

BEYOND FREEDOM

Introduction

DAVID W. BLIGHT, GREGORY P. DOWNS,
AND JIM DOWNS

Emancipation, the idea that lies like a pearl at the center of our understanding of the Civil War, seems simple: it means freedom, the end of slavery. That's how Booker T. Washington saw it. "Finally," he wrote in his landmark autobiography, *Up from Slavery*, "the war closed, and the day of freedom came. Freedom was in the air and had been for months."[1] For a century and a half since, historians have explained the emancipation of four million enslaved people by contrasting their slavery with their newfound freedom. Indeed, for Washington, as for almost everyone who has wrestled with the story of the end of slavery, the idea of freedom did double historical duty: the word was simultaneously slavery's antonym and one of the keywords of the nation's history, embedded in its Bill of Rights. In becoming free, slaves seemed to make not only themselves more American but the rest of the nation as well. Slavery had ended, and the paradox at the heart of American democracy had been resolved.

But contrast Washington's celebration of freedom with an account by Harriet Jacobs, a formerly enslaved woman turned reformer and author. She confronted the many meanings of freedom when she encountered dozens of liberated bondspeople in Duff Green's Row in Washington in 1862. "Many were sick with measles, diptheria, scarlet and typhoid fever," she wrote. "Some had a few filthy rags to lie on; others had nothing but the bare floor for a couch." As Jacobs attempted to comfort them, they looked up at her with "those tearful eyes" that asked, "Is this freedom?"[2]

In recent years Jacobs's question has been echoed by a growing number of historians. Was freedom, narrowly construed, enough? Was freedom simply license, the right to make choices, however constrained, as white planters claimed? Or did freedom extend to the ballot box, to education, to equality of opportunity? Who defined freedom, and what did it mean to nineteenth-century African Americans, both under slavery and after the war?[3]

In raising such questions, historians have begun to place other concepts, like power and belonging, at the center of the story of emancipation. Instead of defining every aspect of postemancipation life as a new form of freedom, scholars have started to examine more carefully the importance of belonging to an empowered government or community in defining the outcome of emancipation. Rather than simply celebrating individual freedom, these studies examine the enormous gap between rights on paper and the capacity to enforce those rights. In doing so, they have cast light on the key role of power and inclusion in shaping the post–Civil War world that emancipation made.

What is at stake in these studies is not only how we understand the Civil War and the end of slavery, but how we understand freedom itself. Reinforced by a hot war against fascism, a cold war against communism, and a forty-year critique of government from both the left and the right, freedom has come to seem the core American value over the last two centuries. But at what cost? By underrating the importance of well-functioning bureaucracies for maintaining civil society, or by reinforcing views of government as freedom's enemy, has the freedom narrative obscured important aspects of what emancipation did and did not accomplish, even as it highlighted others?

Building on W. E. B. Du Bois's 1935 magisterial study, *Black Reconstruction: An Essay Toward a History of the Part which Black Folk Played in the Attempt to Reconstruct Democracy in America, 1860–1880*, Eric Foner is the best-known contemporary scholar to revisit these questions. In both his comparative study of emancipation in the Atlantic world, *Nothing but Freedom* (1983), and his landmark study *Reconstruction: America's Unfinished Revolution* (1988), the most careful elaboration of the freedom narrative, he brilliantly defined the contest over emancipation and Reconstruction as a fight between competing versions of freedom. Since Foner's landmark volume, American historians have turned to the concept of freedom to make sense of the emancipation of four million slaves during and immediately after the Civil War. Drawing on a century and a half of debates over the meaning of freedom, subsequent historians have created one of the most successful paradigms in American history.[4]

Freedom has endured as a paradigm because it became synonymous with black political mobilization. Although freedom echoes across American history, nineteenth-century historians have particularly used emancipation as a window into the shifting, contested meanings of freedom. Never tied to a celebration of either the period or of freedom more generally, the freedom paradigm has always centered around contestation. Scholars who worked within it have always recognized that perfect freedom—if such a thing exists—was not the outcome of emancipation, and they have brilliantly traced the legal, political, and economic fights over the contours of freedom that emerged. In many ways, this process helped capture the conflicting values and political coalitions at the center of American history.

Over the past decade, however, historians have begun to ask whether it continues to make sense to center our discussions around an ever-expansive concept of freedom. In part, this question arises from a growing awareness that literatures on emancipation in other societies do not in fact always place freedom at the heart of analysis. These new directions also emerge from an understanding of the way that the freedom paradigm emerged at a particular Cold War moment, when asserting freedom as a core value helped associate American emancipation with battles against fascism and Stalinism. Parts of the emancipation experience did not easily fit within the freedom paradigm, or could only be made to fit by diminishing central aspects of the story. For example, in March 1868, three years after the close of the Civil War, a North Carolina former slave named Peter Price walked into the local office of the Freedmen's Bureau, a federal agency established to regulate the transition from slavery to freedom by enforcing labor contracts, adjudicating disputes, encouraging education, and, at times, distributing rations. Price's complaint was a common one: his landlord refused to turn over his share of the previous year's crop. Price found a receptive ear in Hugo Hillebrandt, a Hungarian revolutionary who had fought with Garibaldi in Italy before joining the Union cause as a federal agent. After listening to Price's story, Hillebrandt wrote an order demanding that the landlord turn over Price's share of the crop. But when Price carried the order back to the farm, his landlord tore it into pieces, threw it on the ground, and declared, "You might send ten thousand Yankees there and he did not intend to be governed by no such laws."[5] As a judge of practical power, the landlord was right. Hillebrandt could not enforce his orders outside of his office. In desperation, Price asked for help up the bureaucratic ladder, but without success. Some people—such as Hillebrandt—would help him but could not; others perhaps could have but did not. While freedom and its limitations tell us something about cases such as Peter Price's, it may not tell us enough. In ways that cannot fully be contained by ideas of negative or positive freedom, former slaves such as Price asked for and needed not just freedom but force. Self-sufficiency, much less equality, would depend on his inclusion in a group of people the government could commit to successfully assisting. As Price's case demonstrates, defensible legal freedom depended on the ability to be heard by forces strong enough to intervene to help defend rights.

Following in the footsteps of historians of the broader Atlantic world has helped historians of U.S. emancipation to see freedom as a process. If understood as a practice, not a stroke of a pen, emancipation becomes a longer story, one that emphasizes the gulf between the federal government's plans and life on the ground in the postwar South.[6] While it is possible to define those moments through the absence of freedom, it may well be that what former slaves suffered from was not a lack of freedom but a lack of power and belonging.

By asking new questions about the meaning of freedom, the scholars in this volume envision emancipation as a process rather than a shotgun moment of liberation. In studying the distance between legal rights and the capacity to enforce those rights, scholars have centered the shape and power of government as a way of raising questions about emancipation as a test not of liberation but of the process of belonging to a state. By returning to the documents, historians have begun to ask new questions about how emancipation unfolded.

With greater perspective, historians now see some of the costs involved in invoking freedom so continuously. In a paradigm that emphasized the individual, liberatory aspects of emancipation, was there sufficient room to talk about governance or collective belonging? In a paradigm that emphasized contests over freedom, was it possible—peculiarly enough—to actually talk about what freedom was? Instead of treating the problems of emancipation as denials of freedom, scholars have begun once again to ask if those disappointments of emancipation in fact illuminate not freedom's absence but its essence. As scholars have exhausted the meaning of the paradigm and as new circumstances press other concepts of governance or belonging to the forefront, historians are now working toward new ways of organizing the study of emancipation. Others, including Thavolia Glymph in *Out of the House of Bondage* and Susan O'Donovan in *Becoming Free in the Cotton South*, emphasize the constraints on labor contained within freedom. In Steven Hahn's Pulitzer Prize–winning *A Nation under Our Feet*, democratic power, rather than freedom, assumes center stage; his collections of essays suggest the utility of reading the nineteenth century through the lens of not freedom but coercion.[7] What was at stake may not have been a quest for a properly defined freedom but a redefinition of the precise boundaries of coercion in a new economic, political, and ideological moment. More recent work has taken these points even further. Much of it, including Kate Masur's *An Example for All the Land*, explores that troubled relationship between ex-slaves and the federal government. Jim Downs's *Sick from Freedom* used neglected federal records to trace powerful continuities between slavery and freedom and to portray the moment of emancipation as a public health catastrophe. Rather than freedom, many former slaves experienced death. As ex-planters and ex-Confederates regained power, they stepped into the void and created campaigns of political, labor, and sexual terror—vividly rendered in Hannah Rosen's *Terror in the Heart of Freedom* and Carole Emberton's *Beyond Redemption*—to force freedpeople into submission. Others, including Dylan Penningroth in *The Claims of Kinfolk*, emphasize freedpeople's reliance on communal and kinship group claims of power, rather than individual freedom. Gregory P. Downs's *Declarations of Dependence* captured the way that emancipation placed former slaves—such as white North Carolinians—in position to claim dependence on powerful patrons; freedom was not independence but needy people's right to make claims.[8]

This volume, which grew out of a conference organized by David W. Blight, Gregory P. Downs, and Jim Downs through the Gilder Lehrman Center for the Study of Slavery, Resistance, and Abolition, aims to provoke new arguments about the meaning of the period of emancipation. Rather than providing case studies, the volume provides a collection of essays that attempt to raise new questions about the field.

We want to also take full advantage of the benefits that an anthology can offer—to bring together a diverse set of perspectives across the field from both senior and junior scholars to open a conversation and to interrogate the meaning of emancipation by framing it within three distinct categories. The first part of the book, "From Slavery to Freedom," draws on the traditional narrative of this period, coined by the great John Hope Franklin, but introduces new subjects, such as marriage and ritual during the war, and asks new questions about the role of the federal government during this tumultuous period, while the other chapters disrupt the traditional periodization of emancipation by incorporating slavery and the early nineteenth century into the study of freedom more directly. The second part, "The Politics of Freedom," offers both a polemical rendering of emancipation and new interpretations to study the language and politics of democracy. In the third part, "Meditations on the Meaning of Freedom," various historians sidestep the traditional form of academic writing and offer personal accounts of the politics of writing about the history of emancipation and interrogate the use of sources and themes that have informed the scholarship on emancipation over the last fifty years or more.

None of these essays stand as definitive, last words on the subject. They are, instead, efforts to provoke, and to prompt searching discussions about how we organize our approach to the moment of emancipation. The form of some of these essays also departs from traditional scholarly genre in order to capture the utterances, questions, and insights that often get lost in more standard historiographical essays. We hope the essays inspire debate and disagreement; we also hope they help younger scholars entering the field see room to maneuver as they wrestle with the fundamental questions posed by emancipation. By taking on the paradigm of freedom, it may well be that the volume inspires a strong defense of the term; this too would be a welcome result. We do not argue that freedom lacks value as a framework; we argue that the field would benefit from wrestling with its uses and limitations more openly and in competition with other frameworks for understanding the period.

NOTES

1. Booker T. Washington, *Up from Slavery* (Garden City, N.Y.: Doubleday & Company, Inc., 1900), 19.

2. "Life among the Contrabands," *The Liberator*, September 5, 1862. See also Jim Downs, *Sick from Freedom: African American Illness and Suffering during the Civil War and Reconstruction* (New York: Oxford University Press), 162–70.

3. For an excellent overview of how these questions animated recent historical scholarship on emancipation, see Carole Emberton, "Unwriting the Freedom Narrative: A Review Essay," *Journal of Southern History* 82, no. 2 (2016): 377–94. See also Yael A. Sternhell, "Revisionism Reinvented? The Antiwar Turn in Civil War Scholarship," *Journal of the Civil War Era* 3, no. 2 (2013): 239–56.

4. W. E. B. Du Bois, *Black Reconstruction in America, 1860–1880* (New York: Harcourt, Brace, 1935); Eric Foner, *Nothing but Freedom: Emancipation and Its Legacy* (Baton Rouge: Louisiana State University Press, 1983); Eric Foner, *Reconstruction: America's Unfinished Revolution, 1863–1877* (New York: Harper & Row, 1988).

5. As quoted in Gregory P. Downs, *Declarations of Dependence: The Long Reconstruction of Popular Politics in the South, 1861–1908* (Chapel Hill: University of North Carolina Press, 2011), 94–95.

6. For historians in the broader Atlantic world, who imagine emancipation as

a process, see Rebecca Scott, *Slave Emancipation in Cuba: The Transition to Free Labor* (Pittsburgh: University of Pittsburgh Press, 1985); Laurent Dubois, *A Colony of Citizens: Revolution and Slave Emancipation in the French Caribbean, 1787–1804* (Chapel Hill: University of North Carolina, 2004); Aida Ferrer, *Freedom's Mirror: Cuba and Haiti in the Age of Revolution* (Cambridge: Cambridge University Press, 2014); Natasha Lightfoot, *Troubling Freedom: Antigua and the Aftermath of Emancipation* (Durham, N.C.: Duke University Press, 2015).

7. On Hahn's essays on emancipation, see Steven Hahn, *The Political Worlds of Slavery and Freedom* (Cambridge, Mass.: Harvard University Press, 2009).

8. Thavolia Glymph, *Out of the House of Bondage: The Transformation of the Plantation Household* (New York: Cambridge University Press, 2008); Susan Eva O'Donovan, *Becoming Free in the Cotton South* (Cambridge, Mass.: Harvard University Press, 2007); Steven Hahn, *A Nation under Our Feet: Black Political Struggles in the Rural South from Slavery to the Great Migration* (New York: Belknap Press of Harvard University Press, 2003); Kate Masur, *An Example for All the Land: Emancipation and the Struggle over Equality in Washington, D.C.* (Chapel Hill: University of North Carolina Press, 2010); Jim Downs, *Sick from Freedom*; Hannah Rosen, *Terror in the Heart of Freedom: Citizenship, Sexual Violence, and the Meaning of Race in the Postemancipation South* (Chapel Hill: University of North Carolina Press, 2009); Carole Emberton, *Beyond Redemption: Race, Violence, and the American South after the Civil War* (Chicago: University of Chicago Press, 2013); Dylan C. Penningroth, *The Claims of Kinfolk: African American Property and Community in the Nineteenth-Century South* (Chapel Hill: University of North Carolina Press, 2003); Gregory P. Downs, *Declarations of Dependence.*

PART 1

From Slavery
to Freedom

The Grammar of Emancipation

Putting Final Freedom in Context

RICHARD NEWMAN

In the bucolic Mount Hope Cemetery of Rochester, New York, a pair of nineteenth-century graves illuminate the incredible distance American emancipation has traveled since Civil War times. At one end of the cemetery, signs lead visitors to Frederick Douglass's gravesite, where flowers and American flags honor the nation's most important black abolitionist. On the other side, an ordinary headstone marks the burial plot of Dr. John Van Evrie, the most notorious northern racist of the era.[1] With no signs pointing to Van Evrie's grave, few people know that the fire-breathing anti-abolitionist lies near the herald of black freedom. Yet the historical irony of that fact provides lasting satisfaction to those who discover it.

During the 1860s, however, a different story took shape. For Van Evrie spoke to a significant portion of northern as well as southern whites who rejected emancipation nationally. From the U.S. North to the Caribbean, Van Evrie claimed, black freedom had failed. While Douglass mined emancipation's past to make the opposite case, he found Van Evrie's worldview hard to overcome. "It is a sad fact that the people of this country are, as yet, on a plane of morality and philanthropy far below what the exigencies of the cause of human progress demands," Douglass wrote from Rochester in June 1860. Indeed, it "is to be regretted that they will not come up to the glorious work of striking the shackles from four million slaves at a single blow."[2] Van Evrie symbolized the entrenched belief among many white Americans that emancipation was anathema to the thriving republic—and more importantly, perhaps, that previous emancipations regionally and nationally remained problematic. In fact, until his death in 1896—just a year after Douglass—the good doctor remained an intellectual redoubt of anti-abolitionism. Not until a second Reconstruction a century later would his views fade from mainstream American culture.

Along the way, it seems, the world of emancipation that gave shape to Van Evrie's anti-abolitionism has been lost to many historians of Civil War freedom.[3] Though scholars have thoroughly undermined triumphalist narratives of final freedom after 1865, they have largely ignored the contested terrain of early emancipation that engendered Civil War debates over black liberty in the first place.[4] In this sense, they have reified the idea that final freedom was a product of the war years alone. But as the tale of Douglass and Van Evrie shows, mid-nineteenth-century Americans were well attuned to emancipation's embattled past in Atlantic society. From gradual abolition in the North to British and French emancipation in the Caribbean, experiments in black liberty (as many Americans saw them) framed everything from Union confiscation and contraband policies to providential interpretations of southern freedom itself. To even think about American emancipation in the 1860s was to conjure a complex set of ideas about black freedom long since set in motion.

One might call this the grammar of emancipation: a way of conjuring black freedom that was in a very real sense programmed into Civil War Americans. Though embedded in language, the grammar of emancipation transcended mere words. Rather, it was a broad set of ideas and beliefs (codes and rules, in a way) that ordered how many Americans conceived of black freedom.[5] Only by understanding the embattled nature of that grammar can we recover the halting, surprising, and sometimes disappointing roads toward emancipation in the Civil War and beyond.

Early Lessons: The Grammar of Northern Emancipation

Civil War Americans knew that their own emancipation history was nearly a century old by the time sectional battle erupted. While many citizens celebrated the era of northern gradualism that eradicated bondage above the Mason-Dixon Line, others saw early emancipation as problematic. Though glad to see slavery ended, many northerners did not embrace racial equality as an abolitionist corollary. As Joanne Melish has pointed out, concerns about northern freedom shadowed Massachusetts emancipation in the early republic, with whites worrying that blacks would become "slaves to the community"—civic dependents in need of constant governmental support.[6] In Pennsylvania, abolitionist convert Ben Franklin believed that enslaved blacks required white oversight to learn the meaning of freedom. Many African Americans protested these notions. As Richard Allen argued in 1794, liberated African Americans should not have to demonstrate their "superior good conduct" to be treated equally in the North.[7] Yet, with even white reformers exhibiting concerns about black freedom in the early republic, it is little wonder that colonization long remained popular in the North.[8]

With black freedom a contested part of northern society, antebellum abolitionists became well versed in defending it. Philadelphia reformers produced roughly a half dozen major censuses documenting free blacks' economic productivity and communal stability to overcome doubts about abolition (W. E. B. Du Bois later modeled *The Philadelphia Negro,* which launched the field of urban sociology, on these studies). Nevertheless, fears of unruly African Americans led to an era of racial retrenchment: by the 1840s, free blacks were disfranchised in virtually every state above the Mason-Dixon Line while segregation reigned in everything from schools to streetcars. Though opposition to the slave power grew more intense by mid-century, mainstream white northerners still worried about the legacy of early abolitionism. As Pennsylvania congressman Charles Brown noted in 1849, northerners did not believe black equality would be an analog to earlier emancipations. But now, that very prospect—equality as part of abolition—illustrated the true folly of broad emancipation programs in the South.[9]

As Brown's words suggest, lingering doubts about northern emancipation easily spilled over into fears about a second (and much bigger) southern liberation. During the presidential election of 1860, some northern papers predicted that Republican victory would unleash a hoard of enslaved people on the other parts of the nation, many of whom would spread the contagion of racial unrest to the North, Midwest, and West.[10] Such comments flowed not from a lunatic fringe but from years of debate about the "visionary" and "Jacobin" schemes of northern abolitionists and free black activists. Across the early wartime North, a band of emancipation critics argued that abolitionists had fomented sectional strife to expand the failed emancipation policies of earlier times. As George McHenry, the former head of the Philadelphia Board of Trade, claimed in 1862, northern emancipation had produced generations of African American paupers, criminals, and vagabonds and was no model for the South.[11] Paying no heed to abolitionists' studies proving otherwise, McHenry argued vehemently that mass black freedom would ruin the North as well as the South.

The mere discussion of ad hoc black liberty uncovered such fears.

In the early 1860s a host of writers, politicians, and racial scientists argued that confiscation and contraband policies would map the failures of northern abolition onto the nation. The result? White democracy no less than the Confederacy would be endangered if not destroyed. Even when Union fugitive slave policies undercut Confederate strength, some northerners worried that a "sudden" emancipation of southern blacks would harm the nation. In abolition's longtime home, for instance, the pro-Union *Philadelphia Inquirer* wondered if confiscation would lead to the "sudden emancipation" of millions of "semi-savages" inside Union lines. Other Pennsylvania papers believed that contraband and confiscation edicts had already set southern blacks "adrift," with many streaming north.[12] Borrowing from years of northern antiblack discourses, one Pennsylvania correspondent suggested sending "contrabands" to Haiti to "quiet any sensitiveness in relation to too sudden and great increase in our free Negro population." Another paper urged resettling "contrabands in Indian country" as a way of preventing them from moving North and degenerating into "idleness." As Pennsylvania congressman Charles Biddle summed up in 1862, the contraband question was really a "Negro question" and thus a referendum on black liberty north and south. And as a "white man and Pennsylvanian," Biddle rejected black wartime freedom.[13]

No one tilled anti-abolition ground more effectively than New Yorker John Van Evrie. A medical doctor steeped in the new field of racial science, Van Evrie became the North's leading intellectual opponent of black freedom. As he consistently claimed, both science and philosophy proved that blacks occupied a distinct and inferior space in the human chain of being—something he called "savagism." Thus, as abolitionists called for emancipation, Van Evrie pressed harder for "Subgenation": white racial domination north and south. For Van Evrie, "Antislaveryism" was no philanthropic belief but a disease that had been "the cause of secession." If white northerners were not careful, "Antislaveryism" and "Free Negroism" would ruin the country, too. Indeed, as he put it plainly in "Free Negroism," a representative tract from 1862, Civil War Americans could gain a glimpse of the South's potential "free" future by glancing at the North, where black freedom had almost killed white liberty.[14]

Van Evrie's literature and ideas pervaded northern urban areas, where Democrats and conservative Republicans vied for the support of white working men fearful of blacks' impact on the economic order. But they also penetrated the countryside. (Jefferson Davis praised a Van Evrie work that appeared in the mid-Atlantic region before the war.)[15] In Ohio,

Indiana, Illinois, and other midwestern locales, strains of Van Evrie's bald anti-abolitionism remained a powerful part of civic discourse well into the Reconstruction era. Already by the 1860s, however, debates over the meaning of black freedom and white supremacy filtered into seemingly secure antislavery locales such as Iowa. Spawned by African American mobility during the war, as well as black claims to equality in the civic sphere, these debates often (though not always) flowed from white citizens' sense of "entitlements accorded by race": whites' belief in the normative nature of prevailing economic and political structures, where they occupied unquestioned positions of power and control.[16] While some midwestern whites laudably reconsidered their views, others fit black freedom into a neat box that borrowed from the prevailing grammar of emancipation: newly freed African Americans would be treated not as equals but rather a servile class. For this reason, African Americans recognized the need to mobilize anew in the American heartland during and after the war.

Van Evrie's anti-abolitionism was much more crude and vicious than the racism registered in many parts of the American North and Midwest. But in another key sense it was a more elegantly framed and thus appealing explication of black inferiority. Garbed in a discourse of science and statistics, Van Evrie's work did not claim black inferiority in mere philosophical terms but sought to prove it via rigorous study of the known world of emancipation. For this reason, Van Evrie's work would not be dismissed. And it made its mark on the way that wartime emancipation was depicted. It is well to remember that prior to 1863, the Union's proto-emancipation policies were never framed as patriotic and glorious but as pragmatic and necessary. Clearly, Union policy makers worried about the racial dimensions of even limited liberty in the South. And when Lincoln proposed a national plan of compensated gradual emancipation to the border states in early 1862, he carefully calibrated his message to account for these fears. By embracing gradual abolition in the Upper South, Lincoln asserted, Americans everywhere would avoid the bugaboo of "sudden" emancipation; by linking gradualism to colonization, Americans would also drain troublesome free blacks from the white republic.[17] In no small way, the grammar of emancipation dictated the president's talking points about wartime black freedom.

Even after the Emancipation Proclamation took effect, Unionists carefully measured northern support for black liberty. Members of the American Freedmen's Inquiry Commission (AFIC), charged by Secretary of War Edwin Stanton in 1863 with studying emancipation in and beyond the United States, circulated questionnaires about free blacks in the North.

Were free blacks good or bad, industrious or insane, competent or criminal? While many respondents replied that free blacks were a small and genial presence in their midst, these questions conceded northerners' discomfort with their own emancipation history. The grammar of the first emancipation had defined black liberty as inherently problematic and constantly in need of critical investigation. For any Civil War policy maker, black freedom's contested history was easily conjured and not so easily dismissed.

International Grammar: Atlantic Emancipations

If time (i.e., the northern abolitionist past) served as one axis along which Civil War Americans interpreted the potential meaning of national emancipation, then space (emancipation's global geography) served as another key reference point. What were the results of Atlantic emancipations, Union military officials and politicians wondered as wartime liberty loomed? As Samuel Gridley Howe, one of the three AFIC representatives, put it, "Now, when everybody is asking what shall be done with the Negroes—and many are afraid that they cannot take care of themselves if left alone" after a looming southern emancipation, Americans desperately needed information on global black liberty. Howe thought Canada West would illuminate global emancipation's surprising past as well as hopeful future. In present-day Ontario, where Howe and others traveled in the early 1860s, there existed vibrant communities of former slaves. As Howe put it, perhaps "20,000 [former U.S. slaves] are taking care of themselves" in Canada West. A longtime reformer, Howe was well versed in abolitionist defenses of black freedom in the U.S. North. But he knew that white Unionists also wanted international perspectives seemingly free from the contaminated shores of American race prejudice.[18] So he headed farther north.

Though hardly news to race reformers, Howe's positive emancipation report from Canada West targeted an important new audience: Civil War politicians, whose wartime powers might deliver a decisive blow against southern bondage. As Howe put it, free blacks "in Canada earn a living, and gather property; they marry and respect women; they build churches and send their children to schools; they improve in manners and morals . . . [all] simply because they are FREE MEN." To be sure, Howe's pro-emancipation pamphlet contained standard-issue racism (including sections dealing with interracial marriage, which he generally frowned on). Still, Howe's view from Canada West reassured American Unionists that final freedom—liberty for "millions," as he proclaimed—would not result in chaos or race war.[19]

Others remained unsure. Indeed, while Howe's pamphlet celebrated the prospect of mass emancipation in the United States, its very production indicated that Civil War emancipators also had to fight a rearguard action against anti-abolitionists. Here, British Canada was just one spot on an Atlantic world map of emancipations that Civil War politicians studied with great interest. What about Haiti and French imperial emancipation? What about British emancipation in the Caribbean? What about free blacks in Central and South America?[20]

The narrative of emancipation's global failure had been around for much of the nineteenth century, beginning with anti-abolitionist portraits of Haiti as a poor (black) stepchild of Western society.[21] But it intensified on the eve of the Civil War with a burst of pamphlet literature aimed at demonizing both abolitionists and free blacks as Jacobins whose worldwide march had already destroyed great nations and economies.[22] Virginian Albert Bledsoe's *Liberty and Slavery* offered a standard critique of global freedom. Like others, Bledsoe believed that abolition had already failed in Atlantic society. Look no further than Great Britain, he concluded, where black freedom had not only killed the prosperous sugar economy but also harmed "the public good." Bledsoe called global emancipation a "monster," one whose horrible dimensions were clearer than ever by 1860. And wherever that monster traveled, it had ruined white society.[23]

With such dark discourses in mind, it is easy to see why the Civil War era constituted an important moment in the intellectual defense of global black freedom. Indeed, black and white reformers around the world issued stirring defenses of Atlantic emancipation in the early 1860s, knowing full well that they framed the possibility of mass abolition in the war-torn United States. Still, as the *New York Times* commented, "conventional wisdom" dictated that abolition had been a mixed blessing at best and a failure at worst.[24] It fell to one of the *Times*'s own correspondents to challenge mainstream thinking on the eve of the Civil War: William Grant Sewell, whose analysis of free labor successes in the former British West Indies promised to reorient Americans' understanding of global emancipation. Indeed, Sewell showed that key sectors of the Caribbean economy thrived. As fears of a "black republican" revolution swirled in 1861, Sewell's work illustrated that abolitionism elsewhere had not been ruinous.[25]

Abolitionists touted a similar success story in the French Caribbean, where final emancipation took effect in 1848. Though abolitionists hailed French abolition, mainstream Americans pictured it as another visionary—read highly problematic—experiment in black liberty. But in 1862 Boston abolitionist and Republican Party advocate Mary Booth issued a translation of Augustin Cochin's *The Results of Emancipation* to combat such fears.[26] Though it celebrated Francophone freedom, Cochin wrote his book with the United States in mind. In fact, Cochin believed that North Americans held the balance of moral power in mid-nineteenth-century Atlantic society. If they embraced final freedom, then both Brazil and Spanish Cuba would be truly isolated as slaveholding regimes. Yet, he observed sadly, the anti-abolitionist narrative that had shadowed global abolitionism since the 1770s seemed revivified in the United States, so much so that proslavery interests were ready to vanquish emancipation's noble history. Hoping to spur American emancipation, Cochin offered a panoramic study of French freedom that contradicted anti-abolitionist fears. Clearly hoping to influence American policy makers, he asserted that the only lesson of French abolition was that it should have occurred sooner. Little wonder that members of the Lincoln administration eagerly read Cochin's work (via Booth's translation). With sagging war fortunes, the Union might embrace emancipation. And if it did, Cochin's work would shield American emancipation from any detractors.

Even before Cochin's translation became available, race reformers used the lessons of global emancipation to frame wartime black liberty. Edward Atkinson, a cotton manufacturer who supported the Republican Party, used the Caribbean as proof that mass emancipation might work in the United States.[27] Yet once again, the very need to frame American emancipation as a workable experiment suggested the power of anti-emancipation thinking. Here, the specter of Haiti constantly haunted emancipation debate in the Civil War. As Pennsylvanian Charles Biddle put it, Union confiscation and contraband programs might turn the South into Haiti: a place where free blacks ran wild and attacked whites. For Biddle and his allies—Union Democrats, independents, and conservative Republicans—it was all of a piece: the world of emancipation remained a dangerous and disjointed place.[28]

Providence: The Grammar of Emancipation in Civil War America

Debate over emancipation's early history revealed the considerable hurdles Union statesmen, reformers, and politicians had to overcome to secure final freedom in Civil War America. Indeed, as the contested nature of even early wartime emancipation illustrated, Americans could not agree on how to depict black freedom in the past, much less embrace it in the present. In short, there was no progressive narrative guiding Civil War abolition, with members of the Republican war machine moving confidently from antislavery policies in the territories to national abolition. Rather, black wartime liberty was contingent, halting, and always much debated. In fact, it is more accurate to say that American statesmen and military officials did not build on previous (read future-oriented) antislavery policies to secure national abolition so much as they destroyed them. Here, we might call post-1863 emancipation edicts a form of creative destruction: the idea that moving forward required obliterating key parts of the past, in this case many Americans' prevailing fears of abolition. From declaring millions of Confederate blacks free to enlisting black soldiers in the Union war machine to constitutionally banning bondage in American society, Civil War Americans engaged in a series of creatively destructive acts that updated the grammar of emancipation. In this rendering, final freedom would be glorious, patriotic, and providential. As a nearly disbelieving black commentator wrote, even the preliminary Emancipation Proclamation proved that the "world moves" and things could change.[29]

This is a key point, for Americans' providential worldview of Civil War emancipation remains a striking feature of national memory.[30] Yet more than merely a heroic rationalization of the war's horrendous cost—that is, black freedom honored the war dead—providential emancipation accounted for the remarkable ideological shift in Americans' worldviews. How else could one explain Americans' long opposition to, and then quick embrace of, slavery's destruction except by Providence? While Lincoln's second inaugural gave mystical voice to this view, a broad range of Americans resorted to it as well. General Robert Milroy of Indiana offers a representative example. Stationed in Virginia in the first half of the war, Milroy hoped that slavery would end but knew that Unionism remained the rallying cry of northerners. Lincoln's Emancipation Proclamation thrilled Milroy because it blew past the limitations of antebellum times. Now, he wrote to family and friends, the United States was the world's largest liberator. But, he added, emancipation was clearly a "heaven inspired instrument."[31]

By ingeniously turning emancipation's prewar failure into the teleological starting point for final freedom's triumph in the 1860s, Milroy joined others in spinning a providential history of abolition that simultaneously praised the Almighty while absolving northerners of any responsibility for racial problems past, present—or future. As he put it to Lincoln, "future generations" would thank the president for channeling higher powers for the greater good. Who could argue with Providence? Certainly not William Lloyd Garrison, who told British officials feting him in 1867 that providential abolitionism had finally allowed him to wave the American flag proudly overhead.[32] While black activists often dissented, even they agreed that Providence had intervened to emancipate southern slaves. As Frederick Douglass noted, providential freedom gave the United States a moral prestige it never had.[33]

But as perceptive reformers saw all too well, the use of military means to achieve emancipation ends also allowed Americans to misinterpret might for right. Massachusetts abolitionist Lydia Maria Child worried that the wartime destruction of slavery might compel Americans to become self-congratulatory, skimming over racism's power in the antebellum North as well as slavery's vitality in the prewar South. For Child, wartime freedom might very well be seen as the end of history rather than a rejoinder to it—a new phase in the black freedom struggle. Yet even she could not resist celebrating southern slavery's demise in providential terms. There was just no other way to explain it.[34]

Thus, while many Americans celebrated national abolition as a justified consequence of Confederate defeat, others entered the postwar era worried that emancipation's haunted past still predicted a rough future for black freedom. According to a missive from the *Freedmen's Record*, published by the New England Freedmen's Aid Society, liberated blacks now "need[ed] all our help to raise [them] up to education and free civilization." And that would take considerable time.[35] This new form of antislavery gradualism was just one measure of the way that the antebellum grammar of emancipation had survived the war. From the idea that postemancipation blacks needed white oversight to survive liberation to questions about African Americans' very fitness for freedom beyond bondage, white Americans continually drew from the well of emancipation history to understand final freedom's meaning in the future.

In this sense, no idea assumed more power after 1865 than one that had haunted abolition since 1776: emancipation meant not only the absence of bondage but the presence of black liberty. Indeed, Civil War emancipation was not merely an event, or even a process, but an ideology. In its most basic form, emancipation as ideology depicted American liberty as a zero-sum game—whites lost freedom when blacks gained it. Critics of emancipation in the District of Columbia in 1862 claimed that white bondage had replaced black slavery because area masters did not even get to vote on whether or not their property would be liberated. This same fear had surfaced in early American emancipations, when northern masters claimed that black freedom came at the expense of white citizens (who allegedly competed more fiercely for jobs, paid more dearly for government costs to care for liberated slaves, and lost the civic bonds binding them to one another). Repackaged in the antebellum era, this ideology assumed that black freedom undercut northern white economic and political liberty by degrading labor and civic values.

During Reconstruction, negative emancipation ideology would be re-vivified by a new generation of Americans who framed final freedom as a grand experiment in which African American liberty would be compat-ible with white liberty if and only if freed blacks lifted themselves out of their degraded condition. Even abolitionist allies found old discourses—the antebellum grammar of emancipation—compelling. "Abraham Lin-coln decreed your emancipation from slavery," no less a figure than Gov-ernor John Andrew of Massachusetts lectured former slaves in 1865; now "let us complete the work, and emancipate the mind from ignorance." For, as Andrew (who had supported the formation of the famous 54th Massachusetts regiment just a few years earlier) went on, "the enjoyment of every right hangs on education," including such essential civil rights as suffrage. "Thus far," Andrew finished, "the colored people have no-bly fulfilled the hopes of their true friends." But "unless you help your-selves," Andrew warned former slaves, "not even God can make you" truly free and equal.[36] In short, southern emancipation was haunted by the problem—and not just the prospect—of black uplift beyond bondage.

Indeed, as Andrew's words illustrate, Civil War emancipation could easily return to its early national roots of black uplift. From the first emancipations in the U.S. North and Haiti onward, anti-abolitionists depicted blacks as inferiors whose base natures destabilized white soci-ety. Though they vehemently disagreed, even northern abolitionists got pulled into the trap of framing emancipation as part of an uplift process. In this rendering, African Americans deserved freedom not because they were citizens in a republic but because they would prove their moral and intellectual worth once liberated. So too in the 1860s did black and white reformers realize that they had to rationalize even the smallest act of wartime freedom in ways that neutralized white northerners' long-standing concerns about free blacks. In other words, blacks again had to illustrate that they were fit for freedom granted by whites. No sooner had slaves fled to Union lines than black and white abolitionists showed them as busybodies aiding the Union war effort (and not, as critics charged, a drain on Union resources). For white northerners wondering about the broader social impact of wartime freedom, such news was supposed to be reassuring. Still, it contained the seeds of backlash, for if freed blacks were not busy, contained, and controlled, the old grammar of emancipation dictated that freedom would be deemed a failure. White liberty could be boisterous and unruly; black liberty had to be sober and solemn.

And so we return to Douglass and Van Evrie, intellectual enemies who by war's end agreed on one key thing: emancipation's past was still powerful. For as Douglass knew, Van Evrie's anti-emancipation thinking remained very much alive during Reconstruction.[37] While Douglass drew from history to prove African American equality, the rabid New York doctor recycled his earlier pamphlets on blacks' "savagism" in the North to derail race reform nationally. As someone who had escaped southern slavery only to find segregated schools, streetcars, and public facilities in the North, Douglass understood that the struggle for black equality in the United States would be long and grueling. But he was nevertheless chagrined to find Van Evrie's worldview creeping back into national politics in the final decades of the nineteenth century. Providence notwithstanding, Douglass realized that Americans still struggled with the legacies of the first emancipation in the North, when black freedom was unleashed as a troubling presence in an allegedly white republic.

NOTES

1. See introduction to John David Smith, *Anti-Abolition Tracts and Anti-Black Stereotypes* (New York: Garland, 1993).

2. See "The Chicago Nominations," *Douglass' Monthly,* June 1860.

3. The most compelling recent book on American and global abolitionist trends reminds us that black and white antislavery activists had built a formidable transatlantic struggle well before the 1860s. Still, few scholars connect northern and southern emancipation struggles. See Manisha Sinha's magnificent study, *The Slave's Cause: A History of Abolition* (New Haven, Conn.: Yale University Press, 2016).

4. For a trenchant critique of the way American emancipation is subdivided and studied, see especially Edward Rugemer, *The Problem of Emancipation* (Baton Rouge: Louisiana State University Press, 2011), introduction. Several recent and well-regarded studies of Civil War emancipation skim over early American and Atlantic abolitionism prior to the 1860s. See, for instance, Louis P. Masur, *Lincoln's Hundred Days* (Cambridge, Mass.: Belknap Press, 2012). See also these award-winning books: Eric Foner, *The Fiery Trail: Abraham Lincoln and American Slavery* (New York: W. W. Norton, 2010); Allen C. Guelzo, *Lincoln's Emancipation Proclamation: The End of Slavery in America* (New York: Simon & Schuster, 2004).

In *Freedom National: The Destruction of Slavery in the United States, 1861–1865* (New York: W. W. Norton, 2012), James Oakes delves into the Atlantic history of abolition but views the coming of American emancipation in more progressive terms than I do.

5. According to the *Oxford English Dictionary* (*OED*), the historical understanding of "grammar" was quite wide and varied and included metaphorical uses of the term. Thus, in England in the 1600s, one authority noted that "manly sports are the Grammar of Military performance." In this sense, "grammar" is defined as the "fundamental principles or rules of an art or science." See *OED*, 1978 ed., s.v. "grammar."

6. See especially Joanne P. Melish, *Disowning Slavery* (Ithaca, N.Y.: Cornell University Press, 1998), chaps. 2–3 and 5; quote at 84.

7. See Richard Allen and Absalom Jones, "An Address to Those Who Keep Slaves and Uphold the Practice," in *A Narrative of the Black People during the Late Awful Calamity in Philadelphia* (Philadelphia, 1794), reprinted in Richard Newman, Patrick Rael, and Phillip Lapsansky, *Pamphlets of Protest: An Anthology of Early African American Protest Literature, 1790–1860* (New York: Routledge, 2001), 41.

8. On northern emancipation and colonization, see David N. Gellman, *Emancipating New York: The Politics of Slavery and Freedom, 1777–1827* (Baton Rouge: Louisiana State University Press, 2006); Melish, *Disowning Slavery*; Gary B. Nash and Jean R. Soderlund, *Freedom by Degrees: Emancipation in Pennsylvania and Its Aftermath* (New York: Oxford University Press, 1991); Richard S. Newman, *The Transformation of American Abolitionism: Fighting Slavery in the Early Republic* (Chapel Hill: University of North Carolina Press, 2001); Gary B. Nash, *Race and Revolution* (Lanham, Md.: Madison House, 1990); Beverly Tomek, *Colonization and Its Discontents: Emancipation, Emigration, and Antislavery in Early National Pennsylvania* (New York: New York University Press, 2011); Eva Sheppard Wolf, *Race and Liberty in the New Nation: Emancipation in Virginia from the Revolution to Nat Turner's Rebellion* (Baton Rouge: Louisiana State University Press, 2006).

9. See Charles Brown's speech "Abolition and Slavery," in *Cong. Globe*, 30th Cong. 2d Sess. 117–19 (February 19, 1849), quote at 119.

10. See, for instance, the *Clearfield (Pa.) Republican*, October 10, 1860.

11. George McHenry, *Position and Duty of Pennsylvania: A Letter Addressed to the President of the Philadelphia Board of Trade* (London: H. F. Mackintosh, 1863), 72.

12. See *Philadelphia Inquirer*, October 4, 1861; *Franklin County (Pa.) Valley Spirit*, November 27, 1861, June 11, 1862.

13. See *Franklin County (Pa.) Valley Spirit*, November 27, 1861, June 11, 1862; Charles Biddle, *Alliance with the Negro* (Washington, D.C.: L. Towers, 1862), 1–2.

14. *Free Negroism; or, Results of Emancipation in the North and the West India Islands . . .* (New York: Horton, 1863), 1.

15. See "Letters to the Author" in J. H. Van Evrie, *Negroes and Negro Slavery; The First, An Inferior Race—The Latter, Its Normal Condition* (Baltimore: John D. Toy, 1853), 2.

16. See Leslie Schwalm, *Emancipation's Diaspora: Race and Reconstruction in the Upper Midwest* (Chapel Hill: University of North Carolina Press, 2009), 105.

17. Abraham Lincoln, "Message to Congress Recommending Compensated Emancipation," March 6, 1862, available at the American Presidency Project, http://www.presidency.ucsb.edu/ws/?pid=70130.

18. Samuel Girdley Howe, *The Refugees from Slavery in Canada West: Report to the Freedmen's Inquiry Commission* (Boston: Wright and Potter, 1864), iii–iv. See also Matthew Furrow, "Samuel Girdley Howe, the Black Population of Canada West, and the Racial Ideology of the 'Blueprint for Radical Reconstruction,'" *Journal of American History* 97, no. 2 (September 2010): 344–70.

19. Ibid.

20. The literature on Atlantic emancipation is wide and varied. See, for instance, Robin Blackburn, *The American Crucible* (New York: Verso, 2011); Laurent Dubois, *Avengers of the New World* (Cambridge, Mass.: Belknap Press, 2004); Christopher Schmidt-Nowara, *Slavery, Freedom, and Abolition in Latin America and the Atlantic World* (Albuquerque: University of New Mexico Press, 2011); Sue Peabody and Keila Grinberg, eds., "Free Soil in the Atlantic World," special edition of *Slavery and Abolition* 32, no. 3 (2011).

21. See especially Laurent Dubois, *Haiti: The Aftershocks of History* (New York: Henry Holt, 2012), chaps. 3–5.

22. Matthew Clavin, *Toussaint Louverture and the American Civil War* (Philadelphia: University of Pennsylvania Press, 2009).

23. Bledsoe, *Liberty and Slavery*, reprinted in E. N. Elliott, *Cotton Is King* (Augusta, Ga.: Pritchard, Abbott, and Loomis, 1860), esp. chap. 4, "Argument from the Public Good."

24. *New York Times*, March 30, 1861.

25. See William Grant Sewell, *The Ordeal of Free Labor in the British West Indies* (New York: Harper and Brothers, 1861).

26. Augustin Cochin, *The Results of Emancipation* (Boston: Walker, Wise, 1862), introduction.

27. Edward Atkinson, *Report to the Boston Board of Trade on the Cotton Manufacture of 1862* (Boston, 1863), and *The Future Supply of Cotton* (Boston: Crosby and Nichols, 1864), 10–14.

28. *The Alliance with the Negro: Speech of Hon. Charles J. Biddle of Pennsylvania, Delivered in the House of Representatives of the United States, March 6, 1862* (Washington, D.C.: L. Towers, 1862), 8.

29. *Christian Recorder*, October 18, 1862.

30. See especially David W. Blight, *Race and Reunion* (Cambridge, Mass.: Belknap Press, 2001), preface on the competing visions of reunion.

31. See Robert H. Milroy to Abraham Lincoln, January 1, 1864, Indiana Memory Digital Collections, available at http://cdm16066.contentdm.oclc.org/cdm/compoundobject/collection/Milroy/id/2126.

32. See Garrison's remarks of June 29, 1867, in F. W. Chesson, ed., *Proceedings*

at the Public Breakfast Held in Honour of William Lloyd Garrison, Esq. (London: William Tweedie, 1868), 40–50.

33. Douglass, "We Are Not Yet Quite Free," Medina, N.Y., August 3, 1869, in *The Frederick Douglass Papers*, series 1, vol. 4, ed. John W. Blassingame and John R. McKivigan (New Haven, Conn.: Yale University Press, 1991), 220–40.

34. See Lydia Maria Child to Henrietta Sargent, August 24, 1861, in *Letters of Lydia Maria Child* (New York: Houghton Mifflin, 1882), 156.

35. "Prospects for the Future," *Freedmen's Record* 1, no. 11 (November 1865).

36. *Freedmen's Record* 1, no. 10 (October 1865).

37. *White Supremacy and Negro Subordination* (New York: Van Evrie, Horton, 1868) reprinted earlier material from Van Evrie's works.

Writing Slavery into Freedom's Stories

SUSAN O'DONOVAN

When General Joseph Fullerton, a senior Freedmen's Bureau official, returned from a tour through South Carolina, Georgia, and Florida in July 1865, he did not have much good to say. In a pair of lengthy reports, Fullerton rolled out a litany of sins. There were too few agents in too few places, he grumbled. Of those who stood duty, most had no idea what it was they were supposed to be doing, and others would soon be released from federal service. Former slaveholders were proving stubborn, having convinced themselves that the national courts would declare emancipation a sham. Georgia had no assistant commissioner, and neither did Florida; outside of that narrow strip of coast commonly called the Low Country, the federal presence was thin to nonexistent. There was a cavalry command stationed at Macon, Georgia; there was a person who may or may not have been a Freedmen's Bureau official at Augusta, Georgia; and a single army officer had charge of the whole of western Florida. Given the evidence, emancipation was all but stalled, except, importantly, according to those most directly affected: the nation's former slaves. In their minds, they stood on the leading edge of a fresh new world, one in which they would henceforth stand shoulder to shoulder, side by side with their old masters, beneficiaries alike of the legal, social, and political trappings that had long been associated with American citizenship. Reflecting back on his journey through what had been slavery's eastern stronghold, Fullerton had no choice but to conclude that "there are now very few negroes . . . who do not know that the old system of slavery has passed away. Whenever they are asked concerning their present condition the com[mon] reply is 'We have no massa now—We is come to the law now.'"[1]

The conversations relayed by Fullerton in his report shimmered with intellectual rigor and conceptual depth. They called into being a wholly new and revolutionary vision of American social, civil, and political life, one fully shared by the recently freed. These words and the ideas behind them were not uttered by happenstance. Yet while Fullerton could see and hear, he could not bring himself to believe. Like many of his contemporaries (northern as well as southern), the general could not accept that such a sophisticated account of their new position in a fully free nation could possibly have originated in former slaves' heads. No, Fullerton mused as he wrapped up his report, the black people with whom he had talked must have been given those words and the ideas behind them by Union soldiers, or they had appropriated them from old masters and other ex-Confederates, or perhaps they learned them from northerners newly arrived in the former slaveholding states. But whatever the means, Fullerton was convinced that the flow of information was unidirectional, running in a straight line from the always freed to the newly freed. The freedpeople with whom he met might be mimics, but were they intellectuals and political philosophers in their own right? Not hardly, Fullerton says. To quote Martin R. Delany, himself a Freedmen's Bureau agent assigned for a time to the South Carolina Low Country, the recently freed were nothing more than a "simple and childlike people," a population whose civil and political awakening still lay ahead.[2]

A century and a half later, Fullerton's blind spot remains our blind spot. Few scholars of the Reconstruction era are any more prepared today than was Fullerton in 1865 to accept the recently freed as a fully realized political people. Slavery, in other words, is still no training ground for black freedom. It is an assumption that leads to a host of conclusions that trap us within otherwise discredited patterns of thinking. Take, for instance, the wraithlike figures who wander Toni Morrison's imaginary postapocalyptic/postemancipation landscape in *Beloved*, stunned, hungry, tired; memories and minds shattered by slavery's horrors; the enslaved fatalists of Eugene Genovese's *Roll, Jordan, Roll*, a people who can never break away from the deracinating and binary pull of the master-slave dialectic; and the cinematic Solomon Northup, who owes his liberation not to anything intrinsic to slave capabilities but rather to literacy skills acquired before his captivity and to the machinations of learned friends in high places. Slaves did not free Northup; free people did.[3] W. E. B. Du Bois followed a similar line of reasoning in his otherwise brilliant study of *Black Reconstruction*. Anticipating what Orlando Patterson would later make famous as "social death," Du Bois discounted slaves as "absolute subject[s]" of slaveholders' wills. Bondage had rendered them helpless, defenseless, and utterly dependent on the leadership of a very small cadre of "Negroes of the cities, the Negroes who were hired out, [and] the Negroes of intelligence who could read and write." Steeped in an intellectual tradition that rarely if ever considered the enslaved meaningful agents of change, Du Bois ended up in the same logical position that had been occupied by Fullerton before him and a host of intellectuals after. Slaves, he pronounced in his opening chapters, stood apart from those who could and would and have made history.[4]

Such thinking has not only had a pernicious effect on our understanding of slaves and their capacity as agents of change; it has distorted our stories of freedom, too. Anyone who has taught or taken the U.S. history survey knows that nineteenth-century American history is more often than not presented as a serial set: that which happened before the war and that which happened after. An organizational schema whose origins trace back to late nineteenth-century debates about national reunification, the long-standing habit of fracturing the century into two large but unequally sized chunks efficiently dismembers what in truth was a single historical process.[5] It is a trend that is coming under increasing assault, but while those who study crashes, risk, and Indian wars have begun to suggest different starting and ending points for their histories of America's nineteenth century, those of us who study slavery on the one hand and black freedom on the other have generally stuck with the tried and true, no matter how much such a choice still legitimizes old and questionable racist and elitist ideals.[6] With few exceptions (notably Steven Hahn and the past and present editors of the Freedmen and Southern Society Project),[7] historians of nineteenth-century African American life typically focus their inquiries on one side of that wartime divide or the other. It is rare for any of us to do both.[8] To be sure, there is a practical reason to specialize. Freedom and slavery are individually very large subjects of study, and tackling one can be a lifetime's work. Tackling two can be a daunting project. Yet what are we saying when we continue to hold those fields analytically apart? That what women and men managed to make of and for themselves in bondage has no bearing on what they aspired to and accomplished as a free people? That black people drifted out of bondage without a thought in their heads, and no plans for their futures? Our temporalities may make sense in the abstract, but in practice, they carry a message that is chilling in its prejudicial overtones.

Breaking old habits is hard, but we may want to sever the last of our intellectual and conceptual ties with men such as Joseph Fullerton. To drop slaves out or shove them aside implies that they had no history worth studying. Marginalizing them also raises the distinct possibility that we will miss and consequently misunderstand the full range of forces that shaped the post–Civil War nation, never mind the post–Civil War South. How can we hope to know the whole story if we insist on telling only a part? Moreover, to treat black southerners as blank slates defies everything we now know about cognitive processes. People cannot shuck their pasts the same way we delete data from our computers and hard drives. Human memory does not function that way, a phenomenon that sociologists and political philosophers have long acknowledged. In language reminiscent of Karl Marx's, Pierre Bourdieu has reminded his readers that "in each of us, in differing degrees, is contained the person we were yesterday."[9] Because of the lingering presence of the past, the ideas, interests, experiences, and memories forged in slavery became for four million black southerners the materials from which they began to forge new lives in freedom. The two halves are not separable. One bleeds into and informs the other. Thus to overlook, discredit, or downplay as Fullerton did the possibility that black southerners possessed an ideological and political baggage of their own can only add yet another layer of insult to the injuries already done to a people whose lives and labor had in very literal ways underwritten the growth of a nation. If black lives matter today, then so should the whole of the black past.

If ethics is an insufficient reason to write slavery more explicitly into freedom's stories, then maybe empirical evidence will do the trick. The enslaved come alive in slavery's archives, and some of the best evidence of thinking, scheming, and dreaming slaves comes from those who wished otherwise: the women and men who owned them. White southerners' respect for and fear of enslaved people's capacity for learning and conversing, which were almost by definition transgressive activities, was evident early in the flurry of restrictive laws passed in the wake of Nat Turner's revolt, in the rumors of slave rebellion that more generally gobbled up space in the southern press, and in sporadic efforts to halt the sale of so-called ringleaders across state lines.[10] White fears of slaves who saw too much, heard too much, knew too much, and talked too much were also increasingly evident in slaveholders' personal papers, diaries, farm journals, and business correspondence. Indeed, by the 1850s planters had begun abandoning older idioms involving livestock and childhood and replacing them with the more explicitly political lexicon of spies, rebels, and republicans. "Tackeys" was what one disgruntled overseer called the enslaved troublemakers beneath him, making a lightly veiled reference to the eighteenth-century Jamaican who sparked an age of rebellion.[11] Mary Chesnut half-jestingly likened her husband's enslaved valet to a then popular (and fictionalized) international spy, while a Georgia slave-holder, Richard Lyon, dropped all pretense. Slaves, he howled when faced with losing some of his own to a large-scale internal improvement project, were a fully realized political people. Decrying the gathering together of slaves who were strangers, Lyon likened such operations to "regular conventions" at which all a region's slaves would be "abley & fully represented." They will "tal[k] with one another of their wants & their wishes," and then, in time-honored republican fashion, when their work had been completed, "each fellow will go back home thoroughly instructed & charged with mischief."[12]

Slaveholders had no one to blame but themselves for what many saw as a fatal erosion of slavery's order. In their quest for the Golden Fleece and other lucrative commodities, they had managed to plant the seeds of their own destruction. After all, the South's great staples could not make themselves. Successful harvests required vast quantities of labor, and the cheaper that labor, the better. This meant that contrary to popular visions and wisdom, slaves not only sowed, hoed, reaped, and processed vast quantities of crops, they hauled them to market, too. It was a herculean task. By the late 1850s it took better than a half million wagon-loads annually to move cotton alone. Rice, sugar, tobacco, and other commodities had to find their own rides.[13] Slaveholders also needed slaves to build the roads over which all those wagons and later railcars rolled.[14] They needed slaves to pole their rafts, flatboats, and "cotton boxes" on what was often the second leg of a multileg/multinational journey.[15] They needed slaves to feed firewood into the yawning maws of the steamboats that carried towering loads of cotton and other commodities up and down the South's rivers.[16] They needed slaves to run errands, herd livestock, and serve as personal servants, to tend their every need on excursions that frequently carried them across and beyond the continent.[17] Slaves also carried slaveholders' messages and mail, often on top of or in conjunction with other ambulatory occupations. "Dear Sir," wrote Robert Chapman of Fredericksburg, Virginia, to John Newton of Augusta County, Virginia, in well-worn language of the day: "This will be handed to you by Richard a teamster who is in the service of Mr. Thos. Glass one of my neighbors. He is on his way with a load to East Tennessee & will call upon you on his return."[18]

More than the oppressed victims of a capitalist juggernaut (which, of course, they were), enslaved laborers were also the heart and intensely mobile soul of a global market system.[19] Slaveholders knew that to stop slaves in their tracks, to pin them to place, to lock them down into plantations passing as prisons would be to slaughter a very fat, very profitable goose. Capitalism needed to breathe, and for that to happen, antebellum American slaveholders had to have their slaves in near constant motion. Functioning at one and the same time as the lifeblood, the infrastructure, and the lubricant of New World slavery, bound workers were the muscle and machinery that made slavery work. They were the gears that turned the engine of staple production, and though they might fret by day and lose sleep by night, America's slaveholders had no choice but to keep their slaves on a long and loose leash. To bind them too tightly, to hold them too close, to hedge them in behind impenetrable plantation boundaries would have been to commit social, economic, and political suicide. They were, in short, inflexibly dependent on a near infinitely flexible labor force. A mobile workforce generated profit. An immobile workforce would signal the end of an era.

Still, putting slaves into motion was a risky business. Each time a master, mistress, agent, or overseer ordered a slave into the road and on the go, they were willfully plunging their most mobile property into a sea of subversion. This was the paradox at the center of New World bondage, and it is the historical reality with which freedom's scholars must contend. For with every trip made abroad on a master's or mistress's command, slaves entered into an environment that was always ripe with seditious possibility. New people, new ideas, and new opportunities greeted enslaved laborers at every bend of the river or road. It was in running errands for their owner, explains Henry "Box" Brown, that he and his brother came to know "whatever was going on . . . in the world."[20] Living and breathing links in what scholars of early modern Europe describe as "shifting chains of exchange and action," travel allowed slaves to try on new identities, sample new cultures, and experience what it meant to be a masterless man (or woman), if only for a moment. David Dorr took his lessons while out and about on a three-year tour of Europe; William Robinson's came through extended duty on a transcontinental surveyor crew.[21] Travel had an instrumental dimension, too, for it was in making trips abroad that the enslaved were better able to assemble, reassemble, and extend those thickly twisted networks of family, friends, acquaintances, and allies that in their hydralike form often served as slaves' first line of defense against slavery's many offenses.[22] William Webb, a slave who moved back and forth and throughout the Mississippi valley for much of the 1850s, was a master at crafting social connections out of what was for him an always-shifting world of work.[23] So too was the slave Garland H. White. Personal servant to Senator Robert Toombs, White not only accumulated an intimate knowledge of the social and physical topographies of Georgia and Washington, D.C., as a result of his service-induced travel, he also met and befriended a man who, in his later capacity as secretary of state to Abraham Lincoln, was in a position to grant favors to a former slave. "Dear Hon. Wm. H. Seward," White would write at least twice for assistance at the height of the Civil War.[24]

Travel also invited an explicitly political dimension, for where better (and safer) for slaves to enter into, launch, and shape thoroughgoing debates about the state of the nation and their place within it than out of sight and hearing of a master? To be sure, slaves talked (and probably endlessly) in the seclusion of their quarters and whenever else they were out of earshot of a hovering slaveholder. But the privacy granted by the open road, a European street, the deck of an Atlantic steamer, or a crowded riverside wharf provided a fertile environment for a slave's enlightenment. And talk they did. No more discouraged by the lack of literacy than any urban workman, northern mechanic, or recent immigrant, slaves proved themselves to be eager creators as well as consumers of political life. Conversant with the major political parties, their platforms, and their prospects, slaves thrust themselves headlong into what is still too often regarded as a free person's domain.[25]

Seizing the opportunities that opened to them through slavery's work, enslaved men and women rubbed shoulders with theocrats, autocrats, and democrats. They bore witness to republics falling, empires in the making, and bodies politic in violent upheaval: Prior in the mountain West, Dorr in Paris, Peter in Mexico, and the dozens of American slaves whose arrival in Cuba admitted them into a servile insurgency.[26] Those who summered with their owners in coastal New England intermingled with antislavery activists, whalers, free people of color, a dwindling population of Native Americans, and an increasingly radicalized working class, before, of course, returning south for the winter.[27] Georgia slave Houston Hartsfield Holloway gathered up printed litter from the shoulders of roads for delivery to what he dubbed his "reading club," a group of men who helped Holloway come to know "the Democratice partie the Whigg partie the no nothing partie the nulifires and the anteno nothing parties."[28] Farther west, Webb put his sprawling, multistate grid of friends and acquaintances to explicit political purpose. "You ought to single out some men to speak in different places," he advised newfound allies when generating support for John C. Fremont's 1856 presidential campaign.

"Appoint a man to travel 12 miles, and then hand the news to another man, and so on, till the news reache[s] from Louisiana to Mississippi. . . . [We need] to spread the faith. . . . We all must know, before we can make a movement. . . . [We must] tell one another that we expect to be free."[29]

To insist as Fullerton did that the enslaved were nothing more than empty vessels is to miss what is perhaps the best part of freedom's story: the chapters that were written by slaves. To stand on freedom's leading edge and gaze toward the future is also to miss the opportunity to ask what may very well be the most important questions of Reconstruction's history. For if the enslaved were not empty vessels and were instead a cosmopolitan population with more than a passing acquaintance with the political, social, and intellectual leanings of their day—people who like Meme Phebe split her time between coastal Georgia and Providence, Rhode Island; or the seven Tennesseans who were thrust by their master into what another slaveholding '49er described as a "heterogenious comminglement" of human society—what did people like these bring to freedom's table?[30] How did contact with and life among culturally, ethnically, linguistically, and politically diverse populations inform the heated postemancipation debates about freedom's meanings? Thavolia Glymph has introduced us to the well-traveled Rose, the Low Country woman who surfaced during the Civil War to lead her own war.[31] But what about the hundreds of others who likewise traced Meme Phebe's steps north, or the Tennessean slaves' steps west, or Peter's path to Mexico? How did their personal journeys intrude on and interrupt freedom's history? Was it just literacy that set those first black elected officials apart from the bulk of the nation's former slaves? Or was it prior knowledge of different places, different possibilities, different publics, and different futures that caused them to stand at the vanguard of a powerful grassroots mobilization? What about the women of Richmond, Virginia, of whom Elsa Barkley Brown writes; can we trace the origins of their gendered aspirations as a free people back to time spent as slaves on the road and on the go?[32]

These questions and others have the potential to change how we think about what Lincoln famously called the new birth of freedom. But for that to happen, historians need to stop looking forward from freedom's leading edge. We need to retreat deep into black people's pasts, for it is there that we can better observe a people who deftly moved through slavery's horrors with their eyes and minds wide open. Trapped as they were in a system that preyed every day on human mobility, those four million people nevertheless found in their endless cycles of forced migrations means to imagine a world without slavery. To overlook, downplay, or dismiss the accomplishments of slaves is to add new layers of insult to centuries of injury. It is also to risk knowing only a small and distorted part of a much larger story.

NOTES

1. J. S. Fullerton to Maj. Genl. O. O. Howard, July 23, 1865, F-122 1865, Letters Received, ser. 15, Washington Hdqrs., RG 105 [A-5836]; J. S. Fullerton to Maj. Genl. O. O. Howard, July 28, 1865, in *Freedom: A Documentary History of Emancipation, 1861–1867, Series 3, Volume 1: Land and Labor, 1865*, ed. Steven Hahn, Steven F. Miller, Susan E. O'Donovan, John C. Rodrigue, and Leslie S. Rowland (Chapel Hill: University of North Carolina Press, 2008), 145–49; Susan Eva O'Donovan, *Becoming Free in the Cotton South* (Cambridge, Mass.: Harvard University Press, 2007), 113–17.

2. Major M. R. Delany to Bvt. Lieut. Col. W. L. M. Burger, March 5, 1866, Letters and Reports Received Relating to Freedmen and Civil Affairs, ser. 4112, Dept. of SC, RG 393 pt. 1 (filed as C-1401, Freedmen and Southern Society Project, Department of History, University of Maryland, College Park).

3. Toni Morrison, *Beloved* (New York: Knopf, 1987), 78; Eugene D. Genovese, *Roll, Jordan, Roll: The World the Slaves Made* (New York: Random House, 1974), 148–58; Brian Craig Miller, Natalie Zemon Davis, Jim Downs, Susan Eva O'Donovan, and Margaret Washington, "Film Round Table: *12 Years a Slave*," *Civil War History* 60, no. 3 (September 2014): 310–36.

4. W. E. B. Du Bois, *Black Reconstruction in America: An Essay toward a History of the Part which Black Folk Played in the Attempt to Reconstruct Democracy in America, 1860–1880* (1935; reprint, New York: Atheneum, 1962), 6, 9–10, 13, 59. On the continued uses and misuses of Patterson's ideas and the lingering hold of "social death" on the historical imagination, see Vincent Brown, "Social Death and Political Life in the Study of Slavery," *American Historical Review* 114 (December 2009): 1231–49.

5. David W. Blight's *Race and Reunion: The Civil War in American Memory* (Cambridge, Mass.: Belknap Press, 2001) and Cecelia Elizabeth O'Leary's *To Die For: The Paradox of American Patriotism* (Princeton, N.J.: Princeton University Press, 1999) are excellent entry points into a growing body of scholarship on the racial price of reconciliation.

6. Included among those working to reconfigure our temporal landscapes are Scott Reynolds Nelson, *A Nation of Deadbeats: An Uncommon History of America's Financial Disasters* (New York: Knopf, 2012); Jonathan Levy, *Freaks of Fortune: The Emerging World of Capitalism and Risk in America* (Cambridge, Mass.: Harvard University Press, 2012); and Elliott West, *The Last Indian War: The Nez Perce Story* (New York: Oxford University Press, 2009).

7. Steven Hahn draws the most explicit connection between the politics of slaves and the politics of freedpeople in *A Nation under Our Feet: Black Political*

Struggles in the Rural South from Slavery to the Great Migration (Cambridge, Mass.: Belknap Press, 2003); but see also Julie Saville, "Rites and Power: Reflections on Slavery, Freedom, and Political Ritual," in *Slavery to Emancipation in the Atlantic World*, ed. Sylvia R. Frey and Betty Wood (New York: Routledge, 1999), 81–102, and most recently, Thavolia Glymph, "Rose's War and the Gendered Politics of a Slave Insurgency in the Civil War," *Journal of the Civil War Era* 3 (December 2013): 501–32.

8. The list of monographs and articles that fall onto one side or the other is vast, and its growth shows no sign of abating. A 2011 survey of dissertations produced on black Reconstruction since 2003 revealed only one that is explicitly grounded in slavery. The rest pick up their stories in or after the Civil War. Nothing that happened prior to the war is evidently of any account.

9. Pierre Bourdieu, *The Logic of Practice*, trans. Richard Nice (Cambridge: Polity Press, 1990), 56. Karl Marx makes the same point when he writes of men making their own history, but not making it just as they please; see *The Eighteenth Brumaire of Louis Bonaparte*, 3rd ed., trans. Daniel De Leon (Chicago: Charles H. Kerry, 1913), chap. 1.

10. For examples of the laws enacted in the second and third decades of the nineteenth century, see John G. Aiken, comp., *A Digest of the Laws of the State of Alabama: Containing All the Statutes of a Public and General Nature, in Force at the Close of the Session of the General Assembly in January, 1833* (Philadelphia: Alexander Tower, 1833), 391–98; Alexander B. Meek, comp., *A Supplement [to] Aikin's Digest of the Laws of the State of Alabama: All the Unrepealed Laws of a Public and General Nature Passed by the General Assembly since the Second Edition of the Digest, up to the Close of the Called Session in April, 1841* (Tuscaloosa, Ala.: White & Snow, 1841), 208–9, 219–20, 236, 246, 297–301; V. E. Howard and A. Hutchinson, comp., *The Statutes of the State of Mississippi of a Public and General Nature* (New Orleans: E. Johns, 1840), 153–81; Marshall Rachleff, "David Walker's Southern Agent," *Journal of Negro History* 62 (January 1977): 100–103. For a comprehensive primer on antebellum slave rebellions, see Herbert Aptheker, *American Negro Slave Revolts*, 5th ed. (New York: International Publishers, 1983).

11. Wm. Capers to Charles Manigault, September 23, 1859, box 27, folder 254, U. B. Phillips Papers, Sterling Library, Yale University, New Haven, Connecticut.

12. C. Vann Woodward, ed., *Mary Chesnut's Civil War* (New Haven, Conn.: Yale University Press, 1981), 225; Susan Griffin, "The Yellow Mask, the Black Robe, and the Woman in White: Wilkie Collins, Anti-Catholic Discourse, and the Sensation Novel," *Narrative* 12 (January 2004): 55–73 (I am indebted to Julia Stern of Northwestern University for this reference); Richard F. Lyon to Joseph E. Brown, August 9, 1862, Governor's Incoming Correspondence, Georgia State Archives, Atlanta.

13. Basing my calculations on an average load of six 500-pound bales of cotton, it would have required approximately 512,000 wagonloads to move the 1859 crop along the first and overland leg of its farm-to-factory journey. Cotton pro-

duction figures came from Edward E. Baptist, *The Half Has Never Been Told: Slavery and the Making of American Capitalism* (New York: Basic Books, 2014), 114.

14. On the widespread practice of leasing slaves to railroad contractors, see Aaron W. Marrs, *Railroads in the Old South: Pursuing Progress in a Slave Society* (Baltimore, Md.: Johns Hopkins University Press, 2009), esp. chap. 3; for the use of slaves in the construction and maintenance of public roads, see O'Donovan, *Becoming Free*, 38–39.

15. For examples, see Louis Manigault to Charles Manigault, December 31, 1852, in James M. Clifton, ed., *Life and Labor on Argyle Island: Letters and Documents of a Savannah River Rice Plantation* (Savannah, Ga.: Beehive Press, 1978), 134–35; Ulrich B. Philips, *A History of Transportation in the Eastern Cotton Belt to 1860* (New York: Columbia University Press, 1908), 71–72; Edward H. Steel vs. P. Cazeaux, June 1820, Louisiana Supreme Court, New Orleans, case file no. 402, *Slavery, Abolition, and Social Justice* digital archive; Steel v. Cazeaux, June 1820, in Helen T. Catterall, ed., *Judicial Cases concerning American Slavery and the Negro* (New York: Octagon, 1986), 3:462.

16. See Charles Joseph Latrobe, *The Rambler in North America* (London: R. B. Seely & W. Burnside, 1835), 1:289–99, as well as Robert Gudmestad, *Steamboats and the Rise of the Cotton Kingdom* (Baton Rouge: Louisiana State University Press, 2011), 36–44; Thomas C. Buchanan, *Black Life on the Mississippi: Slaves, Free Blacks, and the Western Steamboat World* (Chapel Hill: University of North Carolina Press, 2004), chap. 2.

17. For a tantalizing glimpse of the scope and scale of enslaved people's continental and transcontinental movements, see, for example, Savannah, Georgia: Coastwise Slave Manifests, 1801–1860, and Savannah Coastwise Outward Slave Manifests, 1790–1859, ARC ID 1151775, U.S. Customs Service, Record Group Number 36, National Archives at Atlanta, Georgia; Slave Manifests of Coastwise Vessels Filed at New Orleans, Louisiana, 1807–1860, National Archives microfilm publication M1895, 30 rolls, Records of the U.S. Customs Service, Record Group 36, National Archives, Washington, D.C.

18. Robert H. Chapman to John Newton, October 14, 1824, Newton-Steel Family Papers, Folder 113, Box 10, Ulrich B. Phillips Collection, Manuscripts and Archives, Yale University Library, New Haven, Connecticut.

19. After years of internecine wrangling, scholars of nineteenth-century America have finally come around to a conclusion drawn nearly a century ago by Eric Williams, Edgar Tristram Thompson, and other students of New World plantation societies more generally: that slavery was not only compatible with but also a driving mechanism behind the rise of global capitalism. See Eric Williams, *Capitalism and Slavery* (1944; Chapel Hill: University of North Carolina Press, 1994); Edgar Tristram Thompson, *The Plantation*, ed. Sidney W. Mintz and George Baca (Columbia: University of South Carolina Press, 2010); Joshua D. Rothman, *Flush Times and Fever Dreams: A Story of Capitalism and Slavery in the Age of Jackson* (Athens: University of Georgia Press, 2012); Walter Johnson, *River of Dark Dreams: Slavery*

and Empire in the Cotton Kingdom (Cambridge, Mass.: Belknap Press, 2013); Baptist, *Half Has Never Been Told*; Calvin Schermerhorn, *The Business of Slavery and the Rise of American Capitalism, 1815–1860* (New Haven, Conn.: Yale University Press, 2015).

20. Richard Newman, ed., *Narrative of Henry Box Brown* (New York: Oxford University Press, 2002), 20.

21. David F. Dorr, *A Colored Man Round the World*, ed. Malini Johar Schueller (Ann Arbor: University of Michigan Press, 1999); William H. Robinson, *From Log Cabin to the Pulpit; or, Fifteen Years in Slavery* (Eau Claire, Wisc.: Tifft, 1913), 17; see also Bronwen Wilson and Paul Yachnin, eds., *Making Publics in Early Modern Europe: People, Things, Forms of Knowledge* (New York: Routledge, 2010), 1–19.

22. The geographic reach and complexity of slaves' tangled lives can be seen in the text of the signature books of the Freedmen's Savings and Trust Company, in the runaway advertisements and jailors' advertisements that proliferated in the back pages of the antebellum press, in grand jury presentments, in the narratives produced by the recently freed, in slave hire accounts, in court proceedings and witnesses' statements, and in slaveholders' own accounts.

23. William Webb, *The History of William Webb, Composed by Himself* (Detroit, Mich.: Egbert Hoekstra, 1872), 3–33, http://docsouth.unc.edu/neh/webb/webb.html; see also Susan Eva O'Donovan, "William Webb's World," *New York Times*, February 18, 2011.

24. Garland H. White to Hon. Wm. H. Seward, May 18, 1864, and Garland H. White to Hon. Wm. H. Seward, July 29, 1864, in Garland H. White, Compiled Military Service Records of Volunteer Union Soldiers Who Served with the United States Colored Troops, Records of the Adjutant General's Office, RG 94, National Archives, Washington, D.C.

25. This continued tendency surfaces, for instance, in Stephanie McCurry, *Confederate Reckoning: Power and Politics in the Civil War South* (Cambridge, Mass.: Harvard University Press, 2012), introduction and chaps. 1–2.

26. R. C. Gatlin to Sister, October 18, 1857, R. C. Gatlin to Sister, January 19, 1858, and R. C. Gatlin to Mary, February 27, 1860, all in R. C. Gatlin Papers, mss. 03828, Southern Historical Collection, University of North Carolina, Chapel Hill; Dorr, *Colored Man Round the World*; "Diary kept by Syndenham Moore during the Mexican-American War," 1846–47, Syndenham Moore Family Papers, Alabama Department of Archives and History, Montgomery. Between January 1841 and December 1844 at least sixty-six slaves embarked out of the Port of New Orleans bound for Havana, most of them returning a few weeks or months later; see, for example, Outward Slave Manifest, Port of New Orleans, March 31, 1843, Reel 23, M1895, entries for George and Thom (Frame 662) and Ben Howard and French (Frame 660), and June 2, 1843, Moses, Jim, Albert, and Wesley (Frame 746); Aisha K. Finch, *Rethinking Slave Rebellion in Cuba: La Escalera and the Insurgencies of 1841–1844* (Chapel Hill: University of North Carolina Press, 2015).

27. A good example are the domestic servants who regularly accompanied

their Low Country Georgia owners to the family's summer home in Providence, Rhode Island; see Charles Hoffman and Tess Hoffman, *North by South: The Two Lives of Richard James Arnold* (Athens: University of Georgia Press, 1998).

28. Marie to District Court, West Baton Rouge Parish, Louisiana, 1848, in *The Southern Debate over Slavery*, Volume 2: *Petitions to Southern County Courts, 1775–1867*, ed. Loren Schweninger (Urbana: University of Illinois Press, 2008), 249–50; Dorr, *Colored Man Round the World*; Houston Hartsfield Holloway, Houston Hartsfield Holloway: Autobiography, Houston Hartsfield Holloway Papers, 1894–1932, Manuscript Division, Library of Congress (unpublished transcript by David Paterson), 8–9.

29. Webb, *History of William Webb*, 3–33.

30. For Meme Phebe's semiannual pilgrimages between Georgia and Rhode Island, see Hoffman and Hoffman, *North by South*, xvii–xix, 1–7, 110; Outward Slave Manifest, Port of Savannah, June 7, 1825, May 4, 1826, [April] 1828, May 25, 1829, May 26, 1830, May 23, 1831, May 20, 1833, May 20, 1834, May 24, 1841; Inward Slave Manifest, Port of Savannah, [fall] 1839, all in Slave Manifests of Coastwise Vessels filed at Savannah, Georgia. For Ned and the other enslaved Tennesseans who were ordered west by their owners, see Outward Slave Manifest, Port of New Orleans, March 29, 1850, Ned et al., Frame 607, Reel 25, M1895; L. M. McDowell to My Dear Unkle, February 21, 1853, William G. Dickinson Papers, Southern Historical Collection, University of North Carolina, Chapel Hill. L. M. McDowell went on to elaborate in the same letter what he meant by "heterogenious comminglement." "We have the English, Irish, German, Frenchmen, Welchman, Italians, Portugeas, Polanders, Spainards, Chines, Chilaneans, East Indians, West Indians, The Greaser Mexicans, negroes & Indians, and in short some persons from almost all civilized parts of earth, and judging from their acts, some from uncivilized portions" as well.

31. Glymph, "Rose's War."

32. Elsa Barkley Brown, "Negotiating and Transforming the Public Sphere: African American Political Life in the Transition from Slavery to Freedom," *Public Culture* 7 (Fall 1994): 107–46.

"Us never had no big funerals or weddin's on de place"

Ritualizing Black Marriage in the Wake of Freedom

BRENDA E. STEVENSON

Slavery had destined many awful things, but perhaps the most appalling was its assault on the black family and even the rituals that designated marriage and family life.[1] Those masters who were the most brutal exerted, without discrimination, emotional hardship along with physical and sexual terror on enslaved families. Slave marriage, in their estimation and treatment, was even less than a farce, but rather a site of sadistic control and private, as well as public, dehumanization.

One extreme example must suffice here. Sam and Louisa Everett were born as slaves in tidewater Virginia. Their owner, "Big Jim" McClain, was vicious and voyeuristic, a rapist and slave breeder who did not hesitate to force his slaves to have "orgies" in his presence as a kind of sex show for McClain and his friends, who also were welcome to participate in "choosing for themselves the prettiest of the young women" and "sometimes" forcing "the unhappy husbands and lovers of their victims to look on." When McClain decided that Louisa and Sam should marry, Louisa recounted, he

> ordered Sam to pull off his shirt—that was all the McClain niggers wore—and
> he said to me: "Nor [the name Louisa's owner preferred], do you think you
> can stand this big nigger?" He had that old bull whip flung across his shoulder,
> and Lawd, that man could hit so hard! So I jes said "yassur, I guess so," and
> tried to hide my face so I couldn't see Sam's nakedness, but he made me look
> at him anyhow. Well, he told us what we must git busy and do in his presence,
> and we had to do it. After that we were considered man and wife. Me and Sam
> was a healthy pair and had fine, big babies, so I never had another man forced
> on me, thank God. Sam was kind to me and I learnt to love him.[2]

The only marital ritual they were allowed to perform was that of the sexual act—held in public for their masters and the others of their community to watch.[3]

The abuse of the marriage bed was not nearly all that slave couples endured. There were, of course, institutionalized separations and even lack of choice in a marriage partner. "When I was 21 years old," Jennie Hill of Missouri recalled, "I married. My husband worked on a farm a mile or so from the Fray place." Although they spoke the same vows as whites at their ceremony and Jennie was "proud" of her marriage, "performed by the 'educated nigger,'" the physical separation she, and eventually their children, endured from her husband and their father marked their slave status. "He belonged to another man. He had to stay on his farm and I on mine. That wasn't living—that was slavery," she added bitterly.[4]

Years after he was emancipated, Charles Grandy of Virginia was able to articulate his disappointment in his owner's banal ritualization of slave marriage, but he was especially resentful of the lack of choice in a marriage partner. According to Grandy, if a man desired a wife, his owner would buy one from a trader passing by, regardless of the man's, or woman's, preferences. The "bride" just had to be cheap and bear the physical markings of fertility. His owner's creation of a wedding vow for the two was just as insulting to Grandy's sense of what a marriage ritual should be. According to the former slave, "She would git off de wagon an' he would lead you bof to yo' cab'n an' stan you on de po'ch. He wouldn't go in. . . . He say somepin f'om de Bible an' fnish up wid dis: Dat you wife / Dat yo' huban' / Ise yo' Marser / She yo' Missus / You're married."[5]

Some enslaved persons did not have even the benefit of a few words spoken, or any type of ritual that signified the initiation of a marriage. Former slave woman Dora Franks was clear in her complaints about life before the Civil War in rural Alabama and Mississippi. Enslaved people, Franks complained, were not allowed to celebrate or ritualize family life. According to her, there were no ritualized events that signified either the beginning or end of a family. "Us never had no big fun'als or weddin's on de place," she noted. "Didn' have no marryin' o' any kin'. Folks in dem days jus' sorter hitched up together an' call deyse'ves man an' wife."[6]

When slavery ended, Dora Franks made certain that her new free status included the rituals of respectable citizenship, humanity, and domesticity that previously had been denied her family. In 1867, Dora married freedman Pete Franks. Unlike her mother, who had been forced into a concubinage relationship with a slaveholder, Dora married legally and bore her children legitimately. She had an elaborate wedding, sponsored

"The Marriage." From Emily C. Pearson, *Cousin Franck's Household;*
or, Scenes in the Old Dominion (Boston: Upham, Ford, and Olmstead, 1853),
between pages 168 and 169.

by her employers, followed by a "big supper." According to Dora: "All de
white folks an' de Niggers for miles a-round come to see us git married.
De Niggers had a big supper an' had a peck t'eat." Her husband, in
his own narrative, concurred with Dora's description of their wedding:
"When I was on de Cox place I met Dora an' us married. Dat was a big
weddin' an' a big feas'."[7]

Freedpeople hoped that legal, formalized marriages would allow them
a respected social identity and choice: in their marital partners; in where
the couple, and their children, would reside after marriage; and how
they would structure their households. They also hoped to choose the
ways, both private and public, that they would consummate and celebrate their unions. At the very least, they wanted to participate in a ritual
that publicly and legally recognized their unions. As such, former slaves'
perceptions of the importance of legal marriage linked their ideals of
emancipation to other former bondspersons who had managed to gain
freedom before 1865 in the United States, Canada, Mexico, or beyond.[8]
Hundreds of thousands, if not more, couples who had been married
while enslaved, or wanted to marry after slavery ended, did not hesitate
to participate in legally binding nuptials before the public, black and
white. These rituals pronounced to their families, communities, and the
larger world that they now had a right to claim marital relations, control

over the intimate aspects of their bodies and domestic households, and to bear, take care of, socialize, and maintain their children. Legalized marital rituals, they insisted, drew a line between slavery and freedom.

Slave Marital Rituals: An Overview

There were some marital rituals that masters typically imposed on their bondspeople. The use of the broom as a ritual object that signified marriage between bondswomen and men, for example, was perhaps the most prevalent form of antebellum slave marriage ceremony.[9] "Me and Julie jus' jumped over de broom in front of Marster and us was married. Dat was all dere was to it," Robert Shepherd of Oglethorpe, Georgia, noted. "Dat was de way most of de slave folks got married dem days."[10] Still, some southern slaves, such as Dora Franks, were not required, or allowed, to even jump the broom. Those who were, or chose to do so given that this was their only "option," sometimes found ways to ritualize it that were meaningful to them. As such, not everyone jumped the broom in the same manner; and even those who did ritualize this common household object ascribed different meanings to it. James Bolton, for one, recalled that when slaves married "the couple jined hands and jumped back-uds over the broomstick."[11] Paul Smith, who came from the same county in Georgia as Bolton, noted that "him and de gal come up to de big house to jump de broomstick 'fore deir white folkses. De gal jumped one way and de man de other."[12] Georgianna Gibbs of Virginia recalled that the slaves in her quarters had to jump three times over the broom before they were considered married.[13] Mary Reynolds from Louisiana stated that on her plantation in Concordia Parish, her master and mistress stood inside the door of a slave cabin holding a broom crosswise. As she and her groom stepped from the outside into the interior of the cabin, her mistress placed a flower wreath on Mary's head and the master pronounced the couple married.[14] Likewise, Julia White, from Little Rock, Arkansas, explained that at their "broomstick weddings," their mistress and master each held one end of the broom while the couple jumped over it.[15] At other places, owners mostly were witnesses, not active participants. Josephine Anderson of Florida noted that no one held the brooms at their weddings. She then went on to explain why the broom was so ritually important to those in her community: "Mos folks dem days got married by layin a broom on de floor an jumpin over it," she began. "Dat seals de marriage, an at de same time brings em good luck. Ya see brooms keeps hants away."[16] On Caroline Harris's farm in Virginia, the broom could

THE BROOMSTICK WEDDING.

"Look squar' at de broomstick ! All ready now ! one-two-three-jump ! "

"The Broomstick Wedding." From Mary Ashton Wright Livermore, *The Story of My Life; or, The Sunshine and Shadow of Seventy Years* (Hartford, Conn.: A. D. Worthington, 1897), p. 257. Courtesy of Hargrett Rare Book and Manuscript Library/University of Georgia Libraries.

bring bad luck if, while stepping over it, one touched it. "Ant Sue," Harris noted, "used to say which every one teched de stick was gonna die fust."[17]

The ritual of jumping the broom has not been found in African traditions but rather among Anglo-Saxon and Western European pre-Christian marriage and divorce rituals. Interpretations of the ritualistic meaning have been multiple, even lending itself to sexual analysis: the broomstick as a phallic symbol and the "jumping over" by a female as code for sexual intercourse.[18] Tempie Herndon from North Carolina, however, indicated instead that the broom was used in her marriage ceremony to Exeter as a site of public, gendered competition and ridicule that her owner imposed on the couple, where the ruler of the newly established slave household was determined. She explained that her master began:

> "Come on, Exeter, you and Tempie got to jump over de broom stick backwards. You got to do dat to see which one gwine be boss of your househol'." . . . Marse

George hold de broom about a foot high off de floor. De one dat jump over it backwards, and never touch handle, gwine boss de house. If both of dem jump over without touchin' it, dey won't gwine be no bossin', dey just gwine be congenial. I jumped first, and you ought to seed me. I sailed right over dat broom stick same as a cricket. But when Exeter jump he done had a big dram and his feets was so big and clumsy dat dey got all tangled up in dat broom and he fell headlong. Marse George he laugh and laugh, and told Exeter he gwine be bossed 'twell he scared to speak lessen I told him to speak.

The ruse, of course, was that Tempie's and George's masters remained as the true "bosses" of the slave couple's marital home. Exeter's patriarchal role was roundly usurped by the power George Herndon exercised over his wife Tempie and all of their children, as well as the control that Snipes Durham, Exeter's master, exercised over him. Tempie's role as wife and mother was no more secure. Her children worked for, and had to obey, George and Elizabeth Herndon, not Tempie or Exeter Durham, regardless of who jumped backward the highest.[19]

Tempie Herndon's wedding rituals are an interesting combination of the ceremonial features enslaved persons most typically had to perform and those rituals that many chose to perform, if they could afford them, after they were freed. Not only had Exeter and Tempie jumped the broom—the typical hallmark of a slave marriage—they also were the recipients of an exceptional slave wedding and reception—a clear indication of Tempie's favored status in her master's home. As the bride described it, she was dressed all in white: dress, shoes, long gloves, and a veil her mistress made out of a curtain. Someone even played the wedding march on the Herndon family piano to accompany the couple as they walked down the aisle. Tempie and Exeter then kneeled before a beautiful altar that Tempie's mistress had decorated herself with candles and roses, while Uncle Edmond Kirby, the plantation's black preacher, performed the ceremony. Afterward, there was a reception of barbequed shoat, and an iced white wedding cake, liquor, and dancing.[20] These nuptials, of course, were not legally relevant, and the solemnity of the event soon was undermined by Master Herndon's insistence on the broom-jumping contest. Nonetheless, the exceptional character of the couple's earlier ritual suggested to other black onlookers an alternative nuptial event that included special attire, food, entertainment, and spoken vows.

While this kind of elaborate wedding celebration was rare for slaves, some of the more privileged domestics did experience similar festivities. Former slave James Bolton of Georgia, for example, spoke openly of the different kinds of wedding rituals that indicated an operative plantation class system consisting of field slaves, house slaves, and slaveholding whites. Location, audience, the time spent on and at the event, and the ritualized elements in play were essential variables. Bolton explained that field slaves, who comprised the vast majority of the enslaved, jumped the broom in the quarters with other bondspersons acting as principal witnesses. House slaves, Bolton added, also jumped the broom but sometimes had some religious reading from the Bible, typically located on their owner's back porch or yard, with their master and mistress in attendance. Elite whites, on the other hand, usually exchanged elaborate religious vows in the master's parlor with the white community and family serving as witnesses inside the owner's home, while their slaves stood outside and looked through the window. Field and house slaves' weddings took place on their days off and usually lasted through the evening. Elite slaveholders' wedding rituals, however, were weeklong events, filled with elaborate dinners and even more elaborate gifts. As Ida Rigeley of Arkansas noted: "When the white folks had a wedding it lasted a week. They had a second day dress and a third day dress and had suppers and dinner receptions about among the kinfolks. They had big chests full of quilts and coverlets and counterpanes they been packing back. Some of them would have big dances. A wedding would last a week, night and day."[21] Certainly the symbolism that these comparative locations, vows, timing, clothing, food, and audience indicate abound in James Bolton's and Ida Rigeley's descriptions—even the marriages of slave domestics were considered outside the bounds of legitimacy and importance that the "master's parlor" and days away from work represented.

As Rigeley's description also indicates, the differences between slave and slaveholder weddings and, as such, their status in society were sealed also by the exchange of property as wedding "gifts." Some newly married slave couples, such as Tempie and Exeter, received a slave cabin to live in and the broom they jumped. Some might also have been given a space in the provision grounds and seed. All of these "gifts," however, benefited slaveholders as much as slaves and could be reclaimed by owners whenever they pleased. Slaveholders, conversely, made certain that their children not only had land and appropriate household goods to begin their married lives financially stable, but also labor. Planter weddings wreaked havoc on slave marriages and families because many masters did not hesitate to divide their black "property," married or not, and distribute them as wedding gifts for their own offspring. Bill Homer of Louisiana and Texas explained what happened when his young mistress married: "In de year of 1860, Missy Mary gits married to Bill Johnson and at dat weddin' massa Homer gives me and 49 other niggers to her for de weddin' present. Massa Johnson's father gives him 50 niggers too. Dey has a gran' weddin'. . . . After de weddin' was over, dey gives de couple de infare. Dere's whar dis nigger comes in. I and de other niggers was lined up, all with de clean clothes on and den de massa say, 'For to give my lovin' daughter de start, I gives you dese 50 niggers.' Massa Bill's father done de same for his son, and dere we'uns was, 100."[22]

Freedpeople's Marriage Rituals

Freedpeople brought their experiences with marriage rituals and community and class distinctions, along with their ideals regarding the rights acquired through legal marriage, to bear on the choices they made when they either renewed their vows or took them for the first time. Against the backdrop of the decisions that couples had to make about wedding dresses, cakes, vows, dowries, and dances flowed the changing legal and cultural landscapes that defined black domestic life in the Reconstruction and post-Reconstruction South.

The federal government implemented policies, primarily through military officials and especially the Freedmen's Bureau, that were supposed to regularize the marriage status of the newly freed in accordance with

"Marriage of a Colored Soldier." From *Harper's Weekly*, June 30, 1866.

the ideas and, if possible, the ideals of Christian citizens. Freedmen's Bureau officials, along with northern freedmen's aid and missionary societies who came to the South as early as 1861 to assist in the transition from slavery to freedom, were determined that emancipated blacks should take on the marital constructs to create nuclear, patriarchal families that would project images of a new, civilized black citizenry worthy of freedom and participation in the nation's body politic and society.[23] These cultural pressures intensified as the number of black churches increased throughout the South and membership required a certain adherence to rules of sexual abstinence outside of marriage and monogamy during marriage. All of these organizations exhorted former slaves to try to remain with the spouses and children that they had at the time of their freedom; to abandon multiple liaisons; to seek written documentation, in the form of marriage licenses and certificates, of their marital state; and to live peaceably as husband and wife under one roof, all working for the support and success of family members. Postbellum southern state legislators, via their constitutional conventions and lawmaking abilities, also weighed in on creating rules and regulations to validate, and control, the institution of black marriage. Those legislators with an eye to supporting freedmen's marriages so that white landholders who needed labor might benefit from the work of family groups, rather than individuals, passed laws accordingly. The Georgia legislature, for example, declared that all African American men and women residing together as husband and wife, unless legally married to someone else, were married.[24]

Among this confusing, complicated, and sometimes conflicting patchwork of "instructions" from various sources, most freed couples eagerly sought legitimacy for their relationships and the children that had been, and would be, born of them. While some continued to "jump the broom" even after freedom,[25] and others across the South, such as Malindy Maxwell's parents, who had been married while enslaved, were told that their original "marriage would stand,"[26] it was not unusual for newly freed couples, anxious to legalize their marriage relations, to participate in group or even mass marriages that occurred at military camps, at churches, at the homes of clergy, in Freedmen's Bureau offices, and in district court houses. Tens of thousands, and perhaps more, legally joined in matrimony at these sites and under these conditions.[27] Mary Biddy from Florida explained that soon after emancipation, "A big supper was given, it was early, about twenty-five slave couples attended. There was gaiety and laughter. A barrel of lemonade was served. A big time was had by all, then those couples who desired to remain together were joined in wedlock according to civil custom. The party broke up in the early hours of the morning."[28] Charlotte Forten, while teaching among the freedmen on Saint Helena Island, South Carolina, under the auspices of the Port Royal Relief Association, displayed some of the typical "Yankee" cultural snobbery when she noted in her diary on November 23, 1863:

> Six couples were married to-day. Some of the dresses were unique. Am sure one must have worn a cast-off dress of her mistreses's. It looks like white silk covered with lace. The lace sleeves, and other trimmings were in rather a decayed state and the white cotton gloves were well ventilated. But the bride looked none the less happy for that. Only one had the slightest claim to good looks, and she was a demure little thing with a neat, plain silk dress on. T'was amusing to see some of the headdresses. One . . . was very ridiculous. But no matter for that. I am truly glad the poor creatures are trying to live right and virtuous lives.[29]

The recently freed were not at all put off by "amused" outsiders or irate former masters who resented blacks "putting on airs" and "mimicking" their "betters." Freedpeople went right to the point of why they chose to remarry: "My mother married at Thomas Pope's place," a former South Carolinian slave recalled, "and he had old man Ned Pearson, a nigger who could read and write, to marry 'em. He married lots of niggers den. Atter de war many niggers married over agin, 'cause dey didn't know if de first marriage was good or not."[30] Charlie Davis, also of South Carolina, explained in similar fashion: "My mammy and daddy got married after freedom, 'cause they didn't git de time for a weddin' befo'. They called deirselves man and wife a long time befo' they was really married."[31] Willis Dukes wanted to be certain of the legitimacy of his postbellum marriage, noting: "We didn't jump over no broom neither. We was married like white folks wid flowers and cake and everything."[32] As far as Dukes was concerned, because he and his bride shared the same marital rituals as whites—their marriage had to be legitimate. Former slave Gus Clark, who had lived in both Virginia and Mississippi, also was clear: "I'se had three wives. I didn't have no weddin's, but I mar'ied 'em 'cordin to law. I woan stay with one no other way. My fust two wives is dead."[33] Mildred Graves of Fredericksburg, Virginia, recalled that as a slave, her mistress had given her a cast-off dress and she "stepped over de broomstick," but "arter de war we had a real sho' nuff weddin' wid a preacher. Dat cost a dollar."[34] Mary Reynolds from Texas, who also had been married by stepping across the broom, noted: "After freedom I git married and have it put in the book by the Preacher."[35]

Those who decided, or had the ability, to marry with elaborate rituals and celebrations brought serious thought and planning to the manifestations of their marital bonds. Clothing, food, location, audience, their vows, the license, the celebrant, and the dance celebration were all important items to consider since each was an indication, a declaration, of one's free status. These preparations also suggest the communal efforts and ties, black and white, that shaped black life in the first decades after slavery ended.

Both freedmen and women believed that the clothes they wore when they married were important indicators of their new status as free people who had the right to commit themselves to a legally binding and/or God-ordained union. For women, it also was the opportunity of a lifetime to show off their physical beauty and proclaim their moral purity. These two images stood in stark contrast to popular white ideas of enslaved black womanhood as morally debased and physically unappealing that freedpeople hoped to counter.

Not surprisingly, even decades after their weddings, freedwomen spoke lovingly of their bridal dresses. Their memories were a celebration of the choice, beauty, femininity, and extravagance that freedom manifested in the ritualized clothing they wore on their special day. Some dresses were long and white, and many brides wore white veils as well—symbols of moral and sexual purity. Beneath their veils, some women had powdered faces, but according to Eliza Washington of Arkansas, "no paint."[36] Molly Horn, also from Arkansas, recounted that "Mama bought me a pure white veil. I was dressed all in white."[37] So, too, was Mandy Hadnot of Texas who explained that she "had purty long, black hair and a veil with a ribbon 'round de fron.'"[38] Nellie Smith, a successful cake baker in Athens, Georgia, was delighted to give the details of her first wedding, especially her attire: "I wore a white dress made with a tight-fittin' waist and a long, full skirt that was jus' covered with ruffles. My sleeves was tight at the wrists but puffed at the shoulders, and my long veil of white net was fastened to my head with pretty flowers. I was a mighty dressed up bride." Nellie wore a "very pretty, plain, white dress" when she married the second time.[39] Liza Jones from Texas wore a "white Tarleton dress with de white Tarleton wig." The white dress and wig, Liza explained, were signs "you ain't never done no wrong sin and gwinter keep bein' good."[40]

Other colors and styles for bridal wear also prevailed and suggested that freedwomen's bridal fashion tastes were determined by one's age, generation, previous marital status, locale, religious beliefs, and financial standing. Less elaborate bridal clothing, no doubt, indicated operative class distinctions. Most, for example, certainly could not afford Liza Jones's elaborate "Tarleton" look. Still, the relative "finery" of a woman's wedding ensemble allowed her to claim a physical beauty, femininity, and moral character rarely possible as a slave. Josephine Anderson from Florida recalled that her wedding dress was blue—"blue for true," she explained. "I thought it was the prettiest dress I ever see."[41] "I ain't never seed nothin' lak dat pretty flowerdy weddin' dress dat I wore and I had de prettiest hat and things dat I ever seed," Julia Cole of Georgia recounted.[42] Minerva Edwards of Texas wore a "blue serge suit."[43] "The dress I married in was red silk," Susan MacIntosh of Georgia indicated.[44] Julia Larken, whose financial resources no doubt probably were more typical of most freedwomen, wore a "new calico dress," as did Will Sheets's bride.[45] Nettie McCree of Georgia wore a "black silk dress . . . [that] had a overskirt of blue that was scalloped 'round de bottom." Her husband, Ed, added with pride: "I never will forgit how you looked dat day." Nettie also wore white silk gloves.[46] William McWhorter could not remember precisely what his wife wore, but still he noted: "I'se tellin' you she looked pretty and sweet to me."[47] Few men could have hoped to have their brides beautifully adorned when enslaved, not only because owners tightly controlled clothing allocations, design, and quality, but also because masters retained the most "beautiful" slave women for concubinage.[48]

For most freedwomen, their wedding dress was the most lovely piece of clothing they ever owned. Some even planned to be buried in theirs.[49] Indeed, wedding attire was so important that brides rarely refused assistance in acquiring the various items needed for their presentation/transformation. They reached out to former mistresses, current employers, kin, and grooms for help. Lula Taylor's father, for example, purchased all of his wife's wedding clothing.[50] Bunny Bond recalled that the woman she was keeping house for at the time gave her a "nice white silk dress," while her previous owner "lent" her "one of her chemisette, a corset cover, and a dress that had ruffles around the bottom. It was wide." Bunny also borrowed a used veil from a freedwoman associate.[51] Harriet Jones, of North Carolina and Texas, wore one of her former mistresses' dresses, "red stockin's and a pair of brand new shoes and a wide brim hat," when she married Bill Jones the year after freedom.[52] Betty Curlett's employer, who also was the white woman who raised her, made her wedding dress.[53]

These brides indicated, in the assemblage of clothing that they wore on this most special day, who were operative members of their communities and kinship networks as freedpeople. The necessity to beg, borrow, and, in some instances, steal wedding clothing also suggests the precarious economic status of freedwomen, many of whom could not afford this extraordinary clothing on their own.[54] Grooms often found themselves in the same predicament. Some of this activity indicates as well the fluctuating economic relations between working southern white and black women at the time when fledgling local economies proved burdensome for both. Susan MacIntosh, for example, bought her clothing second-hand from a local white woman.[55] The white silk gloves that Nettie Mc-Cree wore at her wedding were given to her by a local white seamstress whom Nettie patronized. The seamstress may have wanted to thank Nettie for purchasing her wedding dress from her.[56]

Grooms, like their brides, placed great importance on their wedding attire. Dressing for their wedding afforded them the chance to doff their work clothes and take on the look of sophisticated gentlemen, in striking contrast to nineteenth-century racist stereotypes of freedmen being beastlike in manners, intelligence, appearance, and appetite.[57] Ike Derricotte from Athens, Georgia, sported a Prince Albert coat in which he took such pride that he intended to will it to his children.[58] Sam Bond of Arkansas wore a tie, white vest, watch, and gold chain, all borrowed from a local attorney.[59] Nellie Smith's bridegroom stood at the altar in a "real dark-colored cutaway coat with a white vest."[60] Anderson Edwards also wore a Prince Albert cutaway suit,[61] as did Ed McCree, who completed his ensemble with a pair of brown pants, a white shirt, and a vest.[62] Julia Larken's private wedding afforded her groom the opportunity to dress much less formally. Given the expense of formal wear and the inability to acquire it in the rural countryside, Matthew's dress probably was more typical. According to his bride, he "wore some new blue jeans breeches."[63]

Private ceremonies, such as that of Julia and Matthew Larken, usually included the couple, kinfolk, a few close friends, and sometimes employers. The gathering took place at the courthouse or at the home of a preacher, the bride, an employer, or a former owner. Josephine Anderson was married at a local courthouse in Florida.[64] Laura Thornton recalled that she had a marriage license and was married by the local justice of the peace. "I was married right at home where me and my old man stayed. Wasn't nobody there but me and him and another man named Dr. Bryant," she explained.[65] Betty Curlett had a minister marry her in her home.[66] Sylvia Durant of Marion, South Carolina, was married by a minister in the local Bethel Methodist Episcopal Church.[67] Ministers could be black or white, depending on the communal and/or religious affiliations of the couple. Julia Larken was married by "Reverend Hargrove, de white folks preacher."[68] Molly Horn recalled that she had a "colored preacher" marry her in Arkansas.[69]

Fannie Berry also was married by a local black preacher, Elder Williams, in Appomattox County, Virginia. Still, her wedding was hardly a "private affair." Fanny was not the type of freedwoman to perform any important ritual quietly or privately. She boldly splashed her free status and the symbol of her new respectability and social legitimacy for the entire community, black and white, to see. Fannie held her wedding at night at her white employer's house; and she was waited on by two white female friends who accompanied her down the aisle with lighted lanterns. Most of those in attendance at her wedding and reception were black, although Fannie credited her white employers with providing the food and the space for the party. "After marriage de white folks give me a 'ception,'" Fannie explained delightedly. "An', honey, talkin' 'bout a table—hit wuz stretched clean 'cross de dinin' room. We had everythin' to eat you could call for. No, didn't have no common eats. We could sing in dar, an' dance ol' squar' dance all us choosed, ha! ha! ha! Lord! Lord! I can see dem gals now on dat flo'; jes skippin' an' a trottin'. An' honey, dar wuz no white folks to set down an' eat 'fo yo'."[70]

Fannie Berry was hardly the only former slave whose wedding was subsidized by white employers or associates. Those whites who offered assistance usually were longtime associates, often stretching back to the slave era. Their help, on the one hand, no doubt was deemed a blessing, perhaps even an honor by those freedpersons who were their beneficiaries. On the other hand, it also suggests how involved white employers were in the personal lives of the blacks who worked for them. This seeming act of generosity often hid the continued financial exploitation landholding whites imposed on black laborers, leaving them little financial ability to finance their own weddings or to create new, separate households. It also tied their labor, and that of the families derived from the couple or their extended kin, to labor-hungry landholders.[71]

Henry Davis, who resided in South Carolina, recalled that both he and his bride's employers (who had been their owners before emancipation) encouraged them to have a large wedding. Not only did they help with the wedding cost and arrangements, they also provided them with gifts to prepare Henry's new household. "Her white folks give her a trousseau," Henry explained, "and mine give me a bedstead, cotton mattress, and two feather pillows."[72] Molly Horn relied on a local white woman's help for both her wedding and reception.[73] Likewise, Walter Cain and his bride in South Carolina married at "Mr. Walther Spearman's house, a good white man," and "the white folks give us a good supper after the wedding."[74] So, too, did Sam Davis's white "folks." Louisa, Sam's wife, had to complain, however, that the cost of their white patronage was irritating—"they sho' did tease Sam dat day," she recounted.[75] Bunny Bond's white employers and associates provided not only attire for both the bride and groom, but also her wedding cakes.[76] Anderson and Minerva Edwards had a large Texas wedding with more than a hundred people attending. The two had lived on adjoining plantations when they were enslaved. Their former owners gave them an "infair and a big dinner" the day afterward.[77] And Mandy Hadnot noted with pride that "us marry right in de parlor of de mistus house. De white man preacher marry us and mistus give me 'way. . . . De weddin' feas' was strawberry ice cream and yaller cake. Ole mistus giv me my bedstead, one of her purtiest ones, and de set dishes and glasses us eat de weddin' dinner outta."[78] Mandy felt so obliged to her employer, however, that she put off leaving immediately with her husband. "Ole mistus cry so when I hafter leave dat I stay for three weeks after I marry," she explained.[79] Regardless of the ties that employers and former owners tried to strengthen or reestablish with support for freedmen and women's wedding rituals, little could dampen the spirit of celebration derived from these rituals that they largely designed, even if elite whites provided some of the material support for them.

Former slave woman Harriet Gresham recalled gleefully her grand wedding to a member of the First Company, Thirty-fifth Regiment, at a military headquarters in South Carolina.[80] Harriet Jones of Texas also recalled with great detail her large, celebratory wedding and the vows she and her husband took before a biracial crowd under a large elm tree. Her wedding was officiated by a local minister. Two flower girls held her gown's train. The wedding rituals and customs she described from that day drew both on Christian and African indigenous beliefs. They also indicate the important levels of support—material, social, and cultural— that black family members offered their brides and grooms. According to Harriet: "De [Christian] preacher say, 'Bill, does you take dis woman to be you lawful wife?' and Bill say he will. Den he say, 'Harriet, will you take dis nigger to be you lawful boss and do jes' what he say?' Den we signs de book and de preacher say, 'I quotes from de scripture: "'Dark and stormy may come de weather, I jines dis man and woman together. Let none but Him what make de thunder, Put dis man and woman asunder."[81] Bill gave Harriet a gold ring, a ritualistic luxury item, ripe with multiple public declarations of the couple's unending circle of love; Bill's ability to support his wife and future family; and the great value Harriet was to her husband. At the end of their ceremony, the happy couple was regaled with a beautifully set table covered by a white cloth and decorated with red berries, provided by Harriet's former mistress. They feasted on "barbecue pig and roast sweet 'taters and dumplin's and pies and cake." It was at the reception that Harriet's mother presented the bride with a wedding present that symbolized their African past—a rabbit's toe for good luck. According to Harriet, her mother recited to her as she handed over the ritualized animal appendage: "Here take dis lil gift, and place it near you heart; It keep away dat li'l riff What causes folks to part." Harriet's mother offered the bride a gentle reminder of her family's cultural past, one on which they had relied for generations for survival and marital bliss. Bill and Harriet might now be "free," with the ability to marry in the same manner and, hopefully, with the same benefits as whites, her mother indicated, but they should not abandon their traditional ways of ritualizing and protecting marriage bonds. This rabbit's toe, Harriet's mother went on to explain, was so lucky that it was worth much more than the ritualized items typically valued at free people's marriages— monetary gifts and wedding rings—"a million dimes or more. More'n all de weddin' rings." After dinner, the wedding party, led by the bride and groom, paraded to "Marse Watson's saddleshop to dance and dance all night."[82]

Ceremonies and receptions, of course, were integral parts of freedpersons' wedding rituals. Being able to have a legitimate marriage and the rights that it signified were more than ample reasons for the couple, their kin, and their community of freed blacks to celebrate. Night weddings, such as Fannie Berry's, were somewhat popular. Molly Horn in Arkansas also married at night. She "borrowed lamps and had em settin' about." Like Fannie as well, Molly had a sumptuous wedding meal—"roast pork, goose and all sorter pies," along with several cakes.[83] Others had beef, pork, turkey, and antelope.[84] Martha Colquitt, who had a "big weddin" at her sister's house, had two "fine dinners"—one given by her family, and the other by her husband's family, with the help of his former employers.[85] Alex Pope of Georgia recalled that he "had a awful big weddin' de fust time. . . . Us drunk and et and danced and cut de buc most all night long." Even Pope's white neighbor was impressed, commenting that "he never seed sich a weddin' in his life."[86]

Most receptions, undoubtedly, were much more modest and, like those significantly less elaborate wedding clothes and locations, suggested the class differences found among southern freedpeople. These distinctions derived from numerous sources, but primarily diverse levels of access to the southern economy as a result of varying skill and educational levels, the ability to acquire land, tools and work animals, an operative color hierarchy, and the opportunity to take advantage of white patronage or black familial support. Warren McKinney and his bride, for example, had a substantial wedding supper, provided by both of their families.[87] Sylvia Durant of South Carolina,[88] on the other hand, like Susan MacIntosh in Georgia, had "nothing but pound cake en wine."[89]

Wedding cakes, which symbolized the sweetness of the love and commitment between the couple, were particularly important ritual food objects. They were usual fare, even for the most routine marital celebrations. Most cakes probably were plain, like those of Sylvia Durant, but others could be very elaborate. A favorite was a yellow cake with white icing that had the engagement ring baked inside.[90] Nellie Smith from Athens, Georgia, bragged of her special dessert: "I think my weddin' cake was 'bout the biggest one I ever saw baked in one of them old ovens in the open fireplace. They iced it in white and decorated it with grapes."[91]

Former enslaved men and women such as the Durants, Smiths, Horns, and Franks entered their postbellum lives with diverse ideas and ideals of freedom. Most significant was the opportunity to have families beyond the abusive reach of former masters and the state that had supported the slave regime. To be free meant having a legitimate social identity that permitted legal marriages and, through those marriages, parental and patriarchal rights meant to support, protect, and provide a haven for freed families. Freedom, as such, signified taking on the mantle of respectable and respected man- and womanhood and its gendered connotations, symbolized, in part, by the ritualization of marriage. Wedding clothing was supposed to publicly and privately transform the stereotypical image of the beastly, uncouth, simple slave male to that of the proper, if not stately, man ready to lead and support his family and to participate as an equal in southern civic society. Likewise, wedding gowns, gloves, veils, and other finery, often in white, were meant to establish the physical beauty, virginal purity, moral character, and maternal nature of black womanhood, so maligned and savaged by their rampant physical, psychological, and sexual abuse as slaves. The ministers, judges, generals, and literate blacks who pronounced freedpeople's nuptials, handed out marriage licenses and certificates, or recorded the events in Bibles and official rosters helped document a new, "legitimate" freed black social identity. Wedding feasts and dances underscored the social importance of marriage and reaffirmed familial and communal ties in the black populace, even while distinctions in the actual details of the wedding (size, cost, costumes, gifts received, location, and even cultural items chosen to ritualize) may have helped affirm new, or preexisting, class and cultural differentiations. The participation of whites in freedpersons' marriage rituals was a reminder of the lingering economic marginality of freedmen and women and the continuing importance of black labor to employers and former owners. All in all, however, legal marriages, and the rituals that initiated them, were a bright spot in the lives of those free persons after the Civil War struggling against the overwhelming tide of popular southern white determination to deny black citizenship, respectability, masculinity, femininity, and autonomy.

NOTES

1. Regarding slave family life in the antebellum United States, see Brenda E. Stevenson, *Life in Black and White: Family and Community in the Slave South* (New York: Oxford University Press, 1996), 187–257.

2. United States Work Projects Administration, *Slave Narratives: A Folk History of Slavery in the United States from Interviews with Former Slaves* (hereafter cited as *WPA Slave Narratives*), *Florida Narratives*, Kindle Edition, Kindle location 1039–54.

3. *WPA Slave Narratives* (Florida), Kindle location 1079.

4. John Blassingame, ed., *Slave Testimony: Two Centuries of Letters, Speeches, Interviews, and Autobiographies* (Baton Rouge: Louisiana State University Press, 1977), 591–92.

5. Charles L. Perdue Jr., Thomas E. Barden, and Robert K. Phillips, eds., *Weevils in the Wheat: Interviews with Virginia Ex-Slaves* (Charlottesville: University Press of Virginia, 1976), 118.

6. *WPA Slave Narratives, Mississippi Narratives*, Kindle Edition, kindle location 499–536.

7. *WPA Narratives* (Mississippi), Kindle location 590–91.

8. William Still, ed., *The Underground Railroad: A Record of Facts, Authentic Narratives, Letters, &c., Narrating the Hardships, Hair-Breadth Escapes and Death Struggles of the . . . and Others, or Witnessed by the Author*, Kindle Edition, Kindle locations 5604–9, 5896, 7702–5, 8338.

9. For an exception, see *WPA Slave Narratives, Arkansas Narratives*, Part 6, Kindle Edition, Kindle locations 862–63.

10. *WPA Slave Narratives, Georgia Narratives*, Part 3, Kindle Edition, Kindle location 2582–87.

11. *WPA Slave Narratives, Georgia Narratives*, Part 1, Kindle Edition, Kindle locations 987–89.

12. *WPA Slave Narratives* (Georgia, pt. 3), Kindle location 3302–7.

13. Benjamin Drew, ed., *A North-Side View of Slavery, the Refugee; or the Narratives*

of Fugitive Slaves in Canada Related by Themselves with an Account of the History and Condition of the Colored Population of Upper Canada (Boston: John Jewett, 1856), 31.

14. James Mellon, ed., *Bullwhip Days: The Slaves Remember, an Oral History* (New York: Weidenfeld & Nicolson, 1988), 22.

15. *WPA Slave Narratives, Arkansas Narratives*, Part 7, Kindle Edition, p. 74.

16. *WPA Slave Narratives* (Florida), Kindle location 57–62.

17. Perdue et al., *Weevils in the Wheat*, 129.

18. Regarding jumping-the-broom marriage traditions, see Alan Dundes, "Jumping the Broom: On the Origin and Meaning of an African American Wedding Custom," *Journal of American Folklore* 109, no. 433 (Summer 1996): 324–29; Stevenson, *Life in Black and White*, 228–29; Randal Day and Daniel Hook, "A Short History of Divorce: Jumping the Broom—and Back Again," *Journal of Divorce* 10, no. 3/4 (Spring/Summer 1987): 238–47.

19. Norman Yetman, ed., *Voices from Slavery: 100 Authentic Slave Narratives* (Mineola, N.Y.: Dover, 1970, 2000), 164.

20. Ibid.

21. *WPA Slave Narratives, Arkansas Narratives*, Part 6, Kindle Edition, Kindle locations 489–92.

22. *WPA Slave Narratives, Texas Narratives*, Part 2, Kindle Edition, Kindle locations 1827–29.

23. Eric Foner, *Reconstruction: America's Unfinished Revolution, 1863–1877* (New York: Harper & Row, 1988), 82–87; Jacqueline Jones, *Labor of Love, Labor of Sorrow: Black Women, Work, and the Family from Slavery to the Present* (New York: Basic Books, 1985), 62.

24. Susan Eva O'Donovan, *Becoming Free in the Cotton South* (Cambridge, Mass.: Harvard University Press, 2007), 194.

25. Josephine Allen of Florida, for example, noted that "most folks dem days got married by layin a broom on de floor an jumpin over it." *WPA Slave Narratives* (Florida), Kindle location 57–62.

26. *WPA Slave Narratives, Arkansas Narratives*, Part 5, Kindle Edition, pp. 42–43.

27. For a discussion of the roles of the Freedmen's Bureau and other aid and missionary societies in freedmen's marriage, see, for example, Reginald Washington, "Sealing the Sacred Bonds of Holy Matrimony: Freedmen's Bureau Marriage Records," *Prologue* (Spring 2005), http://www.archives.gov/publications/prologue/2005/spring/freedman-marriage-recs.html; Noralee Frankel, "Slave Women to Free Women: The National Archives and Black Women's History in the Civil War Era," *Prologue* (Summer 1997), http://www.archives.gov/publications/prologue/1997/summer/slave-women.html.

28. *WPA Slave Narratives* (Florida), Kindle location 351–63.

29. Brenda E. Stevenson, ed., *The Journals of Charlotte Forten Grimke* (New York: Oxford University Press, 1988), 402.

30. *WPA Slave Narratives, South Carolina Narratives*, Part 1, Kindle Edition, Kindle location 3877–79.

31. Ibid., Kindle location 2984–86.

32. *WPA Slave Narratives* (Florida), Kindle location 1026–28.

33. *WPA Slave Narratives* (Mississippi), Kindle location 255–56.

34. Perdue et al., *Weevils in the Wheat*, 122.

35. *WPA Slave Narratives, Texas Narratives*, Part 3, Kindle Edition, Kindle location 2605.

36. *WPA Slave Narratives, Arkansas Narratives*, Part 7, Kindle Edition, p. 40.

37. *WPA Slave Narratives, Arkansas Narratives*, Part 3, Kindle Edition, Kindle location 3315–20.

38. *WPA Slave Narratives, Texas Narratives*, Part 2, Kindle Edition, Kindle location 1307–11.

39. *WPA Slave Narratives* (Georgia, pt. 3), Kindle location 3125–27.

40. *WPA Slave Narratives* (Texas, pt. 2), Kindle location 2853–55.

41. *WPA Slave Narratives* (Florida), Kindle location 57–62.

42. *WPA Slave Narratives, Georgia Narratives*, Part 1, Kindle Edition, Kindle location 2284–86.

43. *WPA Slave Narratives* (Texas, pt. 2), Kindle location 242–45.

44. *WPA Slave Narratives* (Georgia, pt. 3), Kindle location 906–8.

45. Ibid., Kindle location 461–63, 2399–400.

46. Ibid., Kindle location 655–63.

47. Ibid., Kindle location 1051–52.

48. Sumptuary laws, for example, existed in the colonial era and customarily throughout the antebellum period. See, for example, "An Act for the Better Ordering and Governing Negroes and Other Slaves in This Province," http:// www.teachingushistory.org/pdfs/Transciptionof1740SlaveCodes.pdf. Regarding physically appealing women forced into concubinage, see Brenda E. Stevenson, "'What's Love Got to Do with It?': Concubinage and Enslaved Black Women and Girls in the Antebellum South," *Journal of African American History* 98, no. 1 (Winter 2013): 99–125.

49. *WPA Slave Narratives* (Georgia, pt. 1), Kindle location 1320–24; *WPA Slave Narratives* (Arkansas, pt. 6), Kindle location 2595–99.

50. *WPA Slave Narratives* (Arkansas, pt. 6), Kindle location 2592–99.

51. *WPA Slave Narratives, Arkansas Narratives*, Part 1, Kindle Edition, Kindle location 1919–26.

52. *WPA Slave Narratives* (Texas, pt. 2), Kindle location 2748–57.

53. *WPA Slave Narratives, Arkansas Narratives*, Part 2, Kindle Edition, Kindle location 841.

54. Easter Brown of Athens, Georgia, accused a black woman of stealing her wedding dress. *WPA Slave Narratives* (Georgia, pt. 1), Kindle location 1320–24.

55. *WPA Slave Narratives* (Georgia, pt. 3), Kindle location 906–8.

56. Ibid., Kindle location 661–63.

57. See, for example, Monica L. Miller, *Slaves to Fashion: Black Dandyism and*

the Styling of Black Diasporic Identity (Durham, N.C.: Duke University Press, 2009), 77–136.

58. *WPA Slave Narratives* (Georgia, pt. 1), Kindle location 2703–5.

59. *WPA Slave Narratives* (Arkansas, pt. 1), Kindle location 1925–26.

60. *WPA Slave Narratives* (Georgia, pt. 3), Kindle location 3125–27.

61. *WPA Slave Narratives* (Texas, pt. 2), Kindle location 242–45.

62. *WPA Slave Narratives* (Georgia, pt. 3), Kindle location 655–63.

63. Ibid., Kindle location 461–63.

64. *WPA Slave Narratives* (Florida), Kindle location 57–62.

65. *WPA Slave Narratives* (Arkansas, pt. 6), Kindle location 3163–65.

66. *WPA Slave Narratives* (Arkansas, pt. 2), Kindle location 841.

67. *WPA Slave Narratives* (South Carolina, pt.1), Kindle location 4106–10.

68. *WPA Slave Narratives* (Georgia, pt. 3), Kindle location 461–63.

69. *WPA Slave Narratives, Arkansas Narratives,* Part 3, Kindle Edition, Kindle location 3320.

70. Perdue et al., *Weevils in the Wheat,* 36.

71. Regarding black labor in Reconstruction and post-Reconstruction South, see, for example, Leon Litwack, *Trouble in Mind: Black Southerners in the Age of Jim Crow* (New York: Knopf, 1998), 117–78; Foner, *Reconstruction,* 392–411; Jones, *Labor of Love,* 46–72, 79–109.

72. *WPA Slave Narratives* (South Carolina, pt. 1), Kindle location 3123–27.

73. *WPA Slave Narratives* (Arkansas, pt. 3), Kindle location 3315–20.

74. *WPA Slave Narratives* (South Carolina, pt. 1), Kindle location 2036–37.

75. Ibid., Kindle location 3533–35.

76. *WPA Slave Narratives* (Arkansas, pt. 1), Kindle location 1925–26.

77. *WPA Slave Narratives* (Texas, pt. 2), Kindle location 242–45.

78. Ibid., Kindle location 1307–11.

79. Ibid.

80. *WPA Slave Narratives* (Florida), Kindle location 1323–28.

81. *WPA Slave Narratives* (Texas, pt. 2), Kindle location 2748–55.

82. Ibid., Kindle location 2748–57.

83. *WPA Slave Narratives* (Arkansas, pt. 3), Kindle location 3315–20.

84. *WPA Slave Narratives* (Texas, pt. 2), Kindle location 158–61.

85. *WPA Slave Narratives* (Georgia, pt. 1), Kindle location 2414–17.

86. *WPA Slave Narratives* (Georgia, pt. 3), Kindle location 1743–45.

87. *WPA Slave Narratives, Arkansas Narratives,* Part 5, Kindle Edition, p. 23.

88. *WPA Slave Narratives* (Georgia, pt. 3), Kindle location 906–8.

89. *WPA Slave Narratives* (South Carolina, pt. 1), Kindle location 4106–10.

90. *WPA Slave Narratives* (Arkansas, pt. 7), p. 23.

91. *WPA Slave Narratives* (Georgia, pt. 3), Kindle location 3125–27.

Emancipation as State Building from the Inside Out

CHANDRA MANNING

One day, a Virginia slave owner appeared in Washington, D.C., brandishing a pass signed by the district military commander. Confident in his right to aid from the U.S. government, the slave owner demanded to search for his slaves. The Virginian found the women in one of the contraband camps that sheltered thousands of refugees from slavery, but there his luck ended. One of the women handed a knife to Superintendent of Contrabands Danforth B. Nichols and requested that he "let the wicked blood out of that man." Nichols did not stab the slave owner, but he did prevent him from reclaiming the women. They remained in Washington, D.C., as freedwomen under the protection of the Union army and the U.S. government, simultaneously leaving slavery and reinventing their relationship to the central state.[1]

Historians have long understood the U.S. Civil War as top-down state building in which the president, Congress, and War Department expanded and centralized power, yet the "growth of the central state" means more than how much territory a government controls, how large an army it can place in the field, or how much power any branch amasses.[2] It also means the purposes for which that power is wielded, the purposes for which individual people *expect* that power to be wielded, and the felt results of that power in the daily lives of people under the central state's governance. It means, in short, whether a direct relationship exists between the central government and *some, most, or all* individuals living under its governance, and what purposes that relationship could reasonably be expected to serve.

As the women from Virginia, Superintendent Nichols, and the soldiers of the Union army all participated in the process of Civil War emancipation, they helped build the central state from the inside out, which is to say, beginning at the level of the individual human being and radiating outward through successive orbitals of human relationships to the U.S. government. Specificity is important here: emancipation per se does not necessarily amount to inside-out state building, because emancipation has manumitted individuals into statelessness many times in world history.[3] But in the U.S. Civil War, former slaves who left slavery in the midst of war entered into a new relationship with the Union army, a branch of the U.S. government at that time actively engaged in *saving* the U.S. government. As a result, the wartime emancipation of four million people by federal military and legal action built the central government by placing that government into direct contact with millions of people who formerly lacked any civic presence at all. Moreover, the wartime circumstances under which enslaved African Americans exited slavery placed black women as well as men in newfound positions to call on the federal government to protect and defend individual rights, because the labor and local intelligence rendered by black people to the Union army aided the United States in its struggle for survival. *That* Civil War emancipation happened built the central government by bonding millions more people directly to it. *How* Civil War emancipation happened influenced the strength, nature, and purpose of those new bonds, entailing specific advantages, drawbacks, and limitations.

Thinking about emancipation in this way—by placing the changing relationship between the central state and the individual person at the center—sets aside the conception of state building as a process that operates in a vertical direction between a state at the top and people at the bottom. Yet inside-out state building does not replace a vertical notion of state building with a horizontal model, which would imply an equality of power, because in truth some parties wielded much more power than others. Instead, inside-out state building suggests a circular process, with individual people in the center like the nucleus of an atom. Atomic nuclei are surrounded by orbitals, each of which provides an atom with energy and mass. The outermost orbital, the valence, is the most unstable, and it also bonds the atom to a larger whole. Similarly, an enslaved person was surrounded by orbitals of kin, community, networks, and institutions. Civil War emancipation added new orbitals, starting with the Union army and culminating with the federal government. Ultimately, the federal government bonded to the emancipated individual by a new valence, the part of any atom that is most powerful but also the most unstable.

Conceptualizing emancipation as inside-out state building challenges us to rethink the end of U.S. slavery in three specific ways. First, it attunes us to the role of black women and children in dismantling slavery and reinventing the central state in the United States. Second, it replaces assumptions of emancipation's inevitability with heightened appreciation of its fragility and reversibility. Finally, because state building entails violence, considering emancipation as state building from the inside out offers a framework within which to acknowledge and grapple with violence without gawking at it, minimizing it, or sanitizing it.

Before the Civil War, a black person could not obtain a U.S. passport, legally access courts (at least according to the U.S. Supreme Court), or lay claim to any rights that, as Chief Justice Taney put it, a white man was bound to respect. No enslaved black person could legally own property, move freely, marry, or look to the U.S. government for bodily protection. In 1866 Congress passed the Civil Rights Act, which secured for black people the rights "to make and enforce contracts, to sue, be parties, and give evidence, to inherit, purchase, lease, sell, hold, and convey real and personal property, and to full and equal benefit of all laws and proceedings for the security of person and property, as is enjoyed by white citizens."[4] Recognition of the obvious—that this transition amounted to neither the achievement of full justice nor the fulfillment of all African Americans' hopes—does not eliminate the need to explain a transition as startling as it was disappointing. Viewing emancipation as inside-out state building allows us to see that wartime interactions between slaves and the Union army changed things, because those interactions and the circumstances under which they took place made old presumptions about what the U.S. government should do for whom untenable.

Black men, women, and children labored, laundered, spied, ditched, hauled, and more in Union camps, and in the process they created situations in which officials had to wrestle with previously unimaginable questions of obligation and reciprocity. Suddenly, an ordinary white northern farmer or clerk found himself thrust into a role such as provost marshal or picket sentry, in which his daily duties compelled him to question why the U.S. government should help a white, disloyal property owner, especially when the army and the central state it served could benefit by extending protection to other individuals—such as black nurses, laborers, and launderers—instead. These dilemmas were certainly not planned by the officials who faced them, and the outcomes were neither inevitable nor predictable, but they did help destroy slavery and build the U.S.

government by building new alliances, however tenuous and uneasy, between that government and the formerly enslaved.

There was no unambiguous template for such alliances. The military and the rest of the federal government often shared goals, but sometimes their priorities clashed, and neither had shared interests with enslaved people before. A new script had to be made up as the war went along, which was precisely what Superintendent of Contrabands John Eaton was doing when he sent questionnaires to Union officials throughout the Mississippi Valley directly asking what both men and women were up to in each locale. From Cairo, Illinois, to Louisiana, superintendents of contrabands sent back responses detailing the types and amount of labor that married and unmarried men and women, and even children, personally contributed to the Union. Eaton compiled the responses into charts and tables and wrote up a careful analysis emphasizing that the results clearly demonstrated direct U.S. government obligations not just to black men but also to freedwomen and children on grounds of both "humanity" and "justice"; he might have added expediency, since it was in the army's interest to avail itself of the benefits that former slaves brought to the war effort.[5] As a result, during and after the Civil War, the central government assumed responsibility for securing for more people certain rights—the rights to personal protection, mobility, property, access to courts, and entering into contracts—that it had previously only secured for a smaller number of people.

So what did inside-out state building actually look like, on the ground? For many, it began with personal protection. It is unlikely that Illinois farmer James Jessee had ever thought about black requests for U.S. passports or contemplated the use of the army to protect black people, but he did know that he and his fellow members of the Eighth Illinois Infantry were tired of mollycoddling rebels. When a black woman made her way into camp and told soldiers where to find guns that her Confederate owner had hidden in his house, the men of the regiment concealed her from her master, and Corporal Jessee of the Union army violently challenged the privileged, white, male property owner over his abuse of the woman.[6]

Connected to personal protection was the right to personal mobility. The U.S. government protected this right for white people but circumscribed it for black people before the Civil War, both negatively by not interfering with state and local mandates requiring black people to carry white-signed passes, and positively by authorizing (under the Fugitive

Slave Act) federal commissioners to aid in returning runaways to their owners.[7] Yet in 1865 the U.S. secretary of war issued General Orders No. 129, wielding the authority of the U.S. War Department to invalidate "any system of passes" or other "restraints" on black movement in order to "secure equal justice and the same personal liberty to the freedmen as to other citizens."[8] General Orders No. 129 did not come out of the blue; everybody in the army's path (freedpeople included) chafed at military-imposed restrictions on movement during the war, but black people who enjoyed increased mobility usually did so because they had aided the Union army. A group of enslaved mine workers in Missouri, for example, infuriated the mine foreman by running to Union lines, working as teamsters for the Union army, and then sauntering back through the old neighborhood to demonstrate that instead of being forced to work in the mines, they could come and go at will.[9]

Where protection of property was concerned, the federal government had long been in the business of protecting the property rights of slave owners. Antislavery lawyers and politicians had painstakingly built a case against a constitutional right to property in slaves, but until Lincoln's election, the federal government remained in the hands of leaders who fervently disagreed and who used the power of the federal government precisely to protect such "rights," most obviously in the Fugitive Slave Act of 1850, a breathtaking expansion of federal power on behalf of slave owners.[10]

Bondspeople could not rely on federal protection for any property they might own or claim. Instead, enslaved blacks relied on kin and communal networks to protect claims to property, insofar as such claims could be protected by networks whose lack of legal standing limited their power in the face of white attempts to disrupt them.[11] Communal and extralegal claims grew even more fragile during the Civil War, because the conflict displaced people, scattered communities, and disrupted kin networks. A black mother who picked up her children and fled to Union lines to get away from her owner also left behind her community.

If, once she made it to a contraband camp, that same black woman wanted any possessions protected, she had no choice but to seek the aid of a force never before available to her, the Union army. For its part, the army benefited from any labor or local intelligence that refugees from slavery might bring. Therefore, the U.S. government had reason to extend safeguards to former slaves that would never have been given before the war.

For example, one black man who ran to the Union army in Beaufort, North Carolina, made himself so indispensable to Union soldiers that they presented him with the gift of a hog, a valuable source of nutrition, or cash if the man chose to sell it. The hog thrived under the black man's care, catching the attention of white residents who demanded that the Union provost marshal transfer the hog to a white woman who claimed prior ownership. Instead, the provost marshal called in the black man to give legal testimony as proof of his own ownership and then used that testimony to defend the black man's right to keep the pig and call it rightfully his.[12] This incident, and every incident in which the army protected a former slave's rights to property, helped dismantle slavery and grew the federal government.

The Beaufort pig incident points to additional ways in which the central state changed, for it was not just the pig itself but also the claimant's ability to use legal testimony to retain the pig that mattered.[13] Before the war, black Americans vigorously sought access to courts, with occasional success, but after 1857 the Dred Scott decision by the U.S. Supreme Court denied the right of a black person to avail of the courts. During the war, refugees from slavery behind Union lines fought for and often won access to courts under the auspices of the Union army. After the war, taking cases to court remained a favored strategy and a vigilantly defended right on the part of freedpeople calling on the Freedmen's Bureau, as well as of activist organizations such as the Pennsylvania State Equal Rights League. Black claimants did not consistently win justice, but courts remained a key arena for contesting and defending their claims.[14]

Another specifically legal right, the right to enter into contracts, also grew out of former slaves' direct involvement in the Union war effort. For example, refugees from slavery working as nurses in Union army hospitals sometimes entered into direct contracts with the U.S. government, recorded in a multivolume *Register of Colored Nurses under Contract*.[15]

Open any of those volumes, and you immediately notice the nurses' names—Rachel, Lizzie, Elsie—names that underscore the integral role played by black women in emancipation and inside-out state building, not simply as the addendums or dependents of men but as themselves. A long-standing narrative, advanced during the Civil War by black soldiers and civilians as well as by historians since, argues that black Union soldiers fought for freedom and inclusion within the American republic.[16] Even critical analyses of that narrative, which ask historians to look soberly at its celebration of violence and to attend more diligently to the disappointing version of freedom that black soldiering gained, share the presumption that black enlistment was the only path available.[17] Since women and children could not enlist, they remain invisible.

Historians Stephanie McCurry and Amy Dru Stanley have begun adding some women to the story of emancipation. McCurry argues that the martial route traveled by black soldiers opened a marital route for the black women who married them and gained freedom as soldiers' spouses.[18] For McCurry, the marriage route was an inherently limiting one that reified a narrow gender ideology, in which political society consisted of households headed by men who possessed all the political presence, power, and rights that any household needed, and who mediated between the government and dependents.[19] Amy Dru Stanley posits a similar path for women, but she detects a more expansive ideology at its core, one that asserted the human right to recognition of familial bonds.[20] Yet not even McCurry and Stanley taken together can tell us everything, simply because so many of the black female former slaves encountered by white northerners during the Civil War were not married. Army officials, congressional agents, northern volunteers, missionaries, foot soldiers, and just about every other white northerner who observed freedpeople in the South commented volubly about former slaves' "irregular" domestic arrangements and the high number of unattached black women. White northerners might have wanted to find easily classified black families, but what they found instead were tens of thousands of unattached black women who left Union officials no choice but to see them as individual people, and to question what their relationship to the U.S. government should be as themselves, not as men's dependents.

When we look at emancipation as state building from the inside out, we also become much more alert to its fragility and reversibility. Because we know that the war ended slavery, it is all too easy to assume that once slaves began leaving their masters, slavery was doomed because no earthly power could reinstate it. Republicans in the 1860s brimmed with that optimism, and even the magisterial and anything-but-giddy *Freedmen and Southern Society* project seems to intimate as much in some of the interpretive essays in its invaluable volumes. By thinking about emancipation as a form of state building, we remind ourselves to place Civil War emancipation within the context of contemporary wars, rebellions, and state-making and state-building ventures such as the Revolutionary War, the War of 1812, and wars for independence in Spanish South America. In each of those conflicts, some individuals escaped slavery, but the institution of slavery was not abolished, nor did the relationship between the enslaved and the central state necessarily change. Some of the slaves who escaped to the British during the Revolutionary War gained permanent freedom, but others were sold in the Caribbean after the war. Meanwhile, northern states in the newly independent United States began gradually abolishing slavery at the exact same time that some southern states strengthened slavery. After the War of 1812, slavery actually grew stronger in the United States.[21] In places such as Peru, Ecuador, Bolivia, Chile, and Uruguay, slaves who gained freedom during war were reenslaved afterward. Enslaved veterans of Brazil's Ragamuffin Revolt of 1835 were reenslaved a full ten years after fighting for and achieving their own emancipation.[22] There was no *a priori* reason why the same thing might not have happened in the nineteenth-century United States. Despite the fond hopes of antislavery advocates, emancipation was not an irreversible tide; it did not somehow erase a former master's desire to reenslave or willingness to use force to realize that desire. Unless a former slave could combat that force by exercising or calling on an equal or greater power, emancipation remained a precarious and revocable state. By directly aiding the Union army, black men, women, and children gained access to a force with the power necessary to make emancipation permanent.

Finally, inside-out state building makes room for the violence of the transition from slavery to freedom in the United States, which is to say, refuses to allow us to ignore or whitewash violence but also restrains us from gaping at it like some sort of spectacle. States often do nasty things, and state building often involves war. There is no such thing as "nice" war, and the men, women, and children seeking freedom endured a disproportionate share of the Civil War's cruelty and suffering. Yet if we tell a story only of gratuitous violence, cruelty, and suffering, we run the risk of separating violence out and treating it like a freak show, rather than integral to war and emancipation. Considering emancipation as inside-out state building cannot fully resolve this dilemma (perhaps nothing can), but by understanding states as entities that seek both legitimacy and a monopoly on violence (to temper Max Weber's claim that states *have* legitimate monopolies on violence), we see violence as chillingly central to a contest for legitimacy in which the participants were black and white, male and female.

Amidst violence, the Civil War unmade and remade the worlds in which Americans lived on the largest and smallest of scales. Just as orbitals surrounding atomic nuclei are always unpredictable in their pathways, especially when subject to turmoil, the relationships of kin, community, and membership surrounding the men and women who lived through the war were disrupted by war's upheaval. Civil War emancipation encased the destabilized orbitals that surrounded formerly enslaved men, women, and children with a new valence that bonded them initially to the Union army, and then for the first time to the U.S. central state. Superimposing a new relationship to the central government over other relationships that gave mass and energy to each individual's being also expanded that government. The growth entailed clear advantages for black people, for it meant that their rights to person, mobility, property, and redress enjoyed a legal standing that prewar informal networks lacked.

Yet emancipation as the forging of direct bonds between formerly enslaved individuals and the federal government entailed drawbacks as well. For one thing, the new individualization of freedpeople's relationship to the U.S. government eclipsed some of the communal networks that might have wielded more clout collectively than individuals could once the urgency of war had passed. Moreover, just as valences are the most unstable orbitals, wartime bonds forged between the federal government and the formerly enslaved were also unstable. Legitimizing individuals' claims on the central government on the basis of labor created plenty of room for exploitation and also made it easy to duck reciprocal obligations to women and children after the war, when opportunities for them to contribute directly to U.S. survival were neither abundant nor obvious. It became even easier to forget women's and children's claims because once the war was over, their wartime labor was obscured both by male-dominated black civil rights organizations, who argued chiefly in terms of black soldiers' service, and by federal agencies such as the Southern Claims Commission, whose interrogatories gave whites space to explain their wartime service to the Union but sometimes used truncated forms with no such space for black claimants.[23]

The drawbacks to the process by which U.S. emancipation occurred should not be downplayed, but neither should they allow us to take the destruction of slavery or the newfound ability of black people to make claims on the U.S. government for granted. On the contrary, reversion to slavery and reassertion of prewar status quo were more often the case in an Atlantic context. The process of interaction, obligation, and reciprocity between former slaves and the Union army by which emancipation occurred forged a much more direct relationship between the government and the individual, and it expanded the expectations that each entertained of the other, though these expectations were not always realized. Under these circumstances, escaped slaves (especially formerly enslaved women) and the military invented a new relationship between the U.S. government and individual people, a relationship that took the precise form that it did in response to freedpeople's own priorities, and to the exigencies of war. For black Americans, white Americans, and the U.S. government, emancipation turned the world inside out.

NOTES

1. Testimony of D. B. Nichols, Records of the American Freedmen's Inquiry Commission, File I, National Archives and Records Administration (hereafter NARA) Record Group (hereafter RG) 94 Letters Received by the Office of the Adjutant General (Main Series) 1861–1870 1863-328-0, Microfilm 619 Reel 200, Frames 118–19.

2. The classic statement of the Civil War as top-down state building remains Richard Bensel, *Yankee Leviathan: The Origins of Central State Authority in America, 1859–1877* (New York: Cambridge University Press, 1991). What Washington did with power (such as exercising it to wipe out the billions of dollars of private property that slaveholders assumed they owned in the form of slaves) mattered, and that power did grow, though neither permanently or irreversibly. A burgeoning American political development literature (much of which I find persuasive) seriously challenges easy notions of a small and ineffectual federal government before the war, but not even key voices in that conversation, such as William Novak, Robert Balough, and Gary Gerstle, articulate direct, positive relationships between the federal government and individuals, or demonstrate much positive federal safeguarding for individual rights. Emerging strains of scholarship are beginning to examine changing relationships between central states and the individuals they governed in the context of the U.S. Civil War. Drew Gilpin Faust's *This Republic of Suffering: Death and the American Civil War* (New York: Knopf, 2008) has argued that the war's staggering death toll rendered the U.S. government more immediately accountable to individuals in the Union, while Stephanie McCurry's *Confederate Reckoning: Power and Politics in the Civil War South* (Cambridge, Mass.: Harvard University Press, 2010) has shown how the hardships of war forged much more direct relationships between the central government and individuals, especially women and slaves, in the Confederacy. These accounts tell an important part of the story, in which government responsibility to individuals grew out of what the war did to individuals, and they invite further investigation into what individuals did to the government at war. This essay is one attempt to answer that invitation.

3. In fact, one such instance, the Christie Affair between Britain and Brazil, occurred at exactly the same time as the U.S. Civil War, 1861–65. In this international (and widely reported) incident, a British ship intercepted a vessel sailing from Africa to Brazil with captive Africans bound for the Brazilian slave market aboard and, acting on the authority of antitrafficking codes, liberated the Afri-

cans aboard and disembarked them in Brazil. But once in Brazil, the so-called *emancipados* passed into a status so indistinct that neither of the available designations of *livre* (freeborn) or *libertado* (freed) fit, so they resided in an undefined "not-slave, not-Indian, not-foreigner" category. Historian Daryle Williams is at work on a manuscript about the Christie Affair. My account is drawn from Daryle Williams, "Rethinking the Christie Affair: Free Africans, Citizenship, and Nation during the Anglo-Brazilian Conflict, 1861–1865," unpublished paper presented to the Slavery, Memory, and African Diasporas Seminar at Howard University, December 15, 2012 (cited with permission), and subsequent email correspondence with Daryle Williams, December 2012 and March 2013.

4. 1866 Civil Rights Act, 14 Stat. 27–30, April 9, 1866, http://www.supremelaw .org/ref/1866cra/1866.cra.htm.

5. Records of the American Freedmen's Inquiry Commission, File 6 Testimony from the Department of Tennessee, NARA RG 94 Letters Received by the Office of the Adjutant General (Main Series) 1861–1870 1863-328-o, Microfilm 619 Reel 200. For "Interrogatory 9th" about women's and men's labor, see frame 577. For the tables, see frame 571ff. For the quotations taken from Eaton's analysis of the data, see frames 592–600.

6. Diary of Cpl. James Jessee, 8th Illinois Infantry, August 16, 1862, and October 27, 1862, Jackson, Tennessee, vol. 1, Spencer Research Library, University of Kansas.

7. William Thomas's *The Iron Way: Railroads, the Civil War and the Making of Modern America* (New Haven, Conn.: Yale University Press, 2011) stresses mobility as a key element of citizenship and full personhood in the nineteenth-century United States for white people. Thomas Buchanan's *Black Life on the Mississippi: Slaves, Free Blacks, and the Western Steamboat World* (Chapel Hill: University of North Carolina Press, 2004) also underscores the importance of mobility for black people, though of course that mobility was not guaranteed by the U.S. government. In *The Routes of War: The World of Movement in the Confederate South* (Cambridge, Mass.: Harvard University Press, 2012), Yael Sternhell argues for mobility as the meaning of emancipation for former slaves. The importance of individual mobility reverberates throughout the testimony given by slaves, former slaves, and free blacks to the American Freedmen's Inquiry Commission in 1863 and 1864; it appears over and over in the lists of things that black respondents questioned by the commissioners listed as important to them. See Records of the American Freedmen's Inquiry Commission, NARA RG 94 Letters Received by the Office of the Adjutant General (Main Series) 1861–1870 1863-328-o, Microfilm 619 Reels 199–201. Similarly, in a memorial sent to Congress in 1866, the members of the Pennsylvania State Equal Rights League listed mobility right alongside voting as a chief priority. See Pennsylvania State Equal Rights League Memorial to Congress, February 20, 1866, Papers and Proceedings of the Pennsylvania State Equal Rights League, Leon Gardiner Collection of American Negro His

torical Society Records, Reel 1, Historical Society of Pennsylvania, Philadelphia (hereafter PSERL Papers).

8. General Orders No. 129, July 25, 1865, University of Mississippi Libraries Digital Collections, http://clio.lib.olemiss.edu/cdm/ref/collection/civil_war /id/3291.

9. See correspondence between the mine foreman, John Latty, in Shibboleth, Washington County, Missouri, and the mine owners, the Kennett family, who sat out the war in Saint Louis, from September 1862 to February 1864. Kennett Family Papers, Missouri Historical Society, Saint Louis.

10. For the antislavery case against a constitutional right to property in slaves (which predated the Republican Party but became part of Republican ideology once the party existed) see James Oakes, *Freedom National: The Destruction of Slavery in the United States* (New York: Norton, 2012).

11. Dylan Penningroth, *The Claims of Kinfolk: African American Property and Community in the Nineteenth-Century South* (Chapel Hill: University of North Carolina Press, 2002).

12. James Rumley Diary, December 4, 1862, Beaufort, North Carolina, Levi Woodbury Pigott Collection, North Carolina Department of Archives and History, Raleigh. That the property was a pig seems especially important, in light of the severity with which hog "stealing" by slaves had been treated since colonial days in slaveholding states. See, for example, Eugene Genovese, *Roll, Jordan, Roll: The World the Slaves Made* (New York: Vintage Books, 1976), book 4, part 1, 599ff. If, as *Roll, Jordan, Roll* tells us, "roast pig" in the world the slaves made was "a wonderful delicacy, especially when stolen," roast pig that a court said was yours rather than a white slave owner's must have tasted even better. Thanks to Bryan McCann for reminding me of that subsection title in *Roll, Jordan, Roll.*

13. In fact, one reason why the Beaufort pig incident makes it into the record is that James Rumley, a white Confederate stuck in Beaufort during the Union occupation, was absolutely furious because as he saw it, the notions that a black person could own property or give legal testimony against white people were abominations.

14. Records of the Bureau of Refugees, Freedmen, and Abandoned Lands, NARA RG 105; PSERL Papers, Reel 1. See also Herman Belz, *A New Birth of Freedom: The Republican Party and Freedmen's Rights, 1861–1866* (Westport, Conn.: Greenwood, 1976); Pamela Brandwein, *Rethinking the Judicial Settlement of Reconstruction* (New York: Cambridge University Press, 2011); Martha Jones, "Leave of Court: African-American Legal Claims Making in the Era of *Dred Scott v. Sanford*," in *Contested Democracy: Politics, Ideology, and Race in American History*, ed. Manisha Sinha and Penny Von Eschen (New York: Columbia University Press, 2007); Barbara Welke, "When All the Women Were White, and All the Blacks Were Men: Gender, Class, Race, and the Road to Plessy, 1855–1914," *Law and History Review* 13 (1995): 261–316.

15. See, for example, NARA RG 94 Entry 591, Box 1, Volume 1: *Register of Colored Nurses under Contract [Department of the East] July 16, 1863 to June 14, 1864.* On "home farms" and various other free-labor experiments launched in Union-occupied areas, black workers entered into contracts with white landowners or lessees or sometimes (in cases of confiscated plantations) the federal government; the contracts stipulated wages and limited forms of punishment, and were to be enforced by the United States. See, for example, *Private and Official Correspondence of General Benjamin F. Butler during the Period of the Civil War* (Privately Printed for Jessie Ames Marshall by the Plimpton Press of Norwood, Mass., 1917), 2:439, 487–88. Employees working for planters who reneged were in theory free to hire out their labor to somebody else. That the contract system was widely abused is well known and not in dispute, but what is notable is that the contracts were between landowners or lessees and black workers themselves, a departure from antebellum practices in which white hirers (planters, farmers, railroads, etc.) entered into contracts with white owners to rent black slaves. Rhetorically, at least, the U.S. government assumed the novel responsibility of safeguarding freedpeople's rights under those contracts.

16. See Frederick Douglass, "Address for the Promotion of Colored Enlistments," Philadelphia, July 6, 1863, quoted in David W. Blight, *Frederick Douglass' Civil War: Keeping Faith in Jubilee* (Baton Rouge: Louisiana State University Press, 1991), 161. See also Mary Frances Berry, *Military Necessity and Civil Rights Policy: Black Citizenship and the Constitution, 1861–1868* (Port Washington, N.Y.: National University Publications, 1977); Chandra Manning, *What This Cruel War Was Over: Soldiers, Slavery, and the Civil War* (New York: Knopf, 2007); Joseph Reidy, "The African American Struggle for Citizenship Rights in the Northern United States during the Civil War," in *Civil War Citizens: Race, Ethnicity, and Identity in America's Bloodiest Conflict*, ed. Susannah J. Ural (New York: New York University Press, 2010), 213–36; Christian G. Samito, *Becoming American under Fire: Irish Americans, African Americans, and the Politics of Citizenship during the Civil War Era* (Ithaca, N.Y.: Cornell University Press, 2009); Brian Taylor, "A Politics of Service: Black Northerners' Debates over Enlistment in the American Civil War," *Civil War History* 58, no. 4 (December 2012): 451–80.

17. W. E. B. Du Bois, *Black Reconstruction in America* (1935; reprint, New York: Atheneum, 1969), 110; Carole Emberton, "Only Murder Makes Men: Reconsidering the Black Military Experience," *Journal of the Civil War Era* 2, no. 3 (September 2012): 369–93.

18. Stephanie McCurry, "War, Gender, and Emancipation in the Civil War South," in *Lincoln's Proclamation: Emancipation Reconsidered*, ed. William A. Blair and Karen Fisher Younger (Chapel Hill: University of North Carolina Press, 2012). McCurry does note that black women countered the implication that emancipation had been earned for them with the insistence that they had earned it themselves, but she forecloses the possibility that white officials might have paid any attention to that assessment and therefore denies its efficacy.

19. For a concise exposition of this ideology, see Stephanie McCurry, "The Citizen Wife," *Signs* 30, no. 2 (Winter 2005): 1659–70, and for fuller explication see McCurry's *Masters of Small Worlds* (New York: Oxford University Press, 1995), as well as the titles that the *Signs* article discusses: Norma Basch, *Framing American Divorce: From the Revolutionary Generation to the Victorians* (Berkeley: University of California Press, 1999); Candice Lewis Bredbenner, *A Nationality of Her Own: Women, Marriage, and the Law of Citizenship* (Berkeley: University of California Press, 1998); Nancy F. Cott, *Public Vows: A History of Marriage and the Nation* (Cambridge, Mass.: Harvard University Press, 2000); Hendrik Hartog, *Man and Wife in America: A History* (Cambridge, Mass.: Harvard University Press, 2000); Linda K. Kerber, *No Constitutional Right to Be Ladies: Women and the Obligations of Citizenship* (New York: Hill & Wang, 1998).

20. Amy Dru Stanley, "Instead of Waiting for the Thirteenth Amendment: The War Power, Slave Marriage, and Inviolate Human Rights," *American Historical Review* 115, no. 3 (June 2010): 732–65. Stanley also places more emphasis on the actual number of women and children who gained freedom via the marital route, which in the case of an 1865 law freeing the family members of enlisted black soldiers from the border states was around fifty thousand. There is no question that marriage to soldiers did forge a pathway for many women. "Marriage under the flag" was real, as Union army chaplains' records during the war and piles of widows' postwar pensions attest. But, of course, pension applications by definition privilege the women who married. They do not capture the vast numbers of unmarried women.

21. On the aftermath of the revolution, see Maya Jasanoff, *Liberty's Exiles: American Loyalists in the Revolutionary World* (New York: Knopf, 2011). On northern gradual emancipation alongside southern strengthening of slavery, see Joanne Pope Melish, *Disowning Slavery: Gradual Emancipation and "Race" in New England, 1780–1860* (Ithaca, N.Y.: Cornell University Press, 2000); Arthur Zilversmit, *First Emancipation: The Abolition of Slavery in the North* (Chicago: University of Chicago Press, 1977). On the aftermath of the War of 1812, see Adam Rothman, *Slave Country: American Expansion and the Origins of the Deep South* (Cambridge, Mass.: Harvard University Press, 2005).

22. On South America, see Peter Blanchard, *Under the Flags of Freedom: Slave Soldiers and the Wars of Independence in Spanish South America* (Pittsburgh: University of Pittsburgh Press, 2008). On the Ragamuffin Revolt, I have drawn on Spencer Leitman, "The Black Ragamuffins: Racial Hypocrisy in Nineteenth-Century Southern Brazil," *Americas* 33, no. 3 (1977): 504–18, and conversation with historian of Brazil Bryan McCann.

23. See, for example, List of Local Affiliates of the Pennsylvania State Equal Rights League, 1865; Business Committee Report, Aug. 9, 1865, Proceedings of the Annual Meeting of the Pennsylvania State Equal Rights League, Held in Harrisburg, Aug. 9th and 10th, 1865; Pennsylvania State Equal Rights League Memorial to Congress, Feb. 20, 1866; Proceedings of the Annual Meeting of the

Pennsylvania State Equal Rights League 1866 (and all successive years); William Nesbit and Jacob C. White correspondence (about the Fourteenth Amendment) in 1868; all in PSERL Papers, Reel 1; The Southern Claims Commission Papers: Question Sheet Used in Depositions, The Valley of the Shadow, http://valley.lib .virginia.edu/VoS/claims/SCC_questions.html.

PART 2

The Politics
of Freedom

The Problem of Equality in
the Age of Emancipation

KATE MASUR

By the end of the Civil War, radical Republicans had definitively put the question of equality—by which is usually meant racial equality—on the agenda in politics. There was nothing inevitable about this. Politicians could have seen fit to outlaw slavery and ignore arguments that more must be done to remedy the legal and political disabilities of African Americans, North and South. Indeed, most white Americans might well have favored that course. But those who wanted to see a more dramatic restructuring of American life successfully demanded a conversation about the limits and meanings of equality in the wake of emancipation.

Historians have long recognized this, but they have been surprisingly uninterested. C. Vann Woodward acknowledged, in the aftermath of *Brown v. Board of Education*, just how complex the question of equality had been since the Civil War era. "Equality was a far more revolutionary aim than freedom, though it may not have seemed so at first," he wrote. "Slavery was property based on law. The law could be changed and the property expropriated. Not so inequality. Its entrenchments were deeper and subtler."[1] Yet Woodward was not arguing that historians should study the postemancipation struggle over equality. To the contrary, he was saying that, in the nineteenth century at least, it was largely irrelevant. Only a handful of radicals had pushed for racial equality, he argued; the northern public writ large had been thoroughly opposed. Equality, he said, was a "deferred commitment" that only began to bear fruit in the 1950s.

Subsequent scholars undertook a major reevaluation of emancipation and Reconstruction, but like Woodward they had little to say about the problem of equality. Freedom was their central category of analysis. Emphasizing political economy and viewing slavery's abolition as a problem in labor history, historians focused on the renegotiation of economic relations in the postemancipation South and emphasized competing definitions of freedom among the protagonists—freedpeople, planters, and U.S. government officials.[2] To be sure, the "meanings of freedom" scholarship sometimes touched debates about rights and equality. But between Woodward's dismissiveness and later historians' alternative focus, the postemancipation debate about inequality and possibilities for its remediation has rarely been the subject of serious inquiry.

I propose that we take a new look. As historians have recently begun to demonstrate, activists and politicians frequently succeeded in gaining a hearing for their arguments that governments—whether local, state, or federal—must end racially discriminatory policies and pursue racial equality.[3] Moreover, even if demands for racial and other forms of equality ultimately produced limited results by the late nineteenth century, the arguments they engendered—about space, power, culture, and politics—are revealing. To explore the *problem of equality* is to examine inequality and arguments for its remediation through public policy; it is to explore how people defined appropriate arenas for policy making and how they came to understand some kinds of spaces—such as the market or the domestic sphere—as zones of inequality, as places that were private and characterized by free choice.

Nineteenth-century Americans' use of the category of "the social" and the concept of "social equality" tells us a great deal about their embrace of inequality. Contemporaries often spoke of three realms of human existence: the civil, the political, and the social. The end of southern slavery ushered in a debate about racial equality in all three arenas; among them, however, only the idea of *social* equality carried almost exclusively negative connotations.[4] For most people, calling something a "social" matter meant saying it was private and therefore an area where government had no business trying to intervene to break down racial inequities and injustices. When people invoked "social equality," they were usually making an argument about the limits of legitimate government intervention to promote equality.

In this essay I use controversies surrounding the appointment of the first black cadets at the U.S. Military Academy at West Point, beginning in 1870, to examine how Americans understood the limits of racially egalitarian policy making after the Civil War. I show how white northerners drew on existing ideas about what constituted the social realm to justify discrimination against early black cadets at West Point and how those cadets themselves envisioned social hierarchies. In the conclusion, I offer some thoughts on how postemancipation debates about the boundary between the "social" and other spheres relate to a broader history of race and class inequality in the United States.

We begin with manners, more frequently a topic of exploration in cultural history than in the history of politics and public policy. Cultural historians have long understood that antebellum northerners cared mightily about personal comportment and display. Widely read advice manuals and periodicals offered instructions on good taste and comportment; novelists and others wondered out loud what constituted a lady or a gentleman and whether outward appearance as such signaled inner honor or integrity. In the main, cultural historians have connected such preoccupations with the development of capitalism, arguing in one form or another that new concerns with social distinction and self-presentation emerged as the population became larger and more urbanized, and as the range of consumer goods available for purchase expanded and diversified.[5]

But the world of manners and comportment was not as distant from the world of political democracy as we might imagine. Many writers of conduct manuals, for example, went to some lengths to connect the social sphere, which most preoccupied them, with the political and civil realms, which they defined as separate and distinct from the social. Indeed, etiquette writers often compared the social with the civil, the laws of society with the laws of nations. The "rules of etiquette," one writer argued, "are to society what civil law is to a country." Like a nation, another opined, "society is also an organized association, and has a perfect right to make laws which shall be binding upon all of its members."[6] The comparison was meant to justify and legitimate rules of etiquette. No one would argue that nations should not have laws; social rules were just as necessary.

Comparisons between social laws and public laws also suggested a key distinction, however. Whereas the hallmark of Anglo-American civil law was the idea that it must be enforced equally, without regard to the status of the individuals involved, the signal characteristic of the "code of manners" was that it created and affirmed distinctions among people along lines of status and class. Some commentators believed anyone who learned the proper manners could enter polite society; others held that the highest echelons would always remain closed to even the best-trained parvenus.[7] All, however, seemed to agree that the social realm was (and should be) explicitly and unabashedly hierarchical. In fact, theorists of society often conceived of it in explicit contrast to the political and civil arenas, which were—for better but usually for worse in their view—shaped by more democratic principles. In America, one antebellum writer explained, the "political" and the "social system" were "totally unconnected, and altogether different in character. . . . There is perfect freedom of political privilege, all are the same upon the hustings, or at a political meeting; but this equality does not extend to the drawing-room or the parlour. None are excluded from the highest councils of the nation, but it does not follow that all can enter into the highest ranks of society."[8] Some writers of etiquette books were explicit in their hope that codes of manners would create a bulwark against an increasingly democratic political culture.

We might therefore see the social as in some sense a "private" realm that stood in contrast to the "public" arenas of both civil society and political life. The state's law regulated life in the civil and political arenas, while taste prevailed in the social, which was supposedly characterized by liberty and personal choice. These categories could, to some extent, map onto distinct spaces and bodies. The social world, as contemporaries understood it, was characterized by domestic, interior spaces and their inhabitants. People expressed taste and social distinction not just in choosing decorations for their parlors and dining rooms but also in choosing whom to invite there. The display of manners and proper conduct was crucial in this hierarchical world, as were clothing choices and expectations for mothering and for children's behavior and education. By contrast, the outdoor world of roads, commerce, and polling places was the realm of politics and civil law, a less hierarchical space where men were dominant and where people must interact across class lines whether they wanted to or not.[9]

But the real world did not conform to the neat binaries suggested here: public/private, outdoor/indoor, male/female, and state/society. To the contrary, such distinctions were violated constantly in practice. For instance, men did not consider social relations solely the domain of women; they were thoroughly invested in social distinctions and hierarchy. A host of important intermediate spaces—including railroads, streetcars, schools, and restaurants—could not be readily categorized as either civil or social. And politics itself was fundamentally a "social" activity. Political meetings and debates occurred at barbeques, in pubs, and in homes; political allies referred to themselves as "friends" and members of the same extended family.[10]

In fact, the places where real life challenged the neat boundaries suggested by theories of separate civil, political, and social realms are the most fruitful places to look for conflicts over the meaning and extent of equality. One such place was the U.S. Military Academy at West Point. West Point was a public and political institution, run by the U.S. government for the purpose of producing a corps of army officers. Becoming a student at West Point was a matter of political patronage. Congressmen, War Department officials, and the president could nominate young men—usually the sons of favored constituents—to travel to the academy and sit for its academically rigorous qualifying exams.[11]

Before the Civil War, the idea of a black man training to become an army officer was all but unthinkable. After the war—and after federal Reconstruction measures had defined African Americans as citizens entitled to the same civil and political rights as whites—many Republicans believed black men should also receive equal consideration for cadetships at West Point.[12] As one white advocate of black men's appointment as cadets wrote in 1872, "If it was right under the guarantees of the Fourteenth and Fifteenth Amendments to the Constitution that colored men should be elected as Senators and representatives in Congress, then it was equally right that the representatives of the colored race should be educated at the public expense at West Point—that there should be no discrimination under the general system of equality of citizenship."[13] The logic of appointing black men to West Point had everything to do with civil and political equality.

That logic may sound completely persuasive to our ears, but many contemporaries believed it disregarded something very important. The U.S. Military Academy was more than a public, political institution. It was a place where young men slept, ate, and fraternized together. Life there was full of the kinds of domestic spaces and social situations that so many Americans characterized as part of the "social" sphere, the place where people believed they could choose their own associates and where the laws of society, not government, prevailed. Yet here was the government proposing to place black men in close domestic proximity with white men—perhaps asking them to sleep in the same room and eat at the same tables as equals. When Republican politicians began to nominate African American men for West Point cadetships, the experiment with racial equality in civil and political life came into dramatic tension with white Americans' existing convictions about social inequality and the meanings of race.

The two men at the center of the West Point controversy were James Webster Smith of South Carolina, who arrived at the academy in 1870, and Henry Ossian Flipper of Georgia, who joined him in 1874. Both matriculated amid great publicity, both faced harassment and ostracism by white students, and only Flipper graduated. Perhaps it is not surprising that white cadets' conduct toward the black cadets was worst in the areas of campus life that were most characteristically "social." Outside of classes and drills, white students isolated Flipper and Smith, refusing to acknowledge them or speak to them. The white cadets did not even deign to subject the black men to conventional hazing rituals, for doing so would have recognized them as candidates for admission into the fraternity of West Pointers. "Being without the pale of social recognition," one observer who was sympathetic to the white cadets wrote, the black cadets "have likewise been exempt from all possible annoyance."[14]

Amid the various situations in which Flipper and Smith faced insult and ostracism, dining was especially fraught. There was perhaps no more important ritual of social equality than sitting down to dine with others. James Smith reported that academy officials refused to support white cadets when they balked at sharing a dinner table with him. Yet the formal equality of sitting at the same table was evidently not extended to the enjoyment of the food itself. Smith was about to serve himself one night, he told a friend, when a white cadet demanded to go first, saying, "Do you think I would eat after a d—d nigger?" An officer intervened, but his instruction was that thereafter, Smith "should not touch anything on that table until the white cadets were served." "What I eat I must snatch like a dog," Smith informed his mentor in a letter. Conflicts around meals were so intense—and the sense that the mess table was a "social" institution was so strong—that in 1880, after a decade of racial conflict, the academy's commandant, General John Schofield, expressed special regret that officers had ever demanded that white cadets take their meals with black ones.[15]

White northerners took to the periodical press to discuss the black cadets at West Point and the kinds of equality they could and could not expect. Many asserted that the black cadets should be treated equally to whites in classes and military exercises but not in other facets of life at the academy.[16] One paper commented that although "most of the officers and cadets" were "not over fond" of Smith, they would "treat him with punctilious justice in all their *official* relations—whatever may be their practice in a *social* point of view."[17] A writer for the *North American Review*, published in Philadelphia, affirmed that experience at West Point helped level social distinctions among white people. Young white men arrived at West Point "from all parts of the country, from all ranks of the social scale," he wrote, but they soon became "amalgamated" and graduated "with almost remarkable social equality." Yet the same leveling could not be expected when black cadets were involved, the writer continued, for "it would be expecting too much to hope that the companionship which surmounts or breaks down all the barriers of caste, should tread with equal heel the prejudices of color."[18]

The resort to a language of color "prejudice" was significant because it located the problem not in the institution itself but in the hearts and homes of white people.[19] General Schofield was one of those who insisted that the racial tensions the academy faced were in fact private problems, rooted in the families and homes of whites and blacks alike, and that therefore those problems could not be remedied through public policy. Amid continuing controversy about the treatment of black cadets at West Point, in 1880 Schofield argued that whites' "prevailing 'prejudice'" was neither irrational nor based on anything as superficial as skin color. Rather, it was "a just aversion to qualities which the people of the United States have long been accustomed to associate with a state of slavery and intercourse without legal marriage." "That feeling," he continued, "could not be removed by the simple act of enfranchising the slave" but, rather, required years of work for the elevation of African Americans as a group or "race."[20] Schofield and other like-minded white northerners were prepared to recognize that black cadets were the civic equals of whites. What they refused to acknowledge, Schofield explained, was any demand that young white men must treat young black men as their "social" equals, including at the U.S. Military Academy.

For their own parts, Smith and Flipper were well aware of both the extraordinary hostility they faced from their classmates and the broader debate over "social equality" that swirled around them. One response was to view it as useless and probably humiliating to appear to desire entry into "social" arenas where, whites made clear, they were not welcome. "We cared not for social recognition," Flipper wrote in his 1878 memoir. "We did not expect it, nor were we disappointed in not getting it. We would not seek it. . . . We would not accept recognition unless it was made willingly. These were our resolutions." Whether they knew it at the time, the two men were following the advice of a black newspaper whose editor had publicly counseled them to "study on and acquit themselves like men," regardless of whether they met "social as well as intellectual recognition."[21]

In fact, Flipper and Smith framed white students' disrespectful treatment as evidence of the whites' social inferiority, not their own. There were "many cadets in the corps with whom I think it no honor for any one to associate," Smith wrote, "although they are among the high-toned aristocrats, and will, no doubt, soon be numbered among the 'officers and gentlemen' of the United States Army." Flipper described those who could not bring themselves to be civil to him as "low" and of poor "breeding." In "ordinary civil life," he wrote, "I should consider such people beneath me in the social scale, should even reckon some of them as roughs, and consequently give them a wide berth."[22] Whites tended to impose their ideas about fundamental, immutable "racial" difference onto their convictions that the social realm was a place where equality need not prevail. By contrast, the black cadets insisted that manners and comportment did in fact reflect a person's inner character and that skin color had nothing to do with it.

Holding themselves aloof from white students and understanding themselves as socially superior undoubtedly helped Smith and Flipper survive at West Point, but Smith also provided a glimpse at some of the costs. In a public letter written after his dismissal on academic grounds in 1874, Smith emphasized that he had made quotidian decisions that, while designed to keep white people comfortable, may also have adversely affected his academic career. "I never asked for *social equality* at West Point," he wrote. "I never visited the quarters of any professor, official, or cadet except on duty for I did not wish any one to think that I was in an any way desirous of social recognition by those who felt themselves superior to me on account of color."[23] White cadets could seek academic advice or companionship from teachers or fellow students. Smith and Flipper could rely only on each other.

The social realm had always been a domain of status, hierarchy, and inequality, although class had been more often at issue than race in the antebellum North. When the national conversation turned more intensively to race after the Civil War, northerners adapted existing frameworks to the new context. White people who worried about racial equality advancing into new arenas turned quickly and vehemently to the category of the social, seeking, as others had before them, to counter the expansion of democracy with an energized vision of hierarchical private life as its antithesis. Defensively shoring up, or perhaps even expanding, the social zone was a way of asserting the many forms of inequality that remained perfectly legitimate.

Across the nation in the postemancipation era, when black people and their white allies demanded racial equality in various realms, those who resisted them responded by insisting that what they really sought was "social equality" and that therefore their demands were unreasonable and indeed antithetical to vaunted American traditions of permitting and even encouraging inequality in the social realm. For instance, whites across the country resisted school integration on grounds that it was a social equality measure; they construed public schools not as public institutions but as social or quasi-social ones subject to the authority of parents and reflective of their mores. White southerners attempted to discredit the Knights of Labor by arguing that its biracial conventions and parades were evidence that it promoted social equality. Then there was the matter of political dinners. When Republican editor John Forney hosted a party in Washington in 1870 attended by members of Grant's cabinet and black luminaries from Howard University, it was derided—including in the Republican press—as a "social equality" party. And, of course, when Booker T. Washington ate dinner with Theodore Roosevelt in 1901, white southerners of all stripes cried "social equality" and used the event to undermine the Republican Party's reputation in the South.[24]

Charging "social equality" became a way of discrediting whatever form of racial equality was being claimed—even if it were largely symbolic, as in the case of the infamous Roosevelt-Washington dinner—as unnatural and even un-American. The strategy was effective not so much because "the social" was a vacuous category but because it had long existed as an area (however amorphous) in American life where inequality was completely legitimate, even prized. To argue that demands for racial equality were in fact demands for "social equality" was to argue that such demands attacked the very foundations of collective life. It was to suggest that *all* the accepted hierarchies were under attack—not just traditional structures of racial subordination but also status distinctions within racial groups, relationships within families, and even the social arena itself, which was supposed to be a zone of liberty and personal choice, not of government intervention. The chaos and coercion suggested here helps us understand why black activists and their white allies so consistently denied that they were seeking social equality, even as they made expansive demands for racial equality in a variety of arenas.

By the turn of the century, the advent of new varieties of white supremacy and new ideas about racial biology gave the "social equality" argument an increasingly sexual cast. Whites—particularly southerners—frequently claimed that any recognition of African Americans as social equals would lead directly to sex between black men and white women. But if the early twentieth-century discourse of social equality was notably focused on sex, its nineteenth-century progenitor was not. Although the enrollment of black cadets at West Point engendered a striking conversation about social equality, no one argued that black cadets threatened white women's purity. Rather, the post–Civil War debate about social equality at the military academy and elsewhere concerned the relationship between the government's laws and social conventions; the question of who was responsible for racism and its remedies—individuals, families, or public institutions; and the reassertion, in a new context, of the legitimacy of inequality in ostensibly social or private relationships.

A half century after the 1964 Civil Rights Act and the 1965 Voting Rights Act, we are perhaps more aware than ever of the complexity of equality and inequality, racial and otherwise, in American thought and practice. We can see that the advent of a commitment (however partial) to racial equality in civil and political rights has made a great difference. But it is also clear that amid the stunning economic inequality that encompasses the entire population, racially distinct patterns of inequality continue, particularly in wealth, housing, health, education, and incarceration.

Understanding the persistence of race-based inequality demands that we grasp the relationship between the acceptance of civil and political equality, on the one hand, and the rejection of what was once called social equality, on the other. As historian Matthew Lassiter has shown, for example, after World War II the racial inequities of white suburbanization and black concentration in inner cities were widely perceived as the market-driven result of a myriad of private choices. In fact, these developments were produced in large measure by public policies. Yet, like many white Americans of the Reconstruction era, white suburbanites of the late twentieth century imagined—and insisted—that they inhabited a remarkably capacious "social" or in this case "private" zone, separate from the state, in which liberty prevailed and inequality was acceptable and even desirable. Like their predecessors, they drew on the general acceptance of economic and class inequality to marginalize and diminish demands for racial justice.[25] A critical interrogation of the *problem of equality* after slavery demands that we look for patterns in how Americans have mobilized discourses of individual liberty and private choice to influence, encroach on, and ultimately diminish the few arenas in which they have made a recognizable commitment to racial equality.

NOTES

1. C. Vann Woodward, "Equality: The Deferred Commitment," in *The Burden of Southern History,* updated 3rd ed. with introduction by William Leuchtenberg (Baton Rouge: Louisiana State University Press, 2008), 79.

2. The literature is voluminous but perhaps best defined by the scholarship of Eric Foner culminating in *Reconstruction: America's Unfinished Revolution, 1863–1877* (New York: Harper & Row, 1988) and by that of the Freedmen and Southern Society Project in the series *Freedom: A Documentary History of Emancipation, 1861–1867* and accompanying volumes such as Ira Berlin et al., *Slaves No More: Three Essays on Emancipation and the Civil War* (New York: Cambridge University Press, 1992).

3. For example, Davison M. Douglas, *Jim Crow Moves North: The Battle over Northern School Desegregation, 1865–1954* (New York: Cambridge University Press, 2005); Leslie A. Schwalm, *Emancipation's Diaspora: Reconstruction in the Upper Midwest* (Chapel Hill: University of North Carolina Press, 2009); Stephen Kantrowitz, *More than Freedom: Fighting for Black Citizenship in a White Republic, 1829–1889* (New York: Penguin, 2012); Kate Masur, *An Example for All the Land: Emancipation and the Struggle over Equality in Washington, D.C.* (Chapel Hill: University of North Carolina Press, 2010); Amy Dru Stanley, "Revolutionizing Human Rights: Slave Emancipation and the Civil Rights Act of 1875," in *The World the Civil War Made*, ed. Gregory P. Downs and Kate Masur (Chapel Hill: University of Carolina Press, 2015).

4. Historians who have analyzed "social equality" discourse have mainly explored how it arose in political rhetoric. See, for example, Jane E. Dailey, *Before Jim Crow: The Politics of Race in Postemancipation Virginia* (Chapel Hill: University of North Carolina Press, 2000), 85–93; Nell Irvin Painter, "'Social Equality,' Miscegenation, Labor, and Power," in *The Evolution of Southern Culture*, ed. Numan V. Bartley (Athens: University of Georgia Press, 1988); Richard A. Primus, *The American Language of Rights* (Cambridge: Cambridge University Press, 1999), 153–73; Heather Cox Richardson, *The Death of Reconstruction: Race, Labor, and Politics in the Post–Civil War North, 1865–1901* (Cambridge, Mass.: Harvard University Press, 2001), 122–49; Hannah Rosen, "The Rhetoric of Miscegenation and the Reconstruction of Race: Debating Marriage, Sex, and Citizenship in Postemancipation America," in *Gender and Slave Emancipation in the Atlantic World*, ed. Pamela Scully and Diana Patton (Durham, N.C.: Duke University Press, 2005); Rebecca J. Scott, "Public Rights, Social Equality, and the Conceptual Roots of the *Plessy* Challenge," *University of Michigan Law Review* 106, no. 5 (March 2008): 777–804; Elizabeth Dale, "'Social Equality Does Not Exist among Themselves, nor among Us': Baylies vs. Curry and Civil Rights in Chicago, 1888," *American Historical Review* 102, no. 2 (April 1997): 311–39. J. R. Pole, author of one of the few historical studies of equality, explained his method as follows: "The focus of this study is equality as an issue in public policy. . . . I have not sought to trace the reflections of private individuals; I have used literary evidence only when it is specific in its public implications (and even then very sparingly), and I have allowed the nature of American public preoccupations to dictate the distribution of my own treatment." Pole, *The Pursuit of Equality in American History* (Los Angeles: University of California Press, 1978), xi.

5. John F. Kasson, *Rudeness and Civility: Manners in Nineteenth-Century Urban America* (New York: Hill & Wang, 1990); Richard L. Bushman, *The Refinement of America: Persons, Houses, Cities* (New York: Knopf, 1992); C. Dallett Hemphill, *Bowing to Necessities: A History of Manners in America, 1620–1860* (New York: Oxford University Press, 1999); Karen Halttunen, *Confidence Men and Painted Women: A Study of Middle-Class Culture in America, 1830–1870* (New Haven, Conn.: Yale University Press, 1982); Lawrence W. Levine, *Highbrow/Lowbrow: The Emergence of Cultural Hierarchy in America* (Cambridge, Mass.: Harvard University Press, 1990).

6. Kasson, *Rudeness and Civility*, 60–61.

7. Bushman, *Refinement of America*, 416–24.

8. *The Laws of Etiquette; or, Short Rules and Reflections for Conduct in Society. By a Gentleman* (Philadelphia, 1836), 10.

9. Kasson, *Rudeness and Civility*. It was as if the "republican" side of the United States faced outward, on display for all to see, while the "social" and more explicitly hierarchical side faced inward and was a bit more hidden from view.

10. See, for example, Richard White, *Railroaded: The Transcontinentals and the Making of Modern America* (New York: W. W. Norton, 2010), esp. 93–102; Jean Baker, *Affairs of Party: The Political Culture of Northern Democrats in the Mid-Nineteenth Century* (Ithaca, N.Y.: Cornell University Press, 1983), 110.

11. Stephen E. Ambrose, *Duty, Honor, Country: A History of West Point* (Baltimore, Md.: Johns Hopkins University Press, 1966), 128, 142.

12. Here I am thinking particularly of the 1866 Civil Rights Act and Fourteenth and Fifteenth Amendments.

13. David Clark, in *New York Tribune*, July 31, 1872, in *The Papers of Ulysses S. Grant*, ed. John Y. Simon (Carbondale, Ill.: Southern Illinois University Press, 1998), 21:33.

14. Peter S. Michie, "Caste at West Point," *North American Review* 130, no. 283 (June 1880): 611. The best modern history of early black cadets at West Point is John F. Marszalek, *Assault at West Point: The Court-Martial of Johnson Whittaker* (New York: Maxwell Macmillan International, 1994). During the 1870s and 1880s, twenty-three black men were appointed to West Point. Among them, only three graduated (*Assault at West Point*, 19).

15. Smith's account of the serving incident is in Henry Ossian Flipper, *The Colored Cadet at West Point: Autobiography of Lieutenant Henry Ossian Flipper, U.S.A.*, reprint with introduction by Quintard Taylor Jr. (New York: Homer Lee, 1878; Lincoln: University of Nebraska Press, 1998), 297. For "eat like a dog," see "The Colored Cadet," *Baltimore Sun*, July 8, 1870, 1. For Schofield, see Report of General J. M. Schofield, October 5, 1880, in House Ex. Doc. 1, Part 2, 46th Cong., 3d sess., 230. For additional context, see William P. Vaugh, "West Point and the First Negro Cadet," *Military Affairs* 35, no. 3 (October 1971): 100; George S. Pappas, *To the Point: The United States Military Academy, 1802–1902* (Westport, Conn.: Praeger, 1993), 374.

16. For a critique of the ostracism, however, see *Christian Union*, January 25, 1871, 3, 4.

17. *Christian Union*, November 5, 1870, 2, 18, emphasis added.

18. *North American Review* quoted in Flipper, *Colored Cadet at West Point*, 119.

19. Flipper, *Colored Cadet at West Point*, 119, 319; Rev. E. P. Roe, "Defence of West Point," *New York Evangelist*, February 16, 1871, 42, 7; Report of Schofield, 228–29.

20. Report of Schofield, 229.

21. Flipper, *Colored Cadet at West Point*, 47–48.

22. Ibid., 304, 121.

23. Ibid., 299.

24. Peter J. Rachleff, *Black Labor in the South: Richmond, Virginia, 1865–1890* (Philadelphia: Temple University Press, 1984), 169–78; Daniel Letwin, "Interracial Unionism, Gender, and 'Social Equality' in the Alabama Coalfields, 1878–1908," *Journal of Southern History* 61, no. 3 (August 1995): 518; John K. Severn and William Warren Rogers, "Theodore Roosevelt Entertains Booker T. Washington: Florida's Reaction to the White House Dinner," *Florida Historical Quarterly* 54, no. 3 (January 1976): 306–81; Willard B. Gatewood Jr., "The Roosevelt-Washington Dinner: Accretion of Folklore," in *Theodore Roosevelt and the Art of Controversy: Episodes of the White House Years* (Baton Rouge: Louisiana State University Press, 1970). See also Masur, *Example for All the Land*.

25. Matthew D. Lassiter, *The Silent Majority: Suburban Politics in the Sunbelt South* (Princeton, N.J.: Princeton University Press, 2006); Lassiter, "De Jure/De Facto Segregation: The Long Shadow of a National Myth," in *The Myth of Southern Exceptionalism*, ed. Matthew D. Lassiter and Joseph Crespino (New York: Oxford University Press, 2010); Ariela J. Gross, "Does Colorblind Conservatism Have a Grassroots History?" unpublished paper, cited with author's permission.

When Neighbors Turn against Neighbors

*Irregular Warfare and the Crisis of
Democracy in the Civil War Era*

JUSTIN BEHREND

When Merrimon Howard first learned that white militiamen were on his trail with the intent to murder him, he thought the news was preposterous. "I treated it as a joke and laughed it off," he told a U.S. Senate committee charged with investigating the 1876 political violence in Mississippi.[1] But over many hours, Howard described to the committee the harsh reality behind those warnings. He recalled how white-line clubs began to organize and how club members rode through his home county, spreading fear and terror. He told about how he narrowly averted an ambush, how white-line militias brought a cannon to his hometown and threatened to fire on a large parade of freedpeople, and how white-liners executed thirty black men for attending a politically charged meeting at a rural church. He recounted these events two months after he had fled his home and after warnings of his imminent assassination became too real to ignore. But even at this remove, testifying in Washington, D.C., Howard struggled to understand what had just happened in Jefferson County, Mississippi—the place of his birth. Writing to President-elect Rutherford B. Hayes, Howard expressed his astonishment that the states of Mississippi and Louisiana were "today . . . better prepard for war" and "as much in rebillion . . . as in 1861."[2]

Much of Merrimon Howard's bewilderment stemmed from the intense and sudden rise of paramilitary violence carried out by his neighbors and longtime county residents. Howard had risen from slavery and became a well-regarded political leader in Jefferson County during Reconstruction. He served as justice of the peace, a state legislator, and a county school board member. Beginning in 1871, he won election to three consecutive terms as sheriff, and he counted among his supporters both ordinary freedpeople and white planters.[3] In the eleven years since the Civil War, incidents of collective violence had been exceedingly rare in Jefferson County, and even during the war years, skirmishes between Union troops and Confederate guerrillas were uncommon. In other words, there was no history of warfare, irregular or otherwise, in the county, which helps explain Howard's surprise at the violence of 1876. For eleven years, white Democrats had generally accepted the emancipated social order—a social order that included thousands of black voters and numerous black officials. There were complaints, intimidation, threats, and violence, to be sure, but the scale of opposition to black political power and Republican governance was almost always individual and local. How, then, do we explain the timing and place of these forms of paramilitary violence? How could a seemingly stable county devolve into a condition of lawlessness, terrorism, and murder? Why would some locals take up arms in a warlike manner against their neighbors?

Recently historians have employed a war framework in order to better explain the problem of Reconstruction violence. But to argue that war defined the Reconstruction period is not necessarily new. W. E. B. Du Bois, in his masterpiece *Black Reconstruction in America*, argued that the "civil war . . . never ceased." Because civil wars, he wrote, are "doubly difficult to stop," it becomes all the more likely that "war may go on more secretly, more spasmodically, and yet as truly as before the peace."[4] Only in the last twenty years have scholars returned to this subject in a sustained way. Perhaps inspired by the ways in which wars in Afghanistan and Iraq degenerated into insurgent conflicts and also by the debates on the meanings and contradictions of a war on terrorism, historians have begun to look at Reconstruction violence with new eyes.[5] Some assert, quite plainly, that "'the war' did not end with Lee's surrender" or that the "last battle" took place in 1875 when Redeemers overthrew Mississippi's state government.[6] Others, such as historians James McPherson and Mark Grimsley, claim that one phase of the war ended in 1865 but the second did not conclude until the late 1870s.[7] A variation on this last point is that a "war of Reconstruction" broke out in the wake of Confederate defeat, one characterized by guerrilla warfare and leading to a white southern victory.[8]

A war framework has much to offer as a conceptual approach to understanding the problem of violence and disorder during Reconstruction, but it also has the potential to obscure and flatten the very dynamics that it seeks to explain. The continuity of the Civil War argument rests on a number of parallel developments between the fighting in the first half of the 1860s and the decade that followed. First, there were similar combatants (ex-Union soldiers fighting ex-Confederates). Second, it was a struggle between the federal government and white southerners. And third, the Confederate nation seems similar in orientation to white supremacist militias and politicians.

Yet this perspective elides the vastly different scale of war making in the Civil War and the Reconstruction eras. The Civil War was largely a conflict between nation-states and waged by conventional armies. Although the Union army was deployed during Reconstruction against internal belligerents, the fighting was more akin to irregular warfare and often took the form of guerrilla-style raids.[9] As many historians have noted, the presence of federal troops in the South was minimal, especially after the summer of 1865.[10] And while the army helped protect state leaders in certain southern state capitals, the federal military had negligible impact on the warfare that was often waged across small towns and rural landscapes in the South. The fighting during Reconstruction was local, not sectional, and is better described as a series of conflicts among and between southerners.

One of the defining features of this warfare was the intimacy of the fighting. The belligerents frequently knew each other, as Merrimon Howard knew the men who threatened to kill him. They worked together and rubbed shoulders with each other at markets and in the streets. This spatial context is important not only in explaining the outburst of collective violence but also in understanding the terrain of irregular warfare. Local people took up arms and organized themselves into small, militaristic bands. Some raided other neighborhoods, while others set up defenses against guerrilla attacks.[11] Sometimes the setting was a civic or public space, but more often than not, the fighting took place at private residences and within particular neighborhoods. The fighting that resulted seems to be less a continuation of the Civil War than a series of civil wars on a micro scale.

These violent ruptures in the civic space of local communities raise important questions about the stability and continuity of democracy in the Civil War era. Indeed, these micro civil wars were not just a product of the Reconstruction era; rather, they appear during the Civil War and even before. Many scholars have examined guerrilla fighting between 1861 and 1865, and a few have begun to conceptualize the battles between abolitionists and slave hunters as akin to guerrilla warfare, but these incidents are often treated as just local events without any broader connections.[12] Yet when we step back and look at the entire period from 1850 to 1880, it is clear that collective violence among and between neighbors increased substantially. Rather than conceptualizing the numerous incidents of irregular warfare as episodic and separate occurrences, we ought to see these forms of intimate guerrilla fighting as part of a larger breakdown of democratic values and structures that paralleled national disunion.

It is also difficult to explain this kind of warfare within the traditional freedom narrative. The struggle to attain individual autonomy has provided historians with an important framework to understand secession, war, and Reconstruction, yet it might be useful to shift focus and to think of this era as a struggle over democracy. Local communities depend on mutual respect and trust. In order to conduct day-to-day transactions, whether social or economic, neighbors must rely on an assumption of goodwill.[13] But those assumptions are decisively broken when one group of residents takes up arms against another. When neighbors raised rifles against other neighbors, the intent, as much as can be generalized, was not merely to take away freedoms but to literally expel that group from the body politic or at least to drive them to the margins of society. While it is beneficial to focus our attention on presidential elections, conventional armies, and constitutional amendments to understand the substantial conflicts and destruction of this era, we should not ignore the breakdown of networks of trust and communication that sustain localities, and that in many ways preceded the rupture of the nation. This perspective may help explain why irregular warfare preceded the Civil War and why it persisted well after emancipation.

The 1876 guerrilla raids in Jefferson County denote one particular kind of warfare that plagued many southern communities in this era, but another kind of warfare was on display just a few miles away. In Wilkinson County, Mississippi, a pitched battle broke out between hundreds of militiamen in May 1876; on its surface, this fighting seems to be a continuation of the conventional warfare practiced during the Civil War. However, this conflict, like the many in this era, better resembles irregular warfare because neither side operated within the bounds of state authority, and while military-trained men fought on both sides, the units were loose conglomerations of locals.

Like Jefferson County, Wilkinson County did not have a history of collective violence. A few skirmishes between Confederate guerrillas and Union forces took place during the Civil War, but in subsequent years county residents adjusted to the new political order of biracial Republican governance. In the aftermath of Mississippi's 1875 counterrevolution, Wilkinson County, which had a black population five times as large as its white population, returned a large Republican majority, as it always had since the enactment of black male suffrage.[14] White-line Democrats in and around Wilkinson County, however, judged the so-called Mississippi Plan a success and began to make plans to force Republican politicians out of office. New clubs, loosely affiliated with the Democratic Party, began to appear across the county, referred to as White Men's Clubs, Honest Men's Clubs, and Regulators. These clubs formed the foundation of the white supremacist insurgency.[15]

The belligerence of these Wilkinson County Regulators surprised local black residents because they assumed a warlike posture against their neighbors. When a group of Regulators visited Alfred Black's house, they came at night while he was sick in bed. Black, a freedman, farmer, and labor organizer, had his son answer the Regulators' knocks at the door. The white men not only knew Black personally, but they knew his family well. "Is that you, Charlie Black?" one of them called out from the darkness. "Yes, that is me," the boy told them, demonstrating a measure of familiarity. Later, when another group of Regulators intercepted Alfred Black on a public road as he was returning from a mill, they demanded to know why he was organizing a labor club. Not satisfied with his answers, the Regulators tied a noose around his neck during the interrogation and hoisted him up in the air, back and forth, until he passed out. They made no attempt to conceal their identities and warned Black that they would kill him if he continued to organize black workers. When Black was later called to testify before a U.S. Senate committee about the violence in Wilkinson County, he calmly named eight of the nine men who had nearly lynched him. Asked how he knew these men, Black explained that they lived "just right around me," with one of the Regulators living only three hundred yards from his home.[16]

A few days after Black was attacked, a white merchant was murdered by an unknown assailant in a different part of the county. This incident sent many of Wilkinson's white residents into an uproar. News of the murder quickly crossed the border into West Feliciana Parish to the south and Amite County to the east, prompting white clubs from those counties to move into Wilkinson County. At least one black militia in the eastern part of Wilkinson skirmished with the white paramilitary units.[17] Whites in Woodville then organized pickets to defend against the local black militias whom they believed were intending "to march on the town." Meanwhile, in the densely populated black neighborhoods along the Mississippi River in the western part of the county, the black militias mobilized, not to attack Woodville but to defend their homes and their "rights."[18] Near the river town of Fort Adams, among the bottomlands where black people worked the cotton fields both in slavery and in freedom, locals could see how the events would play out. They knew of the electoral violence that had plagued other parts of the state in 1875. They also recognized their strategic disadvantages. With white-line forces to the south and east and their back to the Mississippi River, they could either make a stand at Fort Adams or escape north to Adams County and Natchez.

The Regulators and other white-line forces also sensed the strategic implications of the impending confrontation. Each day more and more of them, armed and mounted, rode into Woodville looking for a chance to kill black Republicans. "These Regulators in our section of the country," explained Emil L. Weber, a white Republican state senator from West Feliciana Parish, "are better armed to-day, all of them, old and young . . . than they were in confederate times, and they are more violent."[19] According to Hugh M. Foley (a freeborn former state legislator), a force of fifteen hundred armed white men mobilized to attack the black militias in the western half of Wilkinson County.[20]

Local black militias dated back to at least 1869, and Democratic Party leaders had long feared them.[21] Drawing from the ranks of Union army veterans, the militias actually spent more time mobilizing men for elections. For this and other reasons, black witnesses made clear in Senate testimony that these militias were not equivalent to the white paramilitary forces. Alfred Black maintained that freedmen, in general, were not "armed." Incredulous at this response, Senator Angus Cameron (R-Wisc.) countered, "Have not you shot-guns?" Black admitted that he had "an old shot-gun," but this weapon, he insisted, did not make him "armed."[22] Similarly, Merrimon Howard claimed that there were no "armed organizations among the colored people" in Jefferson County. Senator Francis Kernan (D-N.Y.) wondered if it was "not true that the colored people pretty generally had arms." Howard conceded that they had guns, but like Alfred Black he made a distinction between being armed and owning "bird guns."[23] The white forces, by contrast, were "armed" and prepared for war. They possessed the latest and most powerful rifles, including Winchester carbines that could be quickly reloaded and fired with more accuracy and at longer distances than anything the black militias possessed.[24]

Once the irregular white forces headed out from Woodville around May 15, 1876, they assumed the posture of conventional military units attacking reinforced positions. The mounted troops divided into three companies about three to four miles apart and then swept into the southwestern corner of the county in order to pin the black militias against a bend in the Mississippi River known as the "Old River Island." Black militiamen took up defensive positions at various plantations: along a line of thick briar hedges at one place, at the gin house of another, and at the edge of the quarters of a third. "We came upon a line of battle in an old field," one of the white leaders later recalled, "which had been formed by some of the negro ex-soldiers, and promptly charged them in columns of four."[25] The extent of the fighting is unknown, but it carried on for hours and resulted in the deaths of between thirty and fifty black men. In each of these skirmishes, the better-armed and better-organized white forces routed the black militias until, after a series of negotiations, the black forces surrendered. About eleven hundred white men then made camp for the night, as an occupying army, in the midst of the black neighborhoods.

Although some black men wanted to continue the fight into the next day, the battle at Fort Adams marked the end of the irregular warfare in Wilkinson County. It had culminated in an engagement of multiple militias and hundreds of men. White paramilitary forces had even boasted to black Republicans that "we are ready for war," and they had delivered on their promise.[26] But this was not the conventional warfare practiced by the Union and Confederate armies; rather, it resembled the irregular fighting of the Civil War era. Neighbors joined together to make war against other neighbors in loosely organized bands of armed men. As a result, the white-line Regulators forced prominent black and Republican officeholders out of office.[27] Black residents did not lose their freedoms; in fact, they continued to vote despite extensive intimidation and fraud. They even brought in a Republican majority in the November election five months later.[28] But they lost their political voice. With local black leaders unwilling to risk their lives for county offices, the black citizens found themselves pushed to the margins of the body politic.

The intimate nature of the fighting, in that participants knew one another, and the irregularity of the collective violence do not seem unique to these parts of the Natchez District or even to the paramilitary violence of the late 1870s. The Ku Klux Klan and similarly organized units in the late 1860s and early 1870s practiced irregular warfare, in the form of guerrilla fighting.[29] Roving bands of white men attacked their neighbors in a series of clashes, often motivated by criminal or political interests. Local wars broke out in North Carolina, Texas, Kentucky, South Carolina, and other parts of the South. In the Florida Panhandle, the Jackson County War lasted from 1869 to 1871 and included guerrilla attacks against picnickers and the murder of local Republican leaders, among many other violent incidents.[30] Perhaps the most famous local war took place in Colfax, Louisiana, when black Republicans battled white militias for control of the parish courthouse on Easter Sunday 1873. The white forces killed at least eighty-one black men.[31]

These local wars often originated from politically motivated conflicts between black Republicans and white Democrats, but not always. In the 1870s, white Texans resumed their guerrilla raids against Tejano settlements, much as they had done before the Civil War.[32] In northern Alabama, white Unionists, who had fought a low-grade guerrilla war against Confederates during the Civil War, continued to make war until at least 1870.[33]

The more one looks at irregular warfare, the more it becomes clear that fighting during Reconstruction was not all that different from irregular warfare during the Civil War. Recent scholarship on Civil War guerrillas has increasingly demonstrated the centrality of these conflicts to the outcome of the war.[34] Most of the guerrilla activity was either in coordination with conventional armies or targeted against belligerent forces, but as the war entered its "hard" phase in 1863, local guerrilla bands increasingly mobilized to attack other locals.[35] Local wars broke out in western North Carolina, eastern and western Tennessee, northern Alabama, northwestern Arkansas, and in much of Missouri. Historian Noel Fisher reminds us that the Civil War "had many faces," including the conventional fighting between the two main armies, but also the guerrilla struggles between Unionists and secessionists.[36] Rather than a continuity of sectional warfare that spanned the Civil War and Reconstruction eras, there was instead a continuity of irregular warfare at the local level.

Even before secession, instances of irregular warfare dot the landscape, particularly in territorial Kansas and across the border South. Slave hunters, who came north after the Fugitive Slave Act of 1850, operated as guerrilla-style raiders, disguising their actions in the face of potential violence from local abolitionist communities. John Brown and his followers participated in irregular warfare in Kansas, Missouri, and Virginia. Although Brown was largely unknown in Harpers Ferry, townsfolk knew and recognized his advance man, John Cook, who lived there for sixteen months before the guerrilla raid of October 16–18, 1859.[37]

When we refocus our attention from the national to the local and from conventional warfare to guerrilla activity, a different picture of the violence emerges. The irregular warfare was not just about nations, although it was certainly animated by federal policies. These were not merely wars about race, although racial presumptions were in the mix. These were not wars about emancipation, although emancipation seemed to intensify the spread of irregular warfare. It may be that when locals took up arms against their neighbors, they signaled that the state had failed them as a protective force. And while this warfare also reveals a profound disconnect in the shared values that make up a community, the reasons for these ruptures need to be further examined.

Paradoxically, irregular warfare is, in one sense, an expression of democracy but also deeply antithetical to democracy. Local people collectively organized, shared power in a decentralized fashion, and projected their voice, through violence, into the political debates of the day.[38] Yet irregular warfare often targeted democratically elected officials and eligible voters. In many of its variations, it rejected the legitimate paths of protest and disapproval and sought instead to overturn majority rule through force of arms. It might be useful, then, to examine local assumptions about shared governance and popular rule in order to better understand how these local civil wars broke out. The warfare may indicate a much larger ambivalence toward democracy and legitimate authority than is usually ascribed to the so-called golden age of participatory democracy.[39] As we begin to learn more about the fragility of the nation-state, we might find that it rested on a much more fragile social order than we realize.[40]

NOTES

1. Testimony of Merrimon Howard, U.S. Senate, *Testimony as to Denial of Elective Franchise in Mississippi at the Elections of 1875 and 1876*, 44th Cong., 2nd sess., Misc. Doc. 45, p. 160 (cited hereafter as *Denial of Elective Franchise*).

2. M. Howard to President R. B. Hays, February 18, 1877, Rutherford B. Hayes Papers, Rutherford B. Hayes Presidential Center, Fremont, Ohio.

3. Merrimon Howard, sheriff and tax collector, December 7, 1874, Old Bonds, Jefferson County Court House, Fayette, Mississippi. For more on Howard, see Justin Behrend, *Reconstructing Democracy: Grassroots Black Politics in the Deep South after the Civil War* (Athens: University of Georgia Press, 2015), 67–68, 151–53.

4. W. E. B. Du Bois, *Black Reconstruction in America* (New York: Harcourt, Brace, 1935; reprint, New York: Atheneum, 1992), 670.

5. James Hogue, *Uncivil War: Five New Orleans Street Battles and the Rise and Fall*

of Radical Reconstruction (Baton Rouge: Louisiana State University Press, 2006), 4; Stephen Budiansky, *The Bloody Shirt: Terror after Appomattox* (New York: Viking, 2008); Scott Reynolds Nelson, "An American War of Incarceration: Guerrilla Warfare, Occupation, and Imprisonment in the American South, 1863–65," in *Inventing Collateral Damage: Civilian Casualties, War, and Empire,* ed. Stephen J. Rockel and Rick Halpern (Toronto: Between the Lines, 2009), 115–25; Michael Fellman, *In the Name of God and Country: Reconsidering Terrorism in American History* (New Haven, Conn.: Yale University Press, 2010); Mark Grimsley, "Wars for the American South: The First and Second Reconstructions Considered as Insurgencies," *Civil War History* 58, no. 1 (March 2012): 9–10.

6. Paul A. Cimbala and Randall M. Miller, *The Great Task Remaining before Us: Reconstruction as America's Continuing Civil War* (New York: Fordham University Press, 2010), ix; Nicholas Lemann, *Redemption: The Last Battle of the Civil War* (New York: Farrar, Strauss, & Giroux, 2006); Richard Zuczek, "The Last Campaign of the Civil War: South Carolina and the Revolution of 1876," *Civil War History* 42, no. 1 (March 1996): 18–31.

7. James M. McPherson, "War and Peace in the Post–Civil War South," in *The Making of Peace: Rulers, States, and the Aftermath of War,* ed. Williamson Murray and Jim Lacey (New York: Cambridge University Press, 2009), 160–61; Grimsley, "Wars for the American South."

8. Richard Zuczek, *State of Rebellion: Reconstruction in South Carolina* (Columbia: University of South Carolina Press, 1996), 5; James M. Smallwood, Barry A. Crouch, and Larry Peacock, *Murder and Mayhem: The War of Reconstruction in Texas* (College Station: Texas A & M Press, 2003); Lemann, *Redemption,* 179–80; Kenneth W. Howell, ed., *Still the Arena of Civil War: Violence and Turmoil in Reconstruction Texas, 1865–1874* (Denton: University of North Texas Press, 2012), ix, 23; Douglas R. Egerton, *The Wars of Reconstruction: The Brief, Violent History of America's Most Progressive Era* (New York: Bloomsbury, 2014).

9. Scholars use "irregular warfare" as a concept to explain a variety of unconventional fighting that included guerrillas, partisans, raiders, and bushwhackers. In this essay I focus on the guerrilla fighting among and between locals, rather than the asymmetrical attacks on conventional forces more characteristic of partisan warfare. Daniel E. Sutherland, "Sideshow No Longer: A Historiographical Review of the Guerrilla War," *Civil War History* 46, no. 1 (March 2000): 5–23; Robert R. Mackey, *The Uncivil War: Irregular Warfare in the Upper South, 1861–1865* (Norman: University of Oklahoma Press, 2004); Daniel E. Sutherland, *Savage Conflict: The Decisive Role of Guerrillas in the American Civil War* (Chapel Hill: University of North Carolina Press, 2009). On the particularities of civil wars, see Stathis N. Kalyvas, *The Logic of Violence in Civil War* (New York: Cambridge University Press, 2006); Adam Lockyer, "The Dynamics of Warfare in Civil War," *Civil Wars* 12, nos. 1–2 (March–June 2010): 91–116.

10. James E. Sefton, *The United States Army and Reconstruction, 1865–1877* (Baton Rouge: Louisiana State University Press, 1967); Gregory P. Downs, *After*

Appomattox: Military Occupation and the Ends of War (Cambridge, Mass.: Harvard University Press, 2015).

11. Because my interests lie in warfare within bounded local communities, I have excluded the simultaneous wars on the Great Plains. Some scholars characterize Indian fighting as irregular warfare, but their fighting often targeted the U.S. Army, or their raiding served specific economic purposes. Additionally, neither the Native peoples nor American settlers considered themselves part of the same bounded community. For more on Indian warfare, see Pekka Hämäläinen, *The Comanche Empire* (New Haven, Conn.: Yale University Press, 2008), 313–41; Elliott West, *The Last Indian War: The Nez Perce Story* (New York: Oxford University Press, 2009), 152–68; Anthony R. McGinnis, "When Courage Was Not Enough: Plains Indians at War with the United States Army," *Journal of Military History* 76 (April 2012): 455–73.

12. On guerrilla fighting during the Civil War, see Michael Fellman, *Inside War: The Guerrilla Conflict in Missouri during the American Civil War* (New York: Oxford University Press, 1989); Daniel E. Sutherland, ed., *Guerrillas, Unionists, and Violence on the Confederate Home Front* (Fayetteville: University of Arkansas Press, 1999); Victoria E. Bynum, *The Free State of Jones: Mississippi's Longest Civil War* (Chapel Hill: University of North Carolina Press, 2001); Kenneth C. Barnes, "The Williams Clan's Civil War: How an Arkansas Farm Family Became a Guerrilla Band," in *Enemies of the Country: New Perspectives on Unionists in the Civil War South*, ed. John C. Inscoe and Robert C. Kenzer (Athens: University of Georgia Press, 2001), 188–207; Anne J. Bailey, "Defiant Unionists: Militant Germans in Confederate Texas," in Inscoe and Kenzer, *Enemies of the Country*, 208–28; Margaret M. Storey, *Loyalty and Loss: Alabama's Unionists in the Civil War and Reconstruction* (Baton Rouge: Louisiana State University Press, 2004); Jonathan Dean Saris, *A Separate Civil War: Communities in Conflict in the Mountain South* (Charlottesville: University of Virginia Press, 2006); Sutherland, *Savage Conflict*; Clay Mountcastle, *Punitive War: Confederate Guerrillas and Union Reprisals* (Lawrence: University of Kansas Press, 2009); Barton A. Myers, *Executing Daniel Bright: Race, Loyalty, and Guerrilla Violence in a Coastal Carolina Community, 1861–1865* (Baton Rouge: Louisiana State University Press, 2009); Mark W. Geiger, *Financial Fraud and Guerrilla Violence in Missouri's Civil War, 1861–1865* (New Haven, Conn.: Yale University Press, 2010); Michael Fellman, *Views from the Dark Side of American History* (Baton Rouge: Louisiana State University Press, 2011); Barton A. Myers, *Rebels against the Confederacy: North Carolina's Unionists* (New York: Cambridge University Press, 2014). On guerrilla fighting before secession, see Keith P. Griffler, *Front Line of Freedom: African Americans and the Forging of the Underground Railroad in the Ohio Valley* (Lexington: University Press of Kentucky, 2004), 82–87, 122–23; Nicole Etcheson, *Bleeding Kansas: Contested Liberty in the Civil War Era* (Lawrence: University of Kansas Press, 2004), 113–38, 227–45; David Reynolds, *John Brown, Abolitionist: The Man Who Killed Slavery, Sparked the Civil War, and Seeded Civil Rights* (New York: Alfred A. Knopf, 2005); Jeremy Neely, *The Border Between Them: Vio-*

lence and Reconciliation on the Kansas-Missouri Line (Columbia: University of Missouri Press, 2007), 60–85; Stanley Harrold, *Border War: Fighting over Slavery before the Civil War* (Chapel Hill: University of North Carolina Press, 2010).

13. For more on the elements of democracy, see Robert A. Dahl, *On Democracy* (New Haven, Conn.: Yale University Press, 1998); Charles Tilly, *Trust and Rule* (New York: Cambridge University Press, 2005); Charles Tilly, *Democracy* (New York: Cambridge University Press, 2007).

14. On the demographics of the county, see Census 1870, Social Explorer: http://www.socialexplorer.com.

15. For more on these clubs, see the testimony of Hugh M. Foley, U.S. Senate, *Report of the Select Committee into the Mississippi Election of 1875*, 44th Cong., 1st sess., Sen. Rpt., 1535–36, 1539–40 (cited hereafter as *Mississippi in 1875*). For more on the Mississippi Plan, see William C. Harris, *The Day of the Carpetbagger: Republican Reconstruction in Mississippi* (Baton Rouge: Louisiana State University Press, 1979), 650–90.

16. Testimony of Alfred Black, *Mississippi in 1875*, 1583–88. The violence that transpired in Wilkinson County took place while the Senate select committee was investigating the 1875 election. The Senate then extended the investigation to include the events in Wilkinson County. See *Mississippi in 1875*, iv.

17. Testimony of Emil L. Weber, *Mississippi in 1875*, 1567.

18. Testimony of W. H. Noble, *Mississippi in 1875*, 1598, 1603.

19. Ibid., 1570.

20. Testimony of Hugh M. Foley, *Mississippi in 1875*, 1538; *Natchez Democrat*, May 20, 1876.

21. *Woodville Republican*, November 27, 1869. The first reference to a black militia describes at least four "cavalry companies," including one from Fort Adams, attending a large Republican barbecue.

22. Testimony of Alfred Black, *Mississippi in 1875*, 1588.

23. Testimony of Merrimon Howard, *Denial of Elective Franchise*, 189. For more on black gun ownership, see the testimonies of W. H. Noble and James H. Jones, *Mississippi in 1875*, 1607, 1636.

24. On the weapons of the white paramilitary forces, see the testimonies of Hugh M. Foley and Emil L. Weber, *Mississippi in 1875*, 1534, 1573; Gen. Will. T. Martin to Gov. J. M. Stone, May 18, 1876, Gov. Stone correspondence, Series 807: Correspondence and Papers, Mississippi Department of Archives and History (hereafter cited as MDAH), Jackson, Mississippi; James Page et al. to Hon. A. Ames, [n.d.], received November 1, 1875, Gov. Ames correspondence, MDAH.

25. J. H. Jones, "Reconstruction in Wilkinson County," *Publications of the Mississippi Historical Society* 8 (1904): 172.

26. Testimony of Merrimon Howard, *Denial of Elective Franchise*, 189.

27. Testimony of A. M. Hardy, *Denial of Elective Franchise*, 144–45; Hugh M. Foley to U. S. Grant, September 1, 1876, in John Y. Simon, ed., *The Papers of Ulysses S. Grant* (Carbondale: Southern Illinois University Press, 1967–2012), 27:321–22n.

28. Table: "Vote in Mississippi for 1873, 1875, and 1876," *Denial of Elective Franchise*, 813.

29. Allen W. Trelease, *White Terror: The Ku Klux Conspiracy and Southern Reconstruction* (New York: Harper & Row, 1971); George C. Rable, *But There Was No Peace: The Role of Violence in the Politics of Reconstruction* (Athens: University of Georgia Press, 1984), 69–80, 96–99; James M. Smallwood, "When the Klan Rode: Terrorism in Reconstruction Texas," in Howell, *Still the Arena of Civil War*, 214–42; Jim D. Brisson, "'Civil Government Was Crumbling Around Me': The Kirk-Holden War of 1870," *North Carolina Historical Review* 88, no. 2 (April 2011): 123–63; Carole Emberton, *Beyond Redemption: Race, Violence, and the American South after the Civil War* (Chicago: University of Chicago Press, 2013); Michael W. Fitzgerald, "Ex-Slaveholders and the Ku Klux Klan: Exploring the Motivations of Terrorist Violence," in *After Slavery: Race, Labor, and Citizenship in the Reconstruction South*, ed. Bruce E. Baker and Brian Kelly (Gainesville: University Press of Florida, 2013), 143–58; Elaine Frantz Parsons, *Ku-Klux: The Birth of the Klan during Reconstruction* (Chapel Hill: University of North Carolina Press, 2015).

30. Daniel R. Weinfeld, *The Jackson County War: Reconstruction and Resistance in Post–Civil War Florida* (Tuscaloosa: University of Alabama Press, 2012).

31. Charles Lane, *The Day Freedom Died: The Colfax Massacre, the Supreme Court, and the Betrayal of Reconstruction* (New York: Henry Holt, 2008), 265–66. See also LeeAnna Keith, *The Colfax Massacre: The Untold Story of Black Power, White Terror, and The Death of Reconstruction* (New York: Oxford University Press, 2008).

32. Andrés Tijerina, "Foreigners in Their Native Land: The Violent Struggle between Anglos and Tejanos for Land Titles in South Texas during Reconstruction," in Howell, *Still the Arena of Civil War*, 305–25.

33. Margaret M. Storey, "The Crucible of Reconstruction: Unionists and the Struggle for Alabama's Postwar Home Front," in Cimbala and Miller, *Great Task Remaining before Us*, 69–87. See also Scott Reynolds Nelson, "Red String and Half Brothers: Civil Wars in Alamance County, North Carolina, 1861–1871," in Inscoe and Kenzer, *Enemies of the Country*, 37–53; Steven E. Nash, "'The Other War Was but the Beginning:' The Politics of Loyalty in Western North Carolina," in *Reconstructing Appalachia: The Civil War's Aftermath*, ed. Andrew L. Slap (Lexington: University Press of Kentucky, 2010), 105–34; Aaron Astor, *Rebels on the Border: Civil War, Emancipation, and the Reconstruction of Kentucky and Missouri* (Baton Rouge: Louisiana State University Press, 2012); T. R. C. Hutton, *Bloody Breathitt: Politics and Violence in the Appalachian South* (Lexington: University Press of Kentucky, 2013); J. Michael Rhyne, "'The Negroes Are No Longer Slaves': Free Black Families, Free Labor, and Racial Violence in Post-Emancipation Kentucky," in Baker and Kelly, *After Slavery*, 122–42.

34. In particular, see Fellman, *Inside War*; Mackey, *Uncivil War*; Sutherland, *Savage Conflict*.

35. On the "hard" war, see Mark Grimsley, *The Hard Hand of War: Union Mili-

tary Policy toward Southern Civilians, 1861–1865 (New York: Cambridge University Press, 1995).

36. Noel C. Fisher, *War at Every Door: Partisan Politics and Guerrilla Violence in East Tennessee, 1860–1869* (Chapel Hill: University of North Carolina Press, 1997), 3.

37. Griffler, *Front Line of Freedom*; Etcheson, *Bleeding Kansas*; Reynolds, *John Brown*; Neely, *Border Between Them*; Nicole Etcheson, "John Brown, Terrorist?" *American Nineteenth Century History* 10, no. 1 (March 2009): 29–48; Harrold, *Border War*; Steven Lubet, *The "Colored Hero" of Harper's Ferry: John Anthony Copeland and the War against Slavery* (New York: Cambridge University Press, 2015), 91–99, 146–55.

38. Daniel E. Sutherland, "Guerrilla Warfare, Democracy, and the Fate of the Confederacy," *Journal of Southern History* 68, no. 2 (May 2002): 260, 277.

39. For representative works, see Richard L. McCormick, *The Party Period and Public Policy: American Politics from the Age of Jackson to the Progressive Era* (New York: Oxford University Press, 1986); Joel H. Silbey, *The American Political Nation, 1838–1893* (Stanford, Calif.: Stanford University Press, 1991); Glenn C. Altschuler and Stuart M. Blumin, *Rude Republic: Americans and Their Politics in the Nineteenth Century* (Princeton, N.J.: Princeton University Press, 2000); Byron E. Shafer and Anthony J. Badger, eds., *Contesting Democracy: Substance and Structure in American Political History, 1775–2000* (Lawrence: University Press of Kansas, 2001); Sean Wilentz, *The Rise of American Democracy: Jefferson to Lincoln* (New York: W. W. Norton, 2005).

40. On the instability of the state, see Gregory P. Downs, "The Mexicanization of American Politics: The United States' Transnational Path from Civil War to Stabilization," *American Historical Review* 117, no. 2 (April 2012): 387–409; Steven Hahn, *A Nation without Borders: The United States and Its World in an Age of Civil Wars, 1830–1910* (New York: Viking, 2016).

When Everybody Knew

JAMES OAKES

In early 1865 Abraham Lincoln mused about the origins of the Civil War, which was finally coming to an end. When he became president in April 1861, he noted, "One eighth of the whole population were colored slaves," and those slaves "constituted a peculiar and powerful interest. *All knew*," Lincoln added, "that this interest was somehow the cause of the war." Seven decades later, in his monumental study *Black Reconstruction*, W. E. B. Du Bois echoed Lincoln. When the Civil War began, Du Bois wrote, "*They all knew* that the only thing that really threatened the Union was slavery."[1]

What did they all know? What does it mean to say that when the Civil War began everybody "knew" that slavery was "somehow the cause of the war"? These days historians generally agree that when eleven southern states seceded from the Union, they did so to protect slavery. But from what? Was the North, or at any rate were northern Republicans, actually menacing slavery, or was secession a hysterical overreaction to a nonexistent threat? The proslavery origins of the Civil War are widely understood, but were there any antislavery origins that might explain secession as something other than mass hysteria? Historians may agree that the slave states seceded to protect slavery, but few would argue that the victorious Republicans had any intention of undermining slavery in the southern states. Most would say the opposite—that emancipation became a northern war aim only in 1863. When the war started, Republican leaders openly disavowed any desire to free the slaves. Didn't Lincoln declare, in his first inaugural address, that "I have no purpose, directly or indirectly, to interfere with slavery in the States where it exists"? Did he not endorse the so-called Corwin Amendment to the Constitution that would permanently deny to Congress "the power to abolish or interfere, within any State, with the domestic institutions thereof, including that of persons held to labor or service by the laws of said State"? Surely everyone "knew" back in early 1861 that when Lincoln and the Republicans took control of Congress and the presidency, they had no intention of undermining slavery in the southern states.

Except that is not what most people at the time seemed to know. Opposition to slavery was the Republican Party's sole *raison d'être*, and it was widely assumed that Republicans fully intended to use all the power available to them under the Constitution to undermine slavery in the states, even without a civil war. And if there were a war, if the slave states seceded from the Union, the peacetime restraints on the federal government would give way to the war powers allotted to Congress and the president under the Constitution. Those war powers included the authority to directly "interfere" with slavery in the seceded states by emancipating slaves in the disloyal regions of the South. These were among the many things that most Americans seemed to know about by the time Lincoln became president.

How, then, do we explain Lincoln's inaugural promise not to "interfere" with slavery, or the constitutional amendment that he endorsed? These questions have been difficult to answer in large measure because generations of historians have spent so much time dismissing the significance of the northern antislavery movement, repeatedly reducing it to a "tiny group" of marginalized followers of William Lloyd Garrison. So effective has this erasure been that few historians now recognize the assumptions of the broader antislavery movement of which Garrison was but one part. Almost inevitably, we tear Lincoln's first inaugural address and the Corwin Amendment out of their context, not realizing that they both repeated, almost verbatim, the very words most radical abolitionists had been using for decades: the Constitution did not allow the federal government to abolish slavery or directly "interfere" with it in a state. This was the starting premise of the American Anti-Slavery Society, the militant organization founded by Garrison in 1833. "We fully and unanimously recognize the sovereignty of each State, to legislate exclusively on the subject of slavery which is tolerated within its limits. . . . Congress under the present compact, has no right to interfere with any of the slave States in relation to this momentous subject."[2]

Within a decade radical antislavery politicians were saying the same thing. Joshua Giddings, the fearless Ohio Whig, was expelled from Congress in 1842 for proposing a set of antislavery resolutions—the *Creole* resolves. The very first of Giddings's resolutions explained that under both the Articles of Confederation and the Constitution of 1787, "each of the several States composing this Union exercised full and exclusive jurisdiction over the subject of slavery within its own territory, and possessed full power to continue or abolish it at pleasure." Salmon P. Chase agreed, notwithstanding his own radical commitment to abolishing slavery. The founders "did not intend to authorize direct national legislation for the removal of the slavery existing in particular States under their local laws," Chase declared.[3]

By the 1850s even the most radical antislavery politicians were reciting this familiar constitutional refrain. Republicans would like nothing better than to see slavery abolished everywhere, Thaddeus Stevens explained in 1860, but "the Constitution of the United States gives us no power to interfere with the institutions of our sister States. And we do deny now, as we have ever denied, that there is any desire or intention, on the part of the Republican party, to interfere with those institutions." Addressing his southern colleagues in the House of Representatives later in the same year, Ohio's Benjamin Wade insisted that although the Republicans were an antislavery party, "there is no Republican, there is no convention of Republicans, there is no paper that speaks for them, there is no orator that sets forth their doctrines, who ever pretends that they have any right in your States to interfere with your peculiar institution."[4]

No one doubts that these men—Garrison, Giddings, Chase, Stevens, Wade—were radicals committed to the abolition of slavery. Certainly no one in 1860 would have doubted it. They assumed that slavery was a state institution, that it could only be abolished by the states. This was a consensus position that Republican radicals shared with their most conservative allies, including Thomas Corwin. Long before he introduced his amendment prohibiting the federal government from abolishing slavery in a state, he had repeatedly declared that slavery was strictly a state institution, that it "is the creature of local, municipal law."[5] His proposed amendment did nothing more than ratify this "federal consensus." But the antislavery commitments of Republican radicals did not end with the recognition that Congress had no power under the Constitution to "interfere" with slavery in the southern states; rather, that is the premise from which their antislavery commitments *began*. For a conservative such as Corwin, the federal government could do nothing more than ban slavery in a territory, although if a territorial legislature chose to introduce slavery, it would be free to do so. By contrast, radicals assumed that not only could the federal government prevent a territorial legislature from legalizing slavery but Congress should exercise all the constitutional power at its disposal to weaken slavery *in the states*, though stopping short of outright abolition. In Chase's words, the Constitution allowed the federal government to "discountenance and discourage it in the States; and to favor the Abolition of it by State authority."[6]

This was Abraham Lincoln's position. By the time he became president, Lincoln had committed himself not only to a complete ban on slavery in all the territories but also to the abolition of slavery in the District of Columbia, a federal personal liberty law that would guarantee due process rights to slaves arrested as fugitives, and the active suppression of the Atlantic slave trade. He had even hinted that if the slave states seceded the federal government would be under no obligation to enforce the fugitive slave clause of the Constitution. So when he said in his inaugural address that the Constitution did not allow him to interfere with slavery in the states, when he endorsed the Corwin Amendment that merely affirmed this consensus, most Americans understood that he and his fellow Republicans would nevertheless use all the federal power at their disposal to put slavery on a course of "ultimate extinction." What historians have since forgotten, most Americans at the time knew.

The northern Democrats certainly seemed to know. A month before the presidential election of November 1860, a Democratic newspaper in Illinois denounced Lincoln for proposing "to legislate so that slavery must soon be extinguished" in the southern states.[7] The Republicans would not abolish slavery directly, the editors warned. Rather, they would withdraw federal protection from slavery on the high seas, prevent the slave states from expanding into the western territories, and load the federal benches with antislavery judges. If Republicans force the South to secede, northern Democrats also warned, they would then refuse to enforce the fugitive slave clause of the Constitution, and slaves would be "cajoled and coaxed into the North, where no owner could hope to recover them."[8] Were the northern Democrats making this up?

Southern leaders were saying the same things in the wake of the Republican Party's triumph in the recent presidential and congressional elections. The *Kentucky Statesman* warned readers that with control of Congress, Republicans would repeal the Fugitive Slave Act of 1850, prohibit slavery in all the western territories, block the admission of new slave states, and abolish slavery in Washington, D.C.[9] Secessionists waved aside all Republican promises not to interfere directly in the states where slavery already existed. "Where they cannot attack it in the States they will attack it at every other point they can reach," a Louisiana secessionist paper argued. "They will set fire to all the surrounding buildings in the hope that some spark may catch, and everything be destroyed in a general conflagration. They will undermine the pillars of the institution, and then wait quietly for the whole edifice to tumble."[10] "Under the fostering hand of federal power," warned the *Richmond Enquirer*, abolitionism will insidiously plant itself in the border states, "converting them into free States, then into 'cities of refuge' for runaway negroes from the gulf States." Nothing Lincoln said in his inaugural address would have stopped the Republicans from pursuing the policies secessionists warned were coming.

With white southerners talking so openly about what Lincoln and the Republicans would do if they won the 1860 elections, the slaves could hardly remain unaware. During the campaign observers noticed that the "colored population" of Georgia was "manifesting an unusual interest in politics, and the result of the Presidential election." In Macon "every political speech" attracted "a number of negroes" who "managed to linger around and hear what the orators say."[11] Thomas Johnson, a Virginia slave, recalled that in 1860 "there was great excitement in Richmond over the election of Mr. Abraham Lincoln as President of the United States. The slaves prayed to God for his success, and they prayed very especially the night before the election. We knew he was in sympathy with the abolition of Slavery. The election was the signal for a great conflict for which the Southern States were ready."[12] Farther south in Talbot County, Georgia, George Wombly overheard his owner declare that "he was going to join the army and bring Abe Lincoln's head back for a soap dish. He also said that he would wade in blood up to his neck to keep the slaves from being freed."[13] A few weeks after the war began, the governor of Alabama gave an impromptu speech in Montgomery "in which he dwelt on Southern Rights, Sumter, victory, and abolitiondom," while nearby "there were a number of blacks listening."[14] The slaves have "been talking a great deal about Lincoln freeing the servants," a Mississippi mistress worried in her diary in May 1861.[15] The slaveholders made no attempt to disguise the fact that they had seceded because Abraham Lincoln had been elected president. As a young slave in Georgia, Levi Branham, recalled, one of his "young masters" told him about the 1860 election and said "that if Mr. Abe Lincoln was elected the negroes would be free. Then he asked me if I wanted to be free and I told him 'yes.'"[16] However imperfectly, the slaves understood that Abraham Lincoln was the head of an antislavery party, and that when the war began Union soldiers would come into the South as an army of liberation.

It is possible that the slaves were genuinely misguided, that northern Democrats were merely being demagogues, and that the secessionists were in fact responding hysterically to a threat that was not there. Maybe the entire country really did go crazy in late 1860. I doubt it. But as long as we perpetuate the "Lost Cause" tradition that erases and denigrates the broadly popular antislavery movement from the history of the United States, we are left with no plausible way to explain why so many Americans "knew" that the Republicans intended to destroy slavery, whether gradually in peacetime or quickly and brutally as an act of war. The truth is that the reason everybody "knew" what the Republicans intended is because the Republicans had been telling everybody for years.

The organizing principle of Republican antislavery policy was "Freedom National." Because the Constitution recognized slavery as a strictly local institution, Republicans could not directly abolish slavery in the states. But they could make freedom *national* by surrounding the South with a "cordon of freedom"—free states, free territories, and free oceans—a cordon designed to force the slave states to abolish slavery on their own, to put slavery on a course of "ultimate extinction." Long before the constitutional theory justifying this project had been elaborated, pioneering abolitionists such as Benjamin Lundy and his protégé William Lloyd Garrison had specified a number of antislavery policies the federal government could pursue, notwithstanding the ban on direct "interference" with slavery in the states. Congress could ban slavery from the western territories, suppress it on the high seas, and abolish it in Washington, D.C. It could either repeal the Fugitive Slave Act or radically revise it. These policies were supposed to weaken slavery to the point where the slave states themselves would abandon the institution.

As the specific policies were debated and adjudicated in the late 1830s and early 1840s, opponents of slavery formulated a theory of antislavery constitutionalism that justified far more than a simple ban on slavery in the territories. Antislavery constitutionalism, with its broad implications, provided the doctrinal continuity from the abolitionists of the 1830s to the Republican platforms of the 1850s. The specific policies endorsed by the Liberty Party, the Free Soilers, and the Republicans changed over time, but the underlying principles of antislavery constitutionalism persisted. Thus the Republican Party platforms of 1856 and 1860 promised only to ban slavery in the territories, but they justified the ban on the broad principles of antislavery constitutionalism—principles that explain why most Republicans were prepared to go much further. "I am for the *extinction* of slavery," Republican senator George W. Julian declared in 1856. If his party's platform is faithfully carried out, he explained, slavery

> will be abolished in our Federal District; it will be denied the protection of our flag on the high seas, and in its execrable traffic in humanity now carried on by authority of Congress on our southeast coast; our Great National Black Law for the recovery of fugitives will be blotted out; all federal enactments in be-half of slavery will be repealed; the vast power and patronage of the National Government will be rescued from the active and zealous service of the slave interest, and dedicated as actively and zealously to the service of freedom; in short, the peculiar institution, shorn of its "nationality," and staggering under its own weight, will inevitably dwindle and die.[17]

This is the first thing "all knew" when the Civil War began: the Republicans would not violate the "federal consensus" by directly abolishing slavery in any state, at least not until they added the Thirteenth Amendment to the Constitution. Instead, they would make freedom national, by walling off slavery within a cordon of free states, free territories, and free oceans, depriving slavery of all federal support, gradually forcing the slave states to abolish slavery on their own. Hoping to avoid this fate, the slave states began seceding from the Union as soon as the Republican victories in the presidential and congressional elections of 1860 were announced.

But there was something else that everybody "knew" by early 1861. If the slave states seceded from the Union there would be a war, and if that happened Congress and the president could invoke their constitutional war powers and begin emancipating slaves immediately, without compensation, as part of their effort to suppress the rebellion. In offering freedom to slaves who rebelled against their masters by escaping to Union lines, the Republicans threatened to unleash the horrors of "servile insurrection." Making freedom national was conceived as a peacetime program designed to get slavery abolished one state at a time, whereas military emancipation was a war measure and as such took place in the context of violence and social upheaval. Slave rebellion was not something Republicans *wanted* to provoke; all along they hoped to undermine slavery peacefully and gradually. But a revolutionary military emancipation was something they repeatedly warned would happen if the slave states were foolish enough to provoke a war by seceding from the Union.

Throughout history slaves had been armed in wartime, and occasionally an enslaved soldier might even be emancipated as a reward for particularly meritorious service. But over the course of human history, war has far more commonly led to mass enslavement than to mass emancipation. Until the middle of the eighteenth century, slaves in places such as Jamaica and South Carolina were armed for military service and then returned to their plantations as slaves when the war ended or the rebellion was suppressed. This ancient tradition was radically upended during the eighteenth century when, for the first time in history, belligerents on both sides began *offering* freedom to large numbers of slaves as an incentive for them to join the military. Rather than enslave civilians or even prisoners of war, the common practice of the ages, British and American forces emancipated thousands of slaves during the American Revolution, each side hoping to weaken the enemy, win the war, or suppress rebellion. This already radical departure was radicalized still further by the Haitian revolution and the Spanish-American wars of independence, during which all the slaves were freed and slavery as an institution was abolished.[18]

In 1836, citing the Spanish-American precedents and implicitly the revolution in Saint-Domingue, former president John Quincy Adams astonished his colleagues in the House of Representatives by declaring that if the government were called on to suppress a slave rebellion in the southern states, or if a foreign nation occupied the South, the war and treaty-making powers of the Constitution empowered federal authorities to do what the Latin American revolutionaries did—invite the slaves to join forces with the U.S. government by offering freedom not to thousands but to millions of southern blacks. Abolitionists quickly adopted the threat of universal military emancipation to explain why the southern states would never secede from the Union, despite growing antislavery sentiment in the North. Slaves are "dangerous in time of war," Henry Stanton declared. What would happen if "the Union were severed?" he asked. Perhaps the slaves would rise in spontaneous insurrection or be encouraged to rebel by northerners. Or perhaps "a daring leader of Northern forces, inscribing 'freedom' on his banner, might enter the South, and bear off in triumph, thousands of her slaves. Sir, the slave states would be insane to dissolve the Union."[19]

William Jay similarly dismissed southern threats of secession by reciting a litany of problems secession would create for the slave states. After secession, slaveholders could no longer recover their fugitive slaves from the North, and slaves themselves would pour across the Ohio River. The coastwise slave trade would be suppressed as a form of piracy. The slave population itself would soon overwhelm the whites and rise in rebellion.

The civilized world would repudiate the slave South's representatives and resist its imperial expansion. "At length the fatal period would arrive, when, stung with insults and injuries, the new empire would appeal to arms; and should a hostile army land upon its shores," Jay warned, "the standard of emancipation would be reared, and slavery would expire in blood."[20]

Eventually these abolitionist warnings that war would lead to emancipation spread into the political mainstream. "It is but too evident that if the South goes on to disunion on the alleged ground of disaffection, she goes on to civil war," a Boston editorialist explained in 1850. "Who doubts the result of such a contest? The contemplation of it is fearful, terrible in the extreme. The doom of slavery is sealed the day that contest commences."[21] There are three ways to emancipate slaves, Horace Mann explained in 1851. The first two were manumission of individual slaves by individual masters and abolition by the slave states themselves. The third "means of emancipation," Mann continued, was "revolutionary" wartime emancipation such as the founders had "adopted against Great Britain." In those circumstances, the slaves themselves "believe they can obtain their freedom by force." By resisting state abolition and proclaiming that "slavery is eternal," the slaveholders risked making a violent collision over slavery inevitable. "And the ultimate result of collision is as certain as the fulfillment of any natural law." Bloody, violent, wartime emancipation was the only alternative to manumission or state abolition.[22]

Republicans revealed their understanding of the military option by contrasting it with the peaceful alternative of state abolition, and by warning of the consequences of secession. Slavery "will be overthrown," William Seward predicted in 1855, "either peacefully or lawfully, under the constitution, or it will work the subversion of the constitution, together with its overthrow. Then the slaveholders would perish in the struggle." Should the slave states subvert the Constitution by seceding from the Union, they would unleash a "servile war" against which the "American Union is the only defense of the slaveholders—their only protection. If ever they shall, in a season of madness, secede from that Union and provoke that war, they will soon come back again."[23] Any attempt by the slave states to secede from the Union was bound to fail because secession meant war and war would trigger military emancipation. The threat of military emancipation was, in fact, the major reason so many Republicans persisted in the illusion that the slave states would never actually secede from the Union. "It is a principle understood by all intelligent men," the Ohio Republican Joshua Giddings wrote in 1857, "that when war exists, peace may be obtained by the emancipation of all the slaves held by individuals, if necessary."[24]

Giddings was hardly alone. Throughout the secession winter of 1861, Republicans in Congress repeatedly quoted John Quincy Adams, warning that—in the words of one congressman—"the first blast of war will be the trumpet-signal of emancipation." Republican congressman John Bingham of Ohio agreed. In "time of war," he declared in January 1861, the federal government could "interfere with slavery in the States" by "emancipating the slaves." In support of this proposition, he added, "I adopt the words of Mr. John Quincy Adams." James Ashley likewise argued that the federal government, "once involved in war," could undertake "*the removal, by force if necessary, of the cause that produced the rebellion.*" This, he added, "is no new doctrine," for John Quincy Adams had spelled it out "nearly twenty years ago, in the House of Representatives."[25] Before the first shots of the Civil War were fired, before the first slaves ran to Union lines, Republicans were declaring that if the secessionists provoked a war, the federal government would respond by emancipating southern slaves.

Thus Republicans took power and commenced the Civil War already armed with two distinct scenarios for a federal attack on slavery *in the southern states*: concerted federal pressure on those states to abolish slavery on their own, and military emancipation—with its connotations of slave insurrection—justified under enlightenment laws of war and the war powers clause of the Constitution. So what "all knew" in 1861 was that the Civil War had both proslavery *and* antislavery origins. Once those antislavery origins are taken into account, the actual history of slavery's wartime destruction is easier to understand.

To begin with, anyone familiar with the long history of abolitionist agitation would recognize that the antislavery project was substantially a *congressional* project. Historians spend altogether too much time asking questions such as *When did Lincoln decide to free the slaves?* or *What took Lincoln so long to issue the Emancipation Proclamation?* The Lincoln obsession, no matter where it comes from, prevents them from seeing that most of the antislavery policies adopted by the federal government during the Civil War originated in Congress. Congress abolished slavery in Washington, D.C. Congress banned slavery from the western territories. Congress made the abolition of slavery a prerequisite for the admission of new states into the Union. The Thirteenth Amendment did not originate in the White House; it came out of Congress.

Even military emancipation, which Lincoln justified by reference to his authority as commander in chief, required congressional action. When John Quincy Adams first declared that slaves could be freed under the war powers of the Constitution, he attributed the power to Congress. It was Congress that twice determined the scope of federal confiscation of slave "property," with the understanding that the president could then emancipate slaves in federal possession by virtue of his war powers. This is why in September 1861 Lincoln ordered General John C. Frémont to *rewrite* his emancipation order to conform to the letter of the First Confiscation Act, and why he then justified his order by claiming that the scope of emancipation was determined by legislation, not by generals. A few months later Lincoln ordered his secretary of war, Simon Cameron, to remove a recommendation to arm slaves from his annual report on the grounds that it was up to Congress, not the administration, to change the law and allow blacks to enlist in the Union Army. Not surprisingly, it was Congress that made it a crime for anyone in the Union army or navy to participate in the rendition of fugitive slaves, and Congress that eventually did remove the ban on black enlistment in the Union army.

Some antislavery policies did fall exclusively within the domain of the executive branch, and here Lincoln's role was indispensable. Immediately on taking office, the Lincoln administration opened diplomatic negotiations with Britain that resulted in a treaty to suppress the Atlantic slave trade. At the same time, Lincoln's Interior Department undertook the aggressive prosecution of the illegal slave trade, an effort that led to the first-ever execution of a merchant captain convicted of violating federal laws making it a crime for American citizens to trade in slaves. Lincoln said on several occasions that under the Constitution Congress could not actually free a slave in a state, but it could specify which slaves could be "confiscated" from enemy owners. Congress did this twice, in two Confiscation Acts passed in the first two years of the war. Once the slaves had been legally confiscated, the president, acting on his authority as commander in chief, proceeded to emancipate the slaves. In short, military emancipation was a two-step process requiring both congressional and presidential action.

By early December 1861, less than eight months after the war began, the president and his cabinet repeatedly went on record affirming the administration's emancipation policy in a way that conformed to Du Bois's notion of a "general strike." Black workers coming into Union lines from areas in rebellion were voluntarily transferring their labor services from the masters who claimed them as property to federal authorities, who instead employed them as wage laborers. Lincoln administration officials endorsed precisely this policy only weeks after the war began, when slaves escaping to Fortress Monroe offered to work as free laborers for the Union army rather than as slaves for their disloyal masters. As the secretary of the navy explained in his annual report of December 1861, refugees seeking "the shelter and protection of our flag" on Union ships "should be cared for and employed in some useful manner." If neither the navy nor the army had need of their services, "they should be allowed to proceed freely and peaceably without restraint to seek a livelihood in any loyal portion of the country."[26] In his own annual report as secretary of the Treasury, dated December 9, 1861, Salmon Chase explained that the slaves of rebels "may . . . be justly liberated from their constraint, and made more valuable in various employments, through voluntary and compensated service."[27] A few days earlier the secretary of state, William Seward, issued a public letter ordering the Union army to arrest anyone attempting to capture and return slaves escaping into Washington, D.C., from the rebel state of Virginia. Such seizures of fugitive slaves, Seward explained, were a clear violation of the First Confiscation Act. These were not runaway cabinet officers speaking their own minds; they were high-ranking officials making public declarations of administration policy. Lincoln himself had made this clear in his first annual message to Congress. By virtue of the First Confiscation Act, a number of rebellious masters had "forfeited" their claims to the labor of their slaves, and the slaves were "thus liberated."[28] By then Lincoln was already actively pressuring the border states to abolish slavery on their own. In November 1861 he proposed a gradual abolition statute for Delaware, which he saw as a model for other states to follow.

It is sometimes said that Lincoln was committed to nothing more than banning slavery in the territories, that his belated decision to issue an Emancipation Proclamation represented a dramatic shift in his position. But a different interpretation is required to explain Lincoln's extensive record of antislavery policies, all of them in place before he issued his famous proclamation. The territorial ban was actually Congress's to impose, not the president's. But it was up to Lincoln to suppress the Atlantic slave trade, prosecute slave traders, refuse to return slaves escaping to Union lines, emancipate slaves confiscated from disloyal owners, pressure Union generals to implement free labor in occupied parts of the South, and pressure states to abolish slavery on their own.

Obviously the war made it possible for Lincoln and the Republicans to do these things, and no doubt the war created opportunities for slaves to emancipate themselves. But just as the slaves had a long-standing tradition of running to freedom long before the war began, the opponents of slavery had a well-developed understanding of the antislavery policies they could adopt long before they took power. At the outset of the conflict nobody knew how or when slavery would be extinguished, and the Republicans were often hopelessly naïve in thinking the institution of slavery was so weak and vulnerable that it would collapse quickly under the strains of war. But that the Republicans hated slavery, that they intended to undermine it in a variety of ways, that they assumed slaves would claim their freedom by taking advantage of the opportunities war and policy had created—those were the things that all Americans "knew" when the slave states began seceding from the Union in late 1860.

NOTES

1. *Collected Works of Abraham Lincoln*, ed. Roy Basler (New Brunswick, N.J.: Rutgers University Press, 1953), 8:332; W. E. B. Du Bois, *Black Reconstruction* (New York: Harcourt, Brace, 1935), 56.

2. *Declaration of the National Anti-Slavery Convention* (Philadelphia: Matthew and Gunn, 1833).

3. "Address of the Southern and Western Liberty Convention," held in Cincinnati, June 11 and 12, 1845.

4. *Congressional Globe*, January 25, 1860, and December 17, 1860.

5. *Life and Speeches of Thomas Corwin, Orator, Lawyer, and Statesman*, ed. Josiah Morrow (Cincinnati: W. H. Anderson, 1896), 328, 437, 447.

6. "Address of the Southern and Western Liberty Convention."

7. *Springfield Daily Illinois State Register*, September 28, 1860, in *Northern Editorials on Secession*, ed. Howard Cecil Perkins (New York: American Historical Association, 1942), 1:42–43.

8. *New York Daily News*, January 9, 1861, in *Northern Editorials on Secession*, 1:299.

9. *Kentucky Statesman*, January 6, 1860, in *Southern Editorials on Secession*, ed. Dwight Lowell Dumond (New York: American Historical Association, 1931), 3.

10. *New Orleans Daily Crescent*, December 14, 1860, in *Southern Editorials on Secession*, ed. Dumond, 333.

11. Quoted in Clarence L. Mohr, *On the Threshold of Freedom: Masters and Slaves in Civil War Georgia* (Baton Rouge: Louisiana State University Press, 1986), 36–37.

12. Thomas L. Johnson, *Twenty-Eight Years a Slave in Virginia . . .* (Bournemouth, Eng.: W. Mate and Sons, 1909), 27.

13. Quoted in Steven V. Ash, *The Black Experience in the Civil War South* (Santa Barbara, Calif.: Praeger, 2010), 2.

14. William Howard Russell, *My Diary North and South* (Boston: T.O.H.P. Burnham, 1863), 163–64.

15. Quoted in Winthrop D. Jordan, *Tumult and Silence at Second Creek: An In-*

quiry into a Civil War Slave Conspiracy, rev. ed. (Baton Rouge: Louisiana State University Press, 1995), 11.

16. Levi Branham, *My Life and Travels* (Dalton, Ga.: A. J. Showalter, 1929), 45.

17. George W. Julian, *Speeches on Political Questions* (New York: Hurd and Houghton, 1872), 146.

18. George E. Baker, ed., *The Works of William H. Seward* (Boston: Houghton, Mifflin, 1884), 4:248.

19. *Remarks of Henry B. Stanton in the Representatives' Hall* . . . (Boston: Isaac Knapp, 1837), 699ff.

20. William Jay, *A View of the Action of the Federal Government, in Behalf of Slavery* (Utica, N.Y.: J. C. Jackson, 1844), 92.

21. *Boston Courier*, February 5, 1850, quoted in *First Blows of the Civil War: The Ten Years of Preliminary Conflict in the United States* . . . , ed. James Pike (New York: American News Company, 1879), 13.

22. *Proceedings of the Convention of the Colored Freemen of Ohio* (Cincinnati: Dumas and Lawyer, 1852), 19–22. Mann's remarks are contained in a letter he wrote to the convention that is published in the proceedings.

23. *The Works of William H. Seward*, ed. Baker, 4:237, 248.

24. *Congressional Globe*, March 21, 1842.

25. *Congressional Globe*, January 17, 22, and 31, 1861. Southern congressmen denounced these references to the Adams doctrine and demanded that Republicans renounce it, which Republicans refused to do. See, for example, the exchange between Simms and Curtis in *Congressional Globe*, February 26, 1861.

26. *Annual Report of the Secretary of the Navy, December 1861* (Washington, 1861), 20–21.

27. *Report of the Secretary of the Treasury* (Washington, 1861), 13.

28. *Collected Works of Abraham Lincoln*, ed. Basler, 5:48.

PART 3

Meditations on the Meaning of Freedom

Black Women and Children in the Civil War

Archive Notes

THAVOLIA GLYMPH

I am writing a book on black women and children in the Civil War with a particular focus on their experience in refugee camps. Taped over my desk is this prayer of a father: "Our children dyin' fast in de camp, and as we tote dem from one place to udder and bury dem in de cold ground."[1] I found this prayer in a newspaper from 1863. It was the document that finally stopped me in my tracks, that dramatically and profoundly shifted how I read the archives, see my project, and understand history. I am a historian and I am trained to be objective, scientific even, but nonetheless, my heart breaks. Like many scholars, I am also accustomed to seeing and working with heart-wrenching documents of human sorrow, and I have written about the capacity of human beings to do great harm to one another. But this seems, somehow, different. I posted the father's prayer, this document that changed so much, above my desk to keep me going in my despair. From this point my research project enters a new phase, one I initially feel sorely unprepared to take on intellectually. But as I sit and wrestle with the home truths of the "Father's Prayer" always before me, I do come to see that the prayer has rescued me in a sense. This essay is a partial archive of my journey to better understand the work of making freedom in the American South during the Civil War.

By the time I came across the "Father's Prayer," I was deep into a study of black women and children in Civil War refugee camps. I have sat in archives reading the letters and diaries of white southerners and northerners, their journals and published papers, and poring over census records, the official records of the Union and Confederate armies and navies, Treasury Department and other federal records, slave narratives and oral histories. I have transcribed most of the documents and begun writing. But the language in the growing manuscript pages increasingly reads wrong, in tone and meaning, and inadequate to the task. Nothing has made this clearer than the "Father's Prayer."

In the archives and in published reports, I read of black women and children "shut up in their quarters, and literally roasted alive," of "children, only five or six years of age . . . found skulking in the cane break with wounds," of "helpless women . . . found shot down in the most inhumane manner" and "dumped" between railroad tracks. Black women and children were dying on the battlefields of the Civil War. Refugee camps in which they sought refuge and protection had become sites of war. And, too, the southern roads and waterways that carried them there, roads that remained clogged and war torn long after the Civil War was technically over.[2]

My despair, however, is no match for that of a black soldier who writes from Vicksburg in 1865 of freedwomen and their children who after lying outside through a freezing night appear at Union camps in the morning dawn; of black people "being knocked down for saying they are free," of "two colored women . . . found dead side the Jackson road with their throats cut lying side by side," and an attack on a church, burned to the ground with people inside.[3]

But unlike the violence against black people during Reconstruction, which provoked public outcry and sometimes led to the establishment of fact-finding missions, I see that the wartime massacres of black women and children occasion no significant public outcry or congressional investigations despite the reports coming in from every direction.[4] In account after account, military commanders, soldiers, Sanitary Commission and freedmen's aid agents and missionaries, northern planters, chaplains, and the survivors themselves testify to the growing humanitarian crisis.

Though unaccounted for in the literature, memory, and politics of the history of the Civil War, the wartime violence black women and children refugees suffered was a very public affair—witnessed on the ground and reported in military documents and the press. Yet the American Civil War has not generally been associated with refugee camps filled to overflowing with black women and children. Narratives of the war pay them hardly any mind. Until recently, no monuments in their memory troubled the landscape of Civil War memory. In general, they form no significant part of our understanding of the Civil War's human toll or the meanings ascribed to Union victory and emancipation.

Yet for tens of thousands of black women and children, the battlefields that were refugee camps constituted their primary experience of the Civil War. On this terrain, they were reenslaved and died from artillery fire, hunger and malnutrition, disease, overwork on government-sponsored labor camps, and heartbreak. The so-called contraband camps have not lacked for attention, especially in the just-passed moment of 150th-anniversary commemorations of the Civil War. Yet this attention has been largely of the "uplift" kind, focused on camps such as Corinth and Freedmen's Village, compounds distinguished by the incorporation of facilities for religious worship and education. Some of these camps, as Steven Hahn cogently argues, "became the first great cultural and political meeting grounds that the war produced," birthing freedom and providing the space to cultivate notions of belonging and citizenship. In the far more numerous refugee camps, however, the making of freedom unfolded much differently and under more warlike conditions.[5]

As I continue to work on this project, I begin to see what I am trying to do as a kind of re-archiving, and to view my research notes in the way of anthropologists as "field notebooks" that represents, in the words of Michael Taussig, something more than a "mere stepping stone to the next . . . book." I begin to see the "afterthoughts" I jot down as spaces to hold and interrogate ideas, "in wider perspective" and to grapple with the gaps.[6] This project of re-archiving is not just a re-archiving of African American history or African American women's history. It is a re-archiving of U.S. history and the global world of which it is a part. Thinking in this way helps recommit me to the project despite the heartache that as a dispassionate scholar I am not supposed to have.

So I return to my field notebooks and continue to copy and transcribe the evidence of atrocities, the narratives of the struggles refugees faced as they battled hunger, heat and cold, and disease epidemics; their fight to be accorded the rights of citizenship, recognition as the mothers, wives, and daughters of black soldiers, and as human beings generally; their efforts to reconstitute families, communities, and neighborhoods. Still, at times, the afterthoughts that crowd my notebooks keep threatening to derail the project entirely. I think about how I can never adequately capture the voices of women and children screaming and praying as they were "shot down," "inhumanely butchered," or burned alive, the fear that must have gripped children who ran from the slaughter and sought shelter in the swamps of Louisiana as artillery rained down on them, or the absolute astonishment that must have crossed the face and mind of the enslaved woman who, after spending weeks voluntarily cooking for and feeding Union soldiers, was shot down in cold blood by a Union soldier who concluded that she was a threat to her mistress, the wife of a Confederate soldier.[7]

Turning back to my notes, I go over the section on the efforts of the federal government to secure and remove the many thousands of bales of "abandoned" cotton. This is an important initiative that aims to undermine the Confederate project while bringing millions of dollars into the federal treasury. But apparently no one in the federal government thinks to consider this abandoned cotton the fruit of enslaved people's labor that might profitably be put directly to their support. I go back and search the archives for evidence to the contrary. I find none. Rather, the plantation leasing system is lauded as a success despite the easy military target it makes for Confederate attacks on the refugees. I come to understand that despite the violence, the loss of life, and reenslavement, the project is concerned less with answering the loaded question of whether slaves can be transformed into free laborers and more about the profits that can be routed to the federal treasury.

Of course, the profits are also meant to cover the cost of rations for the refugees and a small and often unpaid wage for those who work. In many cases, moreover, the wage is taxed for the support of refugees who are unable to work, including the elderly. A correspondent for the *New York Times* sees and gets it. "This is the whole thing in a nutshell," he writes of the operations of the federal government's plantation labor system, "to protect the commerce of the river and to employ the negroes."[8] A northern lessee of an abandoned plantation in Louisiana writes of his disappointment with leasing agents who had assured him that he would have at his disposal all the hands he desired from among the refugees. He complains that the government has not honored its part of the bargain. Black soldiers interfere when he tries to get the labor of their wives.[9] It is worth recalling that Sherman's 1864 Christmas present telegraphed to President Abraham Lincoln included, in addition to the city of Savannah, 25,000 bales of cotton.[10]

I try to follow the money, as they say. For the year 1863, I find congressional legislation for the support of the army totaling more than $700 million. It includes $50,000 for medicines and medical attendance for "negro refugees, (commonly called contrabands)."[11] I have not yet found where the $50,000 was spent. I am still looking. I do find, however, records of taxes levied on the labor of black women to support the elderly and infirm. One official proudly reports the profits that have accrued to the credit of the federal government from the labor of black women and children. Indeed, it becomes clear that the government had made more from their labor than it spent on their support. Some of the profits would eventually go to funding the Freedmen's Bureau.[12]

As some federal officials and abolitionists continue to decry slavery's destructive impact on black families, the war takes its own devastating toll. Most visible among the refugees are the families of black soldiers and laborers who struggle to be seen as soldiers' wives, mothers, and children. A case in point: by the spring of 1863, the federal government owed black men who had labored on fortifications around Nashville since the summer of 1862 some $112,292.17. Several hundred of the men died before being paid. Efforts by their wives, mothers, and children to claim their back wages were denied. For one group of laborers, the unclaimed wages amounted to more than $42,000. "If a wife comes in with a certificate issued to her dead husband for labor," payment was refused "for the reason that there is no one authorized to sign his name to the receipt-roll."[13]

My despair deepens as I read of Union officers assisting in the return of refugees to slavery despite the illegality of doing so. The summer of 1863 is an especially horrible time for black people in the western theater before and after the fall of Vicksburg. In July, proslavery Union officers are charged by their fellow officers with having repeatedly "connived with slave-hunters by sending forth contrabands on errands so that they might be gobbled up outside the camps." Documents catalog "flagrant injustices" such as mass and open arrests by sheriffs and constables, advertisements offering rewards for the return of escaped slaves, guerrilla forces roaming the country, and black refugees carried off to Kentucky and their free papers destroyed.[14] Elsewhere, nine refugees who had been lucky enough to secure passage aboard a Union vessel were carried to Helena, Arkansas, but there they found their fragile freedom threatened when the provost marshal at Helena issued an order allowing the daughter of the woman who claimed ownership of them, a "young girl," to enter the camp to identify and take them. Samuel Sawyer, superintendent of contrabands at Arkansas, protested this act of reenslavement. The refugees in question, he informed the provost marshal (who must have known this), are "Freed by the President's Proclamation" and, he added, were "loath to risk slavery further. . . . They all aver their unwillingness to go with her." The provost marshal's response revealed how much freedom depended on the views of local commanders. "The General Commanding," the provost marshal responded, "would prefer that they should go, for their own good and that of the Government." And because the Emancipation Proclamation had freed them, he wrote, "it would hardly be returning to slavery."[15]

So must have thought the major general commanding at Nashville in March 1864 when he allowed a Kentucky slaveholder to reenslave three black women refugees and two boys ("if not in the employ of the government") from the area of Clarksville, Tennessee, "without being interfered with by the military authorities." So, too, the Union general who in April 1864 ordered a subordinate to "turn out of your camp (1) negro boy, named Tom, about ten (10) years old, the property of W. W. Allen, of Nashville."[16] Sometimes black women refugees found the enemy closer to home. In January 1864 a Union commander called for the dismissal of several black soldiers on charges of attempted rape of refugee women and threatening to throw them out of camp or take away their jobs if they refused to have sex with them.[17]

In time, I notice that my notes bear a striking resemblance to United Nations reports of refugee camps in the twentieth and twenty-first centuries. "In 30 years in the field," writes Eileen Pittaway in a 2007 United Nations High Commission for Refugees Report, "I have never before been in an established camp where the fear was so palpable and pervasive and where malnutrition and poverty was so rife. Corruption, rape, sexual abuse, abductions, trafficking, organized prostitution, ration fraud and a systematized regime of terror has left a population of at least 26,000 refugees in a state of trauma. . . . Deaths from malnutrition and untreated medical conditions are common."[18] Pittaway's description of life and death in a Bangladesh camp could easily stand in for any number of refugee camps in modern history in places such as Rwanda, Bosnia, Darfur, Syria, Turkey, and Haiti. It could also stand in for Civil War refugee camps in the United States.

The numbers are staggering. "Not less than *thirty-five thousand* are gathered on the banks of the Mississippi from Helena to Natchez," with a third of them concentrated near Vicksburg, a committee of chaplains reported in the fall of 1863. Only five hundred were men. The report called attention to the "fearful mortality" and "destitution of suitable nourishment" in the camps, shortages of physicians and medicines, and "miserable apologies for tents or shelter."[19] In a similar appeal, the members of the Western Sanitary Commission's Standing Committee addressed President Lincoln directly.

> There are probably not less than fifty thousand, chiefly women and children, now within our lines, between Cairo and New Orleans, for whom no adequate

provision has been made. The majority of them have no shelter but what they call "brush tents," fit for nothing but to protect them from night dews. They are very poorly clad—many of them half naked—and almost destitute of beds and bedding—thousands of them sleeping on the bare ground. The Government supplies them with rations, but many unavoidable delays arise in the distribution, so that frequent instances of great destitution occur. The army rations (beef and crackers) are also a kind of diet they are not used to; they have no facilities of cooking . . . and even when provisions in abundance are supplied, they are so spoiled in cooking as to be neither eatable nor wholesome. . . . No language can describe the suffering, destitution and neglect which prevail in some of their "camps." The sick and dying are left uncared for, in many instances, and the dead unburied. It would seem, now, that one-half are doomed to die in the process of freeing the rest.[20]

The Western Sanitary Commission couches its appeal not only on philanthropic and humanitarian grounds "but equally of patriotism, for it would remove an increasing reproach against the Union cause, and by lessening the difficulties of emancipation, would materially aid in crushing the rebellion." Yet, in the end, they placed much of the blame for the problems on the former slaves themselves. Their "helplessness and improvidence . . . forlorn and jaded condition when they reach our lines," the agents wrote, could "easily account for the fact that sickness and death prevail to a fearful extent."[21] Yes, the food was insufficient and there was scarcely any housing. Yes, cold weather seeped into weakened bones and the Mississippi River, their source of water for drinking and washing their bodies—tainted by human and animal carcasses and all manner of detritus from army camps and civilians on the move—fueled outbreaks of disease, and Confederate raiders kept up a traffic in slaves. But the notion that black people were not themselves doing enough remained a potent critique.

Countless references to Civil War "contraband" camps and "refugees" abound in contemporary accounts and secondary sources, but the history of refugee camps as sites of refuge and unspeakable violence remains understudied. To be sure, scholars have explored the plight of black women and children in the Civil War—the well-told story of their expulsion from Camp Nelson, Kentucky, in the dead of the winter of 1864 stands out in this regard, as do references to the loss of life that accompanied Sherman's army across the state of Georgia and through the Carolinas. Still, for the most part, despite what we have learned from recent history about crimes against humanity and refugee populations of predominantly women and children, despite the contemporary reports, we do not associate such matters with the history of the United States or the history of the American Civil War. The dearth of scholarship pales before the wealth of contemporary documentation detailing destitution, malnutrition, reenslavement, and violence of every kind.

There is such discrepancy between the archival papers accumulating in my files and the historiography that it sometimes provokes skepticism among audiences when I give talks on the subject. "If what you say is true," they ask, "why haven't we heard of it before?" How can you even refer to wartime fugitive slaves as "refugees"? a skeptical colleague asks at a seminar workshop. Each time the skepticism sends me back to my field notebooks. I check and recheck my notes from the Official Records of the Rebellion, that mainstay of Civil War military historians. Yes, they are filled with reports filed by Union and Confederate commanders documenting massacres and the reenslavement of women and children. I place these records beside records from the Treasury Department, alongside the glowing letters and reports of superintendents of labor of the profits made from the labor of black women and children, alongside the bills the plantation lessees sent to the federal government to be reimbursed for property and goods lost in Confederate raids. I find no accounting of or payment made to black people for their losses from the raids.

I return to the "Father's Prayer." It is on my mind as I sit in an archive in Pennsylvania reading the letters of a northern white woman who has journeyed to the South to be with her husband, a doctor on the medical staff of the Union army. She is very happy to be in the land of aristocrats. "Our home," she writes her family in the North, "how I wish you could see it. It is as the *old gentleman* says elegant. There is elegance in war times . . . and that I like." She very much likes the accouterments of southern living, especially having her own black cook and waiter. Otherwise, she generally finds black people disgusting.[22]

The prayer haunts me as I sit in an archive in Atlanta and read the letters of a man from Detroit who travels to Hampton Roads, Virginia, in the summer of 1862 to help care for his wounded brother, a soldier in the Union army. The lovely plantations and their gardens and flowers, the wives of Union officers, U.S. Sanitary Commission nurses, and southern white women, too, entrance him. Taking tea at the mansion of a local slaveholder near the shore of the James River reminds him of how he had "always desired to visit a real southern home and here it was," he writes, "the principal feature being darkies—Little niggers."[23]

The prayer slaps up against the voices of northerners such as Maria Mann who journey to the South to help the newly freed but do not see the ways in which they themselves are obstacles to black freedom. "Sometimes I venture on foot, get where advance or retreat is alike impossible," Mann wrote from the camp at Helena, Arkansas, "when some giant of a man either white or colored, passing takes me in his arms & carries me over fences & their private yards to my destination." Unlike the black women refugees, she had a way to get around the dirt and mud, the high waters and dead carcasses in the streets. "The last of my dreams," she writes, "that I should ever be mistress over slaves." She sees nothing amiss when she behaves like one. She was white and seeing her in these dirty, "impassable" streets, men, black and white, picked her up and carried her over the filth to her destination.[24]

I am, of course, accustomed to seeing rank expressions of racism, even among white northerners, and accustomed to its accumulated debris in the works of an older, now discredited, historiography. In *Women in the Civil War* (1966), for example, Mary Elizabeth Massey is willing to admit that black women "died of exhaustion, exposure, or foul play." In the end, though, she impresses on her readers, this must be tempered by the recognition that black women were themselves "brutal." Following Mary Chesnut and Chesnut's contemporaries, she recirculates rumors of black women's indifference to and abandonment of their children, describing them as "indifferent," "brutal," and, ultimately, homicidal.[25] I reread this, grateful for the work of scholars that has done much to demolish such views from the pages of history in recent decades. At the same time, I remain cognizant, to borrow from Rob Nixon, of "the persistence of unofficial hostilities" in new ways and places.[26]

On the ground of war, black women and children experienced freedom's contingency on a multitude of levels. When agents of the federal government looked at black women and children, too many, too often, saw potential laborers and shirkers rather than refugees in need of sanctuary and protection. Confederate raids on refugee camps were often swift and sure.[27] Despite the casualties, these acts of "summary justice" and "extermination," slaveholder William Ravenel wrote, were justified.[28]

Writing the history of black women and children refugees and black resistance to the Confederate state-building project, and placing it in the larger narrative of the Civil War, means that we will have to rethink and rewrite the story of the price paid for Union, freedom, and citizenship, and simultaneously redefine the very term "battlefield." As in most wars, in the Civil War the lines that supposedly separated the spaces of men and guns from those of women and children without either guns or battlefield plans were porous and impossible to hold.[29] By its very nature, war trespasses on and often wipes clean the most carefully drawn lines meant to contain soldiers and their guns. In an important sense, every inch of southern soil was embattled ground as it had always been, and the political and social landscape of the South ensured, in effect, a war without borders. Refugee camps constituted part of this battlefield, and like all battlefields they were spaces that we can map as sites of war and the making of freedom, spaces that constitute an archive in which black women and children are visible—preserved in theaters of war, even in death.[30] Freedom's contingency, as Edward Ayers and Scott Nesbitt have cogently argued, can be mapped in ways that reveal the complexities of emancipation in new ways "better than words alone" can convey.[31]

The narrative evidence is equally compelling. The war had been over a year when in May 1866 Eveline Stuart called at a Louisiana Freedmen's Bureau office stating her desire for "a 'paper' to show that she was permitted to remove from the Stuart plantation." While the Freedmen's Bureau agent informed her "that nothing of this kind is necessary, as no one will probably dispute her right . . . to change her quarters, and take with her what little she may possess," Stuart clearly had reason to doubt this was true. The former slave Nancy who finally escaped to freedom in June 1867 from the man who had held her in bondage for seven years only to be arrested and returned to him just as surely had reason to doubt her right to freedom and mobility was indisputable.[32]

When the Civil War began, slaves began to move on their understanding of its meaning for their lives and freedom—whether that meant fleeing to Union lines, resisting slaveholders' efforts to move them in the opposite direction to more secure Confederate lines, or staying put but taking good notes on slaveholders' behavior and their words and slowly (and sometimes, radically) changing the terms of their enslavement. Behind the Civil War lay 250 years of slavery, 250 years in which black people had pondered the meaning of slavery and freedom and collectively and individually calculated how the structures and mechanisms that upheld human bondage worked—from the federal, state, and police power that girded it to white peoples' claims to racial superiority and the forms these claims took. For 250 years slaves had been at war.

The Civil War represented the intensification of that centuries-old struggle on ground that was both old and new, waged with old weapons forged from the cloth of the struggles that had gone before and retooled for the changed terrain, and new weapons forged on the battlefields of the Civil War. Between 1861 and 1868 enslaved people took many paths to freedom. Historians are today more attuned to the diversity of these paths, the contingency of each grasp at freedom, and the fact that emancipation in the United States was a world of emancipations.[33] In 1862 a cook employed by Treasury Secretary Salmon P. Chase appealed to him for help in finding her daughters who had been sold away to Louisiana before the war. She had little to go on but far more than most African Americans searching for children during and after the war and a powerful ally in the person of her employer. She knew the names of the men who had purchased her daughters and the state to which they had been carried, now back in the hands of the United States. On May 24, 1862, Chase forwarded her inquiry to a Treasury Department employee stationed at New Orleans: "The name of one is Charity Stamps or Stomps and she was a servant when last heard from of Mr. Thomas Jordan," he wrote, "the name of other Grace York, a servant when last heard from of William Horton, Red River Landing, Point Coupee Parish. If you will inquire and have inquiries made of these two women and let me know all that can be ascertained concerning their present situation, whether married or not, whether redeemable or not, you will, by so doing much oblige me."[34] It is interesting that despite Louisiana's radically changed political terrain, the most feasible option that appeared to Chase for securing the freedom of the cook's daughters was to redeem or buy them.

The moment of freedom's arrival varied across the South. It was conditioned by where slaves stood, the kind of work they did, their gender, the timing and nature of contact with Union military forces and other agents of the federal government, and the nature of the war slaveholders waged against them. To be sure, historians have written a great deal about the violence that accompanied the destruction of slavery, which would last for decades to come. The "Father's Prayer," the soldier's letter, Eveline Stuart's request, and the thousands of other stories of slavery's destruction remind us that the antecedents to the postwar violence lay not just in the decades before the Civil War but in the war itself.

The archive accumulating in my file cabinets and on my desk and shelves tells a story difficult to hold and transcribe. It calls for a remapping and re-archiving of the Civil War archive and historiography. The coming of the Union armies and missionaries, a northern doctor wrote, meant that "women in travail and children without parents or friends, were no longer permitted to die in the streets or drag out a miserable life of filth and festering disease in wretched dog-kennels where the eye of humanity never penetrates."[35] For thousands of black women in the Civil War, how-

ever, "the eye of humanity" remained largely focused elsewhere. As scholars our task is to capture as best we can what this meant for their lives
and futures. This is not an easy or pain-free job. It will break your heart.

NOTES

1. "A Father's Prayer," in "Three Months with Contrabands," by a Surgeon,
New York Herald-Tribune, October 21, 1863.

2. On the roads as a path to freedom in Virginia and their meaning for Confederate defeat and black freedom, see Yael A. Sternhell, *Routes of War: The World
of Movement in the Confederate South* (Cambridge, Mass.: Harvard University Press,
2012).

3. Private Calvin Holley to Major General O. O. Howard, December 16, 1865,
Bureau of Refugees, Freedmen, and Abandoned Lands (BRFAL), Mississippi, LR,
M826, Roll 10, RG 105.

4. The American Freedmen's Inquiry Commission (AFIC) appointed by U.S.
Secretary of War Edwin M. Stanton in March 1863 to "inquire into the condition
of the Colored population emancipated by acts of Congress and the proclamations of the president, and to consider and report what measures are necessary
to give practical effect to those acts and proclamations, so as to place the Colored
people of the United States in a condition of self-support and self-defense" was a
notable exception to this trend.

5. Stephen Hahn, *A Nation under Our Feet: Black Political Struggles in the Rural
South from Slavery to the Great Migration* (Cambridge, Mass.: Belknap Press of Harvard University Press, 2003), 73. On the wartime medical crisis, see Jim Downs,
*Sick from Freedom: African American Illness and Suffering during the Civil War and
Reconstruction* (New York: Oxford University Press, 2012), and Margaret Hum-
phreys, *Intensely Human: The Health of Black Soldiers in the American Civil War* (Baltimore: Johns Hopkins University Press, 2008).

6. Michael Taussig, "Writing Culture at 25: Theory, Ethnography, Fieldwork
Conference," talk given at Duke University, October 1, 2011.

7. Lt. Col. Francis M. Drake to Asst. Adjt. Gen. Capt. A. Blocki, Marks Mills,
April 25, 1864, *The War of the Rebellion: A Compilation of the Official Records of the
Union and Confederate Armies*, ser. 1, vol. 34, pt. 1, 715; Matthew Page Andrews,
comp., *The Women of the South in War Times* (Baltimore: Norman, Remington,
1920), 236–45.

8. "The Negroes of the Southwest," *New York Times*, November 28, 1863.

9. H. Wilson to Montross, May 7, 1864, from the holdings of the Freedmen
and Southern Society Project (Q-167).

10. Telegraph from William T. Sherman to Abraham Lincoln, December 22,
1864, Robert Todd Lincoln Papers, Manuscript Division, Library of Congress
(196) Digital ID #Al0196.

11. "A Bill Making Appropriations for the Support of the Army for the year

ending the thirtieth of June, eighteen hundred and sixty four," H.R. 610, 37th Congress, 3d session, in the House of Representatives, December 15, 1862.

12. John Eaton, *Grant, Lincoln, and the Freedmen: Reminiscences of the Civil War* (1907; reprint, New York: Negro Universities Press, 1969), 71; S. B. Holabird, Quartermaster-General, U.S. Army to Hon. J. R. Hawley, Chairman, Committee on Military Affairs, April 5, 1888, U.S. Senate, 50th Congress, 1st Session, Senate Report No. 1040. A similar wage tax was imposed on some black men who worked as laborers for the northern army, prompting challenges to its legality after the war. See Holabird to Hawley.

13. Hon. Thomas Hood and Hon. S. W. Bostwick, "Report of the Commissioners of Investigation of Colored Refugees in Kentucky, Tennessee, and Alabama," Washington, D.C., December 28, 1864, 38th Congress, 2d Session, Senate, Ex. Doc. 28, in *Congressional Series of United States Public Documents* (Washington, D.C.: U.S. Government Printing Office, 1865), 14.

14. Special Correspondent, "From Missouri. A Pro-Slavery Policy—Its Effects—Negroes Seized—Political Schemes—Guerillas, Outrages—Rebel Agents Caught, etc.," St. Louis, *New York Herald Tribune,* July 31, 1863.

15. Correspondent, "Carrying out the Proclamation, Headquarters, Freedmen, Helena, Ark.," *New York Times,* July 1863; Samuel Sawyer et al. to Maj. Gen. Curtis, December 29, 1862, enclosed in Chaplain Samuel Sawyer to Major Gen. Curtis, January 26, 1863, #135 1863, Letters Received Relating to Military Discipline and Control, Series 22, Headquarters of the Army, Record Group 108, National Archives.

16. Hood and Bostwick, "Report of the Commissioners of Investigation of Colored Refugees," 162.

17. Brig. Gen. Wm. Dwight to Brig. Gen. C. P. Stone, January 27, 1864, 76th USCInf, Letters Received, Ft. Jackson, Jan–Feb 1864, from holdings of the Freedmen and Southern Society Project (G-104).

18. E. Pittaway, "Field Notes, UNHCR Mission to Cox's Bazar," 2007, unpublished paper cited in Eileen Pittaway, "The Rohingya Refugees in Bangladesh: A Failure of the International Protection Regime," in *Protracted Displacement in Asia: No Place to Call Home,* ed. Howard Adelman (Hampshire, Eng.: Ashgate, 2008), 83.

19. J. Coles, Jeremiah Porter, and T. M. Stevenson, "Report of the Numbers and Wants of the Contrabands in the Department of the Tennessee, by Committee Appointed by the Chaplains' Association, Vicksburgh, Miss., Oct. 19, 1863," *New York Times,* November 12, 1863.

20. James E. Yeatman, George Partridge, John B. Johnson, Carlos S. Greeley, and William G. Eliot, "Appeal from the Western Sanitary Commission to President Lincoln regarding the condition of freed slaves," November 6, 1863, Broadside, Gilder Lehrman Collection #GLC01545, 11, https://www.gilderlehrman .org/mweb/search?needle=Yeatman%2C%20James%20E.%20%281818 -1901%29&fields=_t301000285.

21. Ibid.

22. Lillie H. Dade to My dear Sisters, Beaufort, SC, Sunday Nov 2nd, 1862, Mrs. Irving H. McJesson Collection No. 1542, Henderson Section, Henderson Letters, 1851–1917, Historical Society of Pennsylvania.

23. Fannie Green Diary, July 4, 1862, Emory University Archives, Collection #636.

24. [Maria R. Mann] to Elisa, February 10, 1863, Letters from Helena, Ark., (Freedman's Camps) 1863 Feb–Apl, Papers of Mary Tyler Peabody Mann, Manuscript Division, Library of Congress.

25. Mary Elizabeth Massey, *Women in the Civil War* (Lincoln: University of Nebraska Press, 1994, orig. pub. 1966 as *Bonnet Brigades*), 275–76. In his introduction to the book Alan Nevins described Massey's work as "a thorough, comprehensive, and impartial history" (xvii). See also Thavolia Glymph, "Mary Elizabeth Massey: Standing with the Master Class," *Civil War History* 61 (December 2015): 412–15, and other essays in this special issue, titled "Historians' Forum: Bonnet Brigades at 50: Reflections on Elizabeth Massey and Gender in Civil War History."

26. Rob Nixon, *Slow Violence and the Environmentalism of the Poor* (Cambridge, Mass.: Harvard University Press, 2011).

27. See, for example, Thavolia Glymph, "Rose's War and the Gendered Politics of a Slave Insurgency in the Civil War," *Journal of the Civil War* 3 (December 2013): 501–32.

28. William Henry Ravenel, Journal Entry for Wednesday, March 22, 1865, in *The Private Journal of Henry William Ravenel, 1859–1887*, ed. Arney R. Childs (Columbia: University of South Carolina Press, 1947).

29. Over the past two decades, studies of the home front have proliferated. See, for example, Elizabeth Leonard, *Yankee Women: Gender Battles in the Civil War* (New York: Norton, 1994); James M. McPherson, *For Cause and Comrades: Why Men Fought in the Civil War* (New York: Oxford University Press, 1997); Jacqueline Glass Campbell, *When Sherman Marched North from the Sea: Resistance on the Confederate Home Front* (Chapel Hill: University of North Carolina Press, 2003); Joan E. Cashin, ed., *The War Was You and Me: Civilians in the American Civil War* (Princeton, N.J.: Princeton University Press, 2002); Catherine Clinton and Nina Silber, eds., *Divided Houses: Gender and the Civil War* (New York: Oxford University Press, 1992); Carol K. Bleser and Lesley J. Gordon, *Intimate Strategies of the Civil War: Military Commanders and Their Wives* (New York: Oxford University Press, 2001); Maris Vinovskis, ed., *Toward a Social History of the Civil War* (Cambridge: Cambridge University Press, 1990); Reid Mitchell, *The Vacant Chair: The Northern Soldier Leaves Home* (New York: Oxford University Press, 1993); Nina Silber, *Daughters of the Union: Northern Women Fight the Civil War* (Cambridge, Mass.: Harvard University Press, 2005); LeeAnn Whites and Alecia P. Long, eds., *Occupied Women: Gender, Military Occupation, and the American Civil War* (Baton Rouge: Louisiana University Press, 2012).

30. I am indebted to Jennifer Morgan for her astute comments on a version of this paper delivered at the 2010 meeting of the American Historical Association. In particular, I wish to thank her for helping me think through the question of mapping and its archival traces.

31. Edward L. Ayers and Scott Nesbitt, "Seeing Emancipation: Scale and Freedom in the American South," *Journal of the Civil War Era* 1, no. 1 (March 2011): 10.

32. Thomas H. Hopwood, Brig, Maj. and Agent FB, Parish of Pt. Coupee, Louisiana, New Roads, Pt. Coupee, Louisiana, May 1866, from the holdings of the Freedmen and Southern Society Project (A-8658).

33. Edward L. Ayers, *In the Presence of Mine Enemies: War in the Heart of America, 1859–1863* (New York: Norton, 2003).

34. Hon. S. P. Chase to My Dear Mr [George S.] Denison, Wash. May 24, 1862, George S. Denison Papers, John Aldrich Stephenson Collection of the Hand, Fiske, and Aldrich Families Papers, Manuscript Division, Library of Congress, Washington, D.C.

35. D. O. McCord, Surg. 63 USCI, Med. Director and Inspector Freedmen, Depts of Miss and Ark "Makes Final Report, Vicksburg, Miss. Aug 3rd 1865" to Col. John Eaton Jr., Gen. Supt. of Freedmen, from the holdings of the Freedmen and Southern Society Project (A-4014).

"Cleaning Up the Mess"

Some Thoughts on Freedom, Violence, and Grief

CAROLE EMBERTON

Violence is not an easy subject for historians to deal with. On the one hand, it is everywhere all the time. Its very ubiquity makes violence, in one sense, ahistorical. This is certainly true for historians of American slavery. Nell Irvin Painter considers the difficulties historians have had writing about violence and slavery when she notes that "any sojourn in southern archives covers the researcher in blood," yet "professionalism prompts historians to clean up the mess before going into print."[1] For Painter, it is not so much the ubiquity of violence that is the problem, but rather the reactions it provokes in the researcher. We are trained to be tidy, to categorize, label, and sort; to compartmentalize and compare; to resolve and rationalize. Historians make the best housekeepers.

Sometimes those efforts to keep the past neat go awry. This was the case in 1998, when a conference on the Atlantic slave trade at William and Mary's Omohundro Institute erupted into controversy over the perceived coldness of white scholars who used statistical surveys and datasets in an attempt to quantify the slave trade's global impact. Audience members, many of whom were black nonacademics, felt alienated by the mostly white presenters' dispassionate delivery of "facts." Criticism that scholars were once again playing the "numbers game" reemerged as many of the nonacademic audience members as well as some of the scholars in attendance took issue with the presenters' unwillingness to address the topics of suffering and redress. Some accused the panelists of "sanitizing one of the ugliest chapters of our history." One attendee summed up the overall dissatisfaction by saying that the presentations lacked "the human touch."[2]

While these criticisms received support from leading academics at the conference, such as Henry Louis Gates Jr. and Bernard Bailyn, who called on historians to recognize the powerful emotions that swirled around slavery and the slave trade, there remained a perceptible unease with the idea that historians should somehow take emotion, particularly pain and suffering, into account. "Are most scholars competent to discuss suffering?" asked one historian on an H-Net discussion board. The answer was a resounding "No." A scholar's responsibility, this discussant wrote, was "the collection and interpretation of knowledge," whereas questions of suffering were better left to artists, religious leaders, and other memorialists. Drawing a sharp line between history and memory, this historian clung to his professional training, which in a peculiar leap of logic, made him unqualified to consider, much less interrogate, the most basic human experiences: pain (both physical and psychological), loss, and grief.[3]

If historians of slavery continue to struggle with these issues, then historians of emancipation should perhaps feel even more torn about how to deal with violence and pain. After all, the narrative of freedom that historians collectively have written in the last thirty years or so is the ultimate cleaning project, sweeping away the vestiges of slavery and mopping up the blood, sweat, and tears of bondage. This historiography hinges on compelling stories of agency, determination, and hope. Even as we acknowledge the continued racial oppression that freedpeople faced in the late nineteenth century, the impulse is to chart the progress of freedom—unfinished but certainly not dead. However, a new subfield within U.S. emancipation studies has emerged that seeks to untidy the story of freedom, as featured at the 2011 "Beyond Freedom" conference sponsored by Yale University's Gilder Lehrman Center. Several of these papers focused on freedpeople's experiences of violence and embraced the unsettling emotions that other scholars have long eschewed. In doing so, they acknowledged a deep-seated need that animated the discord at the earlier Omohundro Conference: to mourn the losses incurred in the transition from slavery to freedom and accept the war's inherent untidiness.

Mourning is hardly an unfamiliar emotion to scholars and audiences of the Civil War era. Who has watched any part of Ken Burns's multi-episode docudrama on the Civil War, accompanied by the anguished chords of the "Ashokan Farewell," and not grieved for the fresh-faced boys who posed proudly with their muskets in their new uniforms before they marched off to die? In her book *This Republic of Suffering* (2008), Drew Gilpin Faust placed these deaths and the mourning rituals they transformed at the center of the period's cultural history. Public mourning for Civil War losses also played an important role in the nation's postwar political history. Southerners put their private feelings of grief to work "redeeming" the region's social and political order. White men and women transformed their personal losses into a movement that valorized the Confederacy and scapegoated former slaves. The literature and iconography of the Lost Cause helped justify the disfranchisement, incarceration, and murder of southern blacks during Jim Crow and, some might argue, continues to inspire discriminatory practices and violent retribution against African Americans to this day.

Eventually, grief became the common ground on which former enemies could meet to mourn their collective losses. Battlefields became places to honor soldiers, whether Union or Confederate, and memorial associations across the nation raised money for monuments commemorating the tragic sacrifice of white men—but they rarely acknowledged the same for black men. A veritable cottage industry for white grief emerged in the last 150 years since the Civil War ended, but collective efforts to remember and grieve black losses have lagged far behind. The war's violent erasure of individual lives on the battlefield that reduced men to numerical statistics of wounded and killed so distressed white soldiers and their families that they went to extraordinary lengths to retrieve and name bodies, bury them in family plots, or build magnificent shrines to their sacrifice. Honored yearly with parades, decorations, and reenactments, white lives have been made grievable by these highly ritualized and scripted mourning performances. Likewise, academic histories recount these efforts and the crippling grief that wracked white Americans for decades. Faust and Mark Schantz collect the tears shed for the white war dead, but the "chattel principle" continues to shape how we understand black suffering in the age of emancipation. Whether a nameless line in a slaver's logbook or an "unknown" entry on a casualty list, black suffering remains largely invisible in the history of emancipation.[4]

One of the most crucial insights to emerge from the "Beyond Freedom" conference is that the manner in which freedom came is as important as the fact that it came at all. That freedom resulted from an act of war mattered, particularly for those people, mostly women and children, caught between two raging armies. Thavolia Glymph's essay in this volume presents an image of the contraband camp as Inferno, a netherworld between slavery and freedom where freedpeople endured countless circles of suffering. With few exceptions, military officials felt little responsibility for contrabands, viewing them largely as burdens on their already-stretched resources and hindrances on their ability to move quickly against the enemy. "Some commanders received them gladly," wrote Adjutant General Lorenzo Thomas, "others indifferently, whilst in very many cases they were refused admission within our lines and driven off by the pickets."[5] Although some army chaplains and missionaries ministered to the contrabands' presumed spiritual and educational needs, even setting up some of the first schools for freedmen within the camps, those efforts were secondary to the army's primary task: waging war. To the extent that contrabands could be mobilized toward this end, they received the military's attention—not always for the better. The "able-bodied" were put to work, sometimes forcibly so, building fortifications, cooking, cleaning, and eventually fighting, but the disabled, the elderly, the very young, and the female were unwelcome encumbrances with little claim to the army's protection. By crossing into Union lines, contrabands hoped they would find safe haven. War offered little sanctuary, however, and they were more likely to find calamity than comfort. The sheer number of contrabands flocking to the Union army overwhelmed the military's resources. Working in a contraband camp in Washington, D.C., abolitionist author Harriet Jacobs, who had herself endured seven years in a cramped attic crawl space to escape slavery, noted the immense task facing the government. Although the army had built barracks to house five hundred escaped slaves, there were 1,500 awaiting shelter. "It is impossible to reach them all," she concluded. Those fortunate enough to be taken under the army's wing found that freedom could have a high price. Having taken to the road as part of the "general strike," whether by choice or out of desperation, these people struggled to keep within the army's reach yet remain safely outside its grasp.[6]

Disease, starvation, and exposure, along with hailstorms of bullets, claimed innumerable lives—deaths that did not make it onto the official casualty lists. When they did, army officials rarely took the time to record their names. General William T. Sherman knew nothing about the "negro" caught in the path of a ricocheting artillery shell while on the march near Savannah. "Some one called to him to look out," recalled Sherman in his *Memoirs*, "but before the poor fellow understood his danger, the ball . . . caught the negro under the right jaw, and literally carried away his head, scattering blood and brains about." Frustrated with the thousands of freedpeople who followed his army as it marched across Georgia in the winter of 1864, Sherman looked on them as unwelcome encumbrances who slowed him down and demanded to be fed from the forage that was intended to keep his soldiers on the move. No wonder that his subordinate, Gen. Jefferson C. Davis, cut loose a pontoon bridge on Ebenezer Creek, leaving hundreds of freedpeople, mostly women, children, and old men, to drown or be slaughtered by the pursuing Confederate cavalry. While working aboard the USS Sachem near Galveston, Texas, at least four unnamed contrabands died when the ship's boiler exploded. The casualty reports listed them only as "a negro contraband, name unknown."[7]

To what extent do historians unconsciously reenact these erasures? Recently, J. David Hacker argued that our estimation of the Civil War dead (620,000) is far too low and should be raised (750–800,000) to include the men who died of their wounds once they were discharged or after the war was officially over. But what about those freedmen who drowned in Ebenezer Creek, or the "unknown" contrabands who died from exploded boilers, or the frequent smallpox epidemics that ravaged contraband camps? Jim Downs (Beyond Freedom's co-organizer) asked these questions in response to Hacker's new figures. Hacker countered Downs's criticism by saying that it is impossible to know how many civilians, black or white, died in the war. Fair enough. Hacker was more incensed with Downs's assertion that he had replicated nineteenth-century terms of categorization that made black suffering invisible. "Perhaps Downs would have been happier if I had wrung my hands for a few paragraphs more," Hacker shot back.[8]

Hacker's dismissiveness of the need to acknowledge the high toll freedom exacted from its recipients exemplifies the discomfort the audience at the 1998 Omohundro conference felt at hearing the slave trade reduced to statistical models. One of the complaints was that there were no names to accompany the numbers. Organizers felt that this was a popular misconception about what the records contained and explained that slave traders rarely recorded names. On arrival in the Caribbean or colonial North America, slaves would be named and renamed at the masters' whim. Thus, just as it is impossible to know with any certainty how many black civilians died during emancipation, it is impossible to recover the true "identities" of these individuals. However, both explanations—perfectly logical and valid in their own right—miss the larger point. History is full of misery and grief, yet historians often do not know how to grieve, or rather, how to create intellectual and emotional spaces within which our audiences—students, the general public, even each other—can mourn the immense losses of the African American past.

The question of which lives are grievable is an important one for all historians but particularly for historians of emancipation. So much of freedpeople's recovered testimony reveals how important it was to publicly grieve for the lives lost to both slavery and freedom. For them, grieving included not only memorializing their lost kin but also acknowledging the ways in which the lives of survivors still teetered on the precipice of annihilation. Take, for instance, the often-cited petition from the Edisto Island freedmen written to Gen. O. O. Howard, the superintendent of the Freedmen's Bureau, in October 1865. As the former owners of the Sea Islands' abandoned plantations began to stream back in attempting to reclaim the property from the freedpeople who had been tending it independently for several years, the federal government reversed its wartime position of supporting ex-slaves' land ownership. Howard had informed the freedmen to abandon their claims on the land and sign labor contracts with their former masters. This proposition outraged the freedmen who, in a moving petition to Howard, framed their vision of postemancipation life through the lens of grief.[9]

"It is with painfull Hearts that we the committee address you," the first line of the petition announced. If we read this announcement not simply as a stylistic convention of nineteenth-century petition writing but as a genuine expression of sadness, how might that transform our understanding of the rest of this document? Typically understood to be an example of the freedmen's belief that land ownership was central to democratic life and governance, the Edisto Island Petition represents a grassroots affirmation of Jeffersonian democracy. But the language of pain, sadness, and grief lends the document an added weight, expanding its historical significance by revealing the writers' emotional burden. "We are at the mercy of those who are combined to prevent us from getting land enough to lay our Fathers bones upon," the petitioners explained. Here the importance of land is not simply for economic independence but for communal rituals of grieving and remembrance. The land is a source of historical continuity that connects present with past and provides the petitioners with both physical and spiritual space in which to remember their departed family members and honor their lives. The freedmen fear being turned out of their ancestral homes not only because it will deprive them of their livelihoods but also because it will sever their bonds with the past and truncate their ability to grieve for those who had gone before.

This is not just historical hand-wringing. These emotions telegraphed much more than the feelings themselves; they also communicated an inherently political message about the role of the state and its attempt to regulate feeling in postemancipation America.[10] In an extended denunciation of Howard's admonition to forgive their former masters for past wrongs, the Edisto Islanders decried the government's callousness when it came to questions of black suffering and grief: "You ask us to forgive the land owners of our Island. You only lost your right arm In war and might forgive them. The man who tied me to a tree & gave me 39 lashes & who stripped and flogged my mother & my sister & who will not let me stay in His empty Hut except I will do His planting & be Satisfied with His price & who combines with other to keep away land from me well knowing I would not have any thing to do with Him If I Had land of my own—that man, I cannot well forgive. Does it look like he has forgiven me, seeing How He tries to keep me In a condition of Helplessness." The petitioners rejected the imposition of Howard's desired emotional response—forgiveness—and instead demanded that the government recognize and accept the feelings of anger, grief, and resentment that the freedmen believed were more than justified. By pointing to Howard's missing arm, which he lost at the Battle of Fair Oaks, the freedmen simultaneously acknowledged the general's pain and reminded him that, despite his physical limitation, he remained in the eyes of the state *whole*. "You *only* lost your right arm," they say, while freedpeople continued to lose ("He tries to keep me In a condition of Helplessness") and are forced to live with the psychic wounds of having to watch their loved ones brutalized with no recourse or justice. Replacing forgiveness with outrage, the freedmen attempted to reconfigure the affective bonds that tied them to the nation. And why not? Hadn't outrage—southerners' outrage at Lincoln's election followed by the reaction to secession as the "essence of anarchy," as Lincoln called it in his first inaugural address— propelled the nation into war? Hadn't outrage over the hundreds of thousands of deaths and amputated limbs of white soldiers such as Howard convinced the beleaguered Union to endure in the war effort "until every drop of blood drawn by the lash shall be paid with another drawn by the sword"? Why was it permissible for white men to express outrage and sadness over their war dead, which now included the martyred president, but freedmen were prohibited from the same expressions of grief for their own people? Why were their expressions of grief interpreted as tantamount to "race war" and a threat to social order? Not surprisingly, Howard dismissed their claims to righteous outrage. "The whipping post you complain of is abolished forever," he proclaimed; "the duty of forgiveness is plain and simple. Forgive as we hope to be forgiven of Him who governs all things."[11]

By attempting to make their own grief visible to agents of the state, the Edisto Islanders articulated a vision of citizenship premised on what critic and philosopher Judith Butler calls "the precariousness of life." "Precariousness implies living socially," explains Butler, "that is, the fact that one's life is always in some sense in the hands of the other." By pointing out Howard's injury, the freedmen asked him to recognize their mutual vulnerability as living beings, but at the same time, they resisted the tendency evidenced in much of the sentimental writing on slavery in this period to flatten the experience of suffering and equate Howard's with their own. Instead, by highlighting the differences in their vulnerability, the Islanders aimed to elicit an emotional response from Howard that would propel him into action on their behalf and fulfill the social obligations implicit in the idea of precariousness. Howard, however, did not find their lives grievable. As he would later remark in a decision to restrict ration distribution to freedpeople in order to keep them from being too dependent on the government, "suffering is a necessary condition of freedom." Likewise, grief is a necessary condition of democratic reform, for without it "there is no life, or, rather, there is something living that is other than life," according to Butler. "Only under conditions in which the loss would matter," and thus be grieved, "does the value of life appear." In other words, a life not grieved is a life not lived. Therefore, the cultural regulation of grief, exposed in Howard's response and the Freedmen's Bureau policy on everything from labor contracts to vagrancy, apprenticeships, and ration distribution, revealed the myriad ways in which black lives still did not count for very much in the new old world of freedom.[12]

As historians, it is important for us to see that grieving—or refusing to grieve—is a political act, not only as we analyze how people in the past mourned but also how in our own work we might perpetuate the same aversions or denials when it comes to tidying up our narratives. Do we take time as we research and write to consider the nameless souls whose misfortune provides our intellectual fodder? To what ends do we work when we recreate brutal scenes of dehumanization in our writing? When we treat the war as tragedy, whose losses do we mourn? Is there a way to make space in our work to grieve for freedpeople as well as enslaved ones? These are difficult questions but ones that those of us who write about emancipation and its legacy must ask ourselves.

NOTES

1. Nell Painter, *Southern History across the Color Line* (Chapel Hill: University of North Carolina Press, 2002), 6.

2. "Numbers Abound, but Not Names," *Richmond Times-Dispatch*, September 14, 1998.

3. http://h-net.msu.edu/cgi-bin/logbrowse.pl?trx=vx&list=h-high-s&month=9810&week=a&msg=BNyqiThSP1CTu7d2JarlaQ&user=&pw=.

4. Walter Johnson described the "chattel principle" as the reduction of a person to a price in *Soul by Soul: Life in the Antebellum Slave Market* (Cambridge, Mass.: Harvard University Press, 2000). On death and mourning practices during the Civil War, see Drew Gilpin Faust, *This Republic of Suffering: Death and the American Civil War* (New York: Knopf, 2008) and Mark Schantz, *Awaiting the Heavenly Country: The Civil War and America's Culture of Death* (Ithaca, N.Y.: Cornell University Press, 2008).

5. Adj. Gen. Lorenzo Thomas to Edwin Stanton, October 5, 1865, *The War of the Rebellion: A Compilation of the Official Records of the Union and Confederate Armies*, ser. 3, vol. 5, p. 118.

6. Jacobs quoted in the *Liberator*, April 10, 1863.

7. William T. Sherman, *Memoirs of General W. T. Sherman* (New York: Library of America, 1990 [1875]), 671; http://exhibits.library.rice.edu/items/show/768.

8. J. David Hacker, "A Census-Based Count of the Civil War Dead," *Civil War History* 57, no. 4 (December 2011): 306–47; http://blog.oup.com/2012/04/black-white-demographic-death-toll-civil-war/.

9. Henry Bram et al. to Major General O. O. Howard, [October 20 or 21, 1865], B-53 1865, Letters Received, ser. 15, Washington Headquarters, Bureau of Refugees, Freedmen, and Abandoned Lands, Record Group 105, National Archives.

10. For more on how emotions telegraph larger meanings, see Barbara Rosenwein, "Worrying about Emotions in History," *American Historical Review* 107 (June 2002): 821–45.

11. Maj. Genl. O. O. Howard to the Committee of the Colored People of Edisto Island, October 22, 1865, vol. 64, pp. 415–16, Letters Sent, ser. 2, Washington Headquarters, Bureau of Refugees, Freedmen, and Abandoned Lands, Record Group 105, National Archives.

12. Judith Butler, *Frames of War: When Is Life Grievable?* (London: Verso, 2009), 14–15.

In the Moment of Violence

Writing the History of Postemancipation Terror

HANNAH ROSEN

Scholarly treatments of violence following emancipation in the southern United States have traditionally been preoccupied with the before and after. That is, they have focused on the perceived causes of the extensive white-on-black political violence of the postemancipation period and on its effects.[1] Only recently have historians begun to scrutinize instead the moment of violence itself. By that I mean the specific content of violent encounters—the language used, the gestures made, the scenes coerced by assailants.[2] And yet, despite a general lack of interpretation, the particular forms taken by postemancipation violence were neither inevitable nor self-evident in origin. In fact, violent attacks in this period frequently involved surprisingly elaborate performances of brutality not explained by the overt political aims of the assailants. These, I contend, cry out for analysis.

Even if historians have rarely focused their analysis on the moment of violence, they have frequently described the abuse that occurred during terroristic assaults in the postemancipation years. And the repetition of such description has been subject to criticism by others. The "endless recitations of the ghastly and the terrible," literary scholar and cultural historian Saidiya Hartman has argued, only "exacerbate the indifference to suffering that is the consequence of the benumbing spectacle." Hartman offers a powerful warning against indulging the narrative appeal of stories of violence that "exploit the shocking spectacle" of an abused black body, especially given "the precariousness of empathy and the uncertain line between spectator and witness."[3] Narrating violence—and especially repeating details of abuse for the purpose of creating drama—runs the risk of normalizing suffering as well as appealing to the worst of voyeuristic tendencies. But this kind of narration is not the same as analysis, and the particular forms in which political violence was enacted remain important terrain for scholarly interpretation. Specifically, I am advocating close reading of the details of violent encounters as a window onto the political culture and conflicts of their time.

This essay explores such an approach to interpreting the moment of violence by treating closely three incidents of sexual violence suffered by African American women at the hands of white men following emancipation in the southern United States.[4] Representations of sexual violence seem particularly vulnerable to the concerns expressed by Hartman, due to the potentially sensationalist character of stories of rape. Indeed, often in the past, scholars considering postemancipation political violence recounted experiences of rape and other forms of sexual abuse primarily for the purpose of dramatizing the extremes of terror. More recent treatments by some feminist historians have taken a more analytical approach, arguing that rape was a conscious strategy intentionally deployed by white men in order to shore up a white supremacist patriarchy challenged by the outcome of the Civil War.[5] I am advocating a third approach, one that might help us move beyond both sensationalist and conspiratorial or purely instrumentalist readings of violence. This approach emphasizes the discursive dimensions of violent attacks. Sexual violence during Reconstruction was not simply an instrument of force, a tool white southerners used intentionally to intimidate opponents and assure their desired outcomes in elections or labor disputes. It also worked as a form of brutal political expression. Through their words and actions, assailants staged meanings for race that contested the rights and identities being claimed by African Americans in freedom. These scenes involved enormous performative excess, content seemingly unrelated to the stated political aims of the assailants, which drew on gendered imagery circulating in white political discourse at the time. This imagery depicted African American women and men as lacking what were considered to be honorable gender norms, sexuality, and family relationships and thus as supposedly unfit for citizenship and suffrage. I argue that focusing on these aspects of postemancipation violence reveals how specific attacks can best be understood as both a manifestation of and a participant in discursive contests over what race was going to mean in a society without slavery. This approach may better our chances of avoiding the dangers of sensationalist and exploitative renderings of black suffering. It aims instead at developing useful interpretations of the symbolic universe of the assailants that made particular kinds of violence both meaningful and legitimate to the perpetrators, and that shaped in part the experience of the victims.

My emphasis on the discursive dimensions of sexual violence during Reconstruction has been shaped in part by debates among feminist historians regarding the "linguistic turn" in historical scholarship. A number of feminist social historians in the 1990s were critical of or at least cautious about applying poststructuralist methods to women's history, arguing that deconstructing categories such as gender would not help bring the experiences and struggles of women to light. These scholars were responding to contentions of Joan Wallach Scott and others that historians do not have unmediated access to the "real" experience of historical actors, and that social-historical sources illuminate not so much experience in the past as the discourses by which people represented and through which they came to understand their experience. Scott's feminist critics claimed that privileging language and representation made it impossible to analyze the actual material experiences of women in the past and present. And some of these critics invoked women's experiences with rape and other forms of violence as an example of something "real," a harsh, physical reality that existed outside of discourse and that could not be captured by an emphasis on meaning.[6]

The approach I am advocating for analyzing sexual violence began as an attempt to bridge this divide between poststructuralist and more empirical and materialist feminist scholars. By fusing the methods of cultural analysis with the practice of social history, my work on the subject of sexual violence seeks to show, in a historically grounded, concrete fashion, how rape, a "real," material, physical act of violence, happened through language, was intensely symbolic, and was a product of and participant in political discourse. Specifically I find that one cannot understand well the history of rape and other forms of sexual violence—and their political force—during Reconstruction without considering the discourses that invested that violence with meaning for its assailants as well as its victims.

The incidents of sexual violence explored in this essay were part of the larger history of terror that followed the Civil War, when bands of white men, often called "night riders" by freedpeople,[7] roamed especially rural areas of the South, disarming black Union soldiers and threatening and killing black community leaders. After the enfranchisement of black men under the Reconstruction Acts, vigilante gangs commonly sought to prevent new black voters from participating at the polls. Testimony about sexual violence that African American women suffered in the context of this political terror has been preserved in government archives. This testimony contains details about assailants' actions and about exchanges between assailants and victims that are extremely disturbing. Though it risks "exploit[ing] the shocking spectacle" warned against by Hartman, I will nonetheless recount these disturbing details to the extent necessary for my analysis. I do so in hopes of highlighting the dilemmas involved in writing about violence while also suggesting a possible way to move beyond them.

The first of three violent encounters I will consider occurred in Robertson County, Tennessee, in late October 1866. Here, one afternoon, members of a family of former slaves named Willis watched as three white men approached the fence around their yard. These men called for the mother of the family (whose first name was not saved in the record) to come to the fence. Mrs. Willis responded but went no farther than the front door. Mrs. Willis's son, Henry, later reported to the Freedmen's Bureau that these men then "used the most obscene language" in addressing his mother. Henry also repeated how "one of them asked her if she had connection with a man lately. She said she was not in the habit of doing it. . . . He then said, God damn you I will make you do it." The man then drew his pistol and jumped over the fence into her yard. He stopped there, though, and did not follow through on his threat. A few days later, this time at night, the same men returned to the Willis home, beat Mrs. Willis's husband Sanford, plundered their belongings, and burned their house to the ground. According to affidavits left with the Freedmen's Bureau by both Henry and his sister Amanda, one of these men also led Amanda "down into the woods" and raped her.[8]

The second case occurred in Cherokee County, Alabama, in 1869. There a seventeen-year-old former slave named Cynthia Bryant was staying at the home of freedman George Moore, his wife, and his mother, whose name was Rina Barry. In the middle of the night, while Cynthia was sleeping in a bed with Rina, several disguised men burst into the home. The men dragged George out of the house and beat him. George later told a lieutenant at a nearby camp of federal troops who was collecting information on the activities of the local Klan that while several of these men "guarded me . . . others went in and ravished a young girl who was visiting my wife." Rina Barry herself described to a sympathetic white neighbor what had happened to Cynthia Bryant, and this neighbor wrote down Rina's story and sent it to the same army lieutenant: "One came to the bed where she [Rina] and a neighbor woman were sleeping, and wanted to get in bed with them. . . . They refused him, but he said if the girl that was in bed with Reaner [Rina] did not submit to him, he would shoot her, and had a gun in his hand. The girl commenced crying and said she did not want to die; and then he set his gun down by the bed and stripped off the cover and got on the girl in bed with Reaner." Rina also recounted how another assailant "tried to get George's wife out doors to some of the other men and let them have to do with her." George's wife dissuaded the attackers of this plan, however, by telling them "she had just miscarried and couldn't."[9]

Finally, the third assault also occurred in 1869, this time in Rockingham County, North Carolina. Here we have no direct testimony about the attack, only the report of a local court clerk sent to a state supreme court justice, which the justice in turn sent on to the governor. We do not know how the clerk learned of the attack, but we can presume the details of this incident were reported to him by freedpeople who were either victims of the assault or witnesses to it. According to this report, a group of disguised men whipped a black man while forcing him to pretend he was having intercourse with a black girl. The assailants furthermore insisted that the girl's father be a witness to the scene.[10]

How can we as scholars write about and interpret such disturbing accounts of sexual violence and terror? How can the record of such moments of tense exchange and physical and psychic brutality expressed in sexual and gendered form be described and analyzed in a way that makes them part of a useful history? Alternatively, if these moments of violence cannot be interpreted in an illuminating and useful way, does repeating their details risk either reproducing the indignity that these women and their families suffered or effacing their suffering by making it simply an object of analysis? These questions arose for me as I was researching sexual violence during Reconstruction, and especially when the cold-blooded brutality I have occasionally discovered in the archives stopped me in my analytical tracks.[11] Even when not stymied by the record of brutality, I have still found myself in the uncomfortable and ethically challenging position of having a successful research day amount to the discovery of evidence of another person's pain. And with Saidiya Hartman's critique in mind, I have often feared that these stories might serve as much as combat racist and sexist ends.

Yet my hesitancy to pursue histories of sexual violence inspired by these ethical dilemmas was counterbalanced by the overwhelming evidence of the lengths to which many black women and men living through Reconstruction had themselves gone to make their experiences of violence part of the public record. Freedpeople traveled great distances and risked retaliation by white vigilantes in order to testify before congressional investigating committees, federal grand juries, and the Freedmen's Bureau, white officials whom freedpeople no doubt suspected were as likely to receive them with skepticism as sympathy.[12] And still, they went to testify. Thus we know that, at that time at least, they wanted their stories told.

Also compelling my efforts to write useful histories of sexual violence was the fact that the way the history of racial violence after emancipation had traditionally been interpreted could not account, for instance, for the "obscene language" directed at Mrs. Willis, or the freedman forced to simulate sex with a child. Histories of postemancipation violence had tended to emphasize not what historian Thomas Holt has called "the inexplicable excesses of racial phenomena [and] their seeming irrationality" but rather violence's more materialist aims and effects.[13] To some degree, this is understandable. White gangs had clearly directed their violence at those people who most visibly exercised, promoted, or enabled the empowerment of former slaves—soldiers, militia members, ministers, teachers, and those who bought land or resisted white efforts to control their labor. Indeed, night-rider violence was so seemingly instrumental and so explicitly targeted for political ends that it is difficult to resist reducing its meaning entirely to its function. And yet, violence also took striking forms seemingly unrelated to function. Most saliently, this politically targeted and instrumental violence was suffused with imagery of gender and sexuality beyond anything necessitated by the explicit political ends of its assailants. Trying to understand this, I have come to see night-rider violence not simply as an instrument of force but also as a complex rhetoric of power and a stage for articulating racial meanings that contested the rights and identities claimed by African Americans in freedom.

Returning to the violent encounters described above, and contextualizing and attempting to read them more closely, may help elaborate this point. Mrs. Willis was crudely propositioned and her daughter Amanda was raped in a region of Tennessee where in 1866 freedpeople were facing starvation. Planters had neither rations nor wages to pay them, so laborers began refusing to work in their fields and were seeking alternative means of subsistence. In frustration with this assertion of autonomy on the part of their former slaves, local planters allowed a band of ex-Confederate guerrillas, known as Colonel Harper's gang, essentially to take over the region. A broadside allegedly drafted by the gang, here calling themselves the "I Am Committee," was posted on doors and read aloud to freedpeople in this area. Notably, among the regulations for former slaves' conduct that this document contained were the rules that not only all black men but also all black women and children had to be in the employ of a white person and that all black families were to continue to live on their former owners' land.[14] These rules effectively refused any appearance of independent domestic life for former slaves and insisted on white men's control over the allocation of the labor in black families.

The white vigilantes who attacked the Willis home in October 1866, one of whom claimed to be Colonel Harper himself,[15] further dramatized an alleged impossibility of independent black households. Their actions communicated to the audience for the attack—both themselves and their victims—that the norms and identities associated with a supposedly protective patriarchy did not apply to black families. Simply by asking Mrs. Willis "if she had connection with a man lately," her assailants forced her into an exchange in which she was positioned not as a proper wife standing at the front door of the home she shared with her husband but rather as a loose or lewd woman. The fact that the man who propositioned her failed to do as he threatened—he menacingly jumped over the fence, a symbol of the boundaries of a man's private and protected domain,[16] but he did not in the end "make her" have forced "connection" with him—highlights the importance of the verbal exchange, and of an almost scripted posturing that was frequently evident in night riders' attacks. The assertion of black women's depravity contained within this exchange was made more visceral and concrete when these men returned a few nights later, separated Amanda from the protective space of her home and family, and forced her to engage in sex with a white stranger.

The other two assaults I described occurred after black men had secured the right to vote and night riding became a common strategy to keep black men from the polls. Indeed, the attack during which Cynthia Bryant was raped occurred just before an election in Alabama, and the intruders had first demanded to know for whom George had voted in the last presidential election. They cursed and beat him when he defiantly replied that he had voted for Republican president Ulysses S. Grant. When George testified about the attack, he reported, "the cause of this treatment, they said, was that we voted the radical ticket."[17] Part of that "treatment" was to enter and behave in the Barry-Moore household as if they were in a house of ill repute, a place in which women were available to have sex with strange white men on demand. Rather than physically forcing sex, the man who raped Cynthia Bryant first asked for her submission—he said he wanted to get in bed with her. He overwhelmed her initial refusal by threatening to kill her, but once he had obtained her acquiescence, signaled to him when she said, "she did not want to die," he put his gun down. He compelled her to perform her consent, and thus her depravity, and this allowed him to maintain the fantasy that he was engaging in illicit but consensual sex, sex that marked the Barry-Moore household not as a virtuous domestic sphere that served as the basis of a legitimate political authority for its patriarch but rather as a space of vice, marginal to any community of upstanding citizens.

We know far less about the scene of simulated sex coerced by night riders in North Carolina, except that it occurred in an area where disguised white men had been assaulting freedpeople almost nightly for a month. But we do know that the Klan often circulated rumors of unruly domestic relations and illicit sexual practices among former slaves as rationales for attacks. Such misrepresentations of African American sexuality were invoked in the midst of actual assaults, suggesting that fantasies of black sexual transgression played an important role in shaping the specifics of individual incidents of violence. The Klan appears to have reveled in accusing black men and women of inappropriate conduct within their families, for instance when they beat a black woman in Gwinnett County, Georgia, telling her she was being punished because she had been "knocking about" with a man other than her husband.[18] I see the otherwise inexplicable forcing of a man to pretend he was having sex with a child in this context. By forcing freedpeople to perform transgressive and possibly violent sex or by forcing them to appear to allow it to occur in their families, vigilantes coerced black men and women into participating in white fantasies representing them as incapable of proper domestic relationships and virtuous gender identities, relationships and identities that were key to many white men's own depiction of the legitimacy of their political power.[19] Night riders employed patriarchal logic along with vivid pornographic imagination to construct gendered representations of racial difference.

African American women were not, of course, the authors or choreographers of these gendered scenes. Nonetheless, from their words—both the words they and others attributed to them in the moment of violence and the words they chose to describe assaults when they testified after the fact—we can at times discern the ways that they understood and reacted to the assaults. Also evident are women's efforts to convey opposing meanings for the scenes in which they were forced to participate. In a variety of ways, for instance, women refused assailants' idea that they were participating in consensual, casual sex. When Cynthia Bryant declared that she "did not want to die," she told the assailant, the other intruders who were present in the room, Rina Barry who lay by her side, and other members of the Barry-Moore household with whom she stayed that yes, she was acquiescing to this man's demands, but she did so only under the threat of deadly force. Despite the pretense this man seemed to want to enact when he put his gun down, she was not agreeing to have sex. Rather, she told all around her, she was trying to save her life.[20]

When Rina Barry recounted the events of that night to her neighbor, at least as he recorded them in his letter, the majority of her words focused on exchanges between the attackers and women regarding demands for sex. This was despite the fact that the assailants were responsible for a wide range of criminal acts.[21] Something similar can be observed in Amanda Willis's testimony. In her affidavit before the Freedmen's Bureau agent, Willis foregrounded the fact that she had been raped while only briefly mentioning other acts of violence against her family and their home. Following longer and more detailed affidavits made by her father and brother, Amanda Willis testified this way:

> On or about the 23rd day of October 1866, I saw three men at Mother's house, and after putting all of us out of the house and our clothes, one of the men got me by the arm and told me to follow him. he brought me down into the woods and had forcible connection with me.
>
> They all left immediately afterwards.
>
> They burned up father's house.[22]

The emphasis on sexual violence in Willis's and Barry's accounts of the attacks on their homes may have been the result of questioning. Perhaps Barry's neighbor asked her to elaborate on an initial report that Bryant had been raped. And Amanda Willis may have testified less about the theft, beating of her father, and arson for which the attackers were also responsible because the Freedman's Bureau agent before whom she spoke, already in possession of affidavits describing these crimes, asked her to speak specifically about the rape. We will never know for sure. Regardless, the fact that these women willingly offered testimony focused on rape indicates that foremost in their minds regarding the horrors of their experience thus far as free people was that black women still were not living free of sexual assault. Their testimony suggests not only the importance of bodily integrity and lives free of sexual abuse to freedwomen's expectations for freedom but also that they understood the centrality of sexuality to the racist practices seeking to exclude them from fully realizing a free life. They may well have felt a particular urgency to protest this aspect of postemancipation terror.

We may never be able to circumvent entirely the perils of sensationalism and, obversely, the potential numbing of readers to African American pain through the telling and retelling of stories of white-on-black violence. But analyzing sexual violence, and the politics and discourse that gave it meaning, also helps us deconstruct—and if possible counter—the racist and sexist scripts that mobilized rape.[23] By reading closely the moment of violence, I seek to foreground its symbolic dimensions without either detaching ourselves from or exploiting for dramatic purposes the pain and horror of the experience of that violence. This approach to analysis can help us make sense of that "inexplicable excess" of racial violence to which Thomas Holt refers by situating it, in the case of rape, in the ways meanings for race were articulated with and through discourses of gender and sexuality. This approach may also help us make sense of the highly sexualized racism with which we continue to struggle to this day. Thus, I hope that by analyzing stories of violence, with caution and care, we can contribute to the building of useful history.

NOTES

I thank Gregory Downs, Jim Downs, and David Blight for inviting me to participate in "Beyond Freedom," where this essay began, and especially Jim for encouraging me to use this conference as an opportunity to reflect on approaches to analyzing violence.

1. The extensive literature on postemancipation racial violence in the United States includes W. E. B. Du Bois, *Black Reconstruction in America: An Essay toward the Part Which Black Folk Played in the Attempt to Reconstruct Democracy in America, 1860–1880* (New York: Meridian, 1962 [1935]), esp. 674–84; John Hope Franklin, *Reconstruction: After the Civil War* (Chicago: University of Chicago Press, 1961), chap. 9; Allen W. Trelease, *White Terror: The Ku Klux Klan Conspiracy and Southern Reconstruction* (Baton Rouge: Louisiana State University Press, 1971); George C. Rable, *But There Was No Peace: The Role of Violence in the Politics of Reconstruction* (Athens: University of Georgia Press, 1984); Eric Foner, *Reconstruction: America's Unfinished Revolution* (New York: Harper & Row, 1988), esp. 425–44; Michael Perman, "Counter Reconstruction: The Role of Violence in Southern Redemption," in *The Facts of Reconstruction: Essays in Honor of John Hope Franklin*, ed. Eric Anderson and Alfred A. Moss Jr. (Baton Rouge: Louisiana State University Press, 1991), 121–40; Catherine Clinton, "Bloody Terrain: Freedwomen, Sexuality and Violence during Reconstruction," *Georgia Historical Quarterly* 76 (Summer 1992):

313–32, and "Reconstructing Freedwomen," in *Divided Houses: Gender and the Civil War,* ed. Catherine Clinton and Nina Silber (New York: Oxford University Press, 1992), 306–19; Martha Hodes, "The Sexualization of Reconstruction Politics: White Women and Black Men in the South after the Civil War," in *American Sexual Politics: Sex, Gender, and Race since the Civil War,* ed. John C. Fout and Maura Shaw Tantillo (Chicago: University of Chicago Press, 1993), 59–74; Martha Hodes, *White Women, Black Men: Illicit Sex in the Nineteenth-Century South* (New Haven, Conn.: Yale University Press, 1997), chap. 7; Scott Reynolds Nelson, "Livestock, Boundaries, and Public Space in Spartanburg: African American Men, Elite White Women, and the Spectacle of Conjugal Relations," in *Sex, Love, Race: Crossing Boundaries in North American History,* ed. Martha Hodes (New York: New York University Press, 1999), 313–27; Scott Reynolds Nelson, *Iron Confederacies: Southern Railways, Klan Violence, and Reconstruction* (Chapel Hill: University of North Carolina Press, 1999); Stephen Kantrowitz, *Ben Tillman and the Reconstruction of White Supremacy* (Chapel Hill: University of North Carolina Press, 2000); Stephen Kantrowitz, "One Man's Mob Is Another Man's Militia: Violence, Manhood, and Authority in Reconstruction South Carolina," in *Jumping Jim Crow: Southern Politics from Civil War to Civil Rights,* ed. Jane Dailey, Glenda Elizabeth Gilmore, and Bryant Simon (Princeton, N.J.: Princeton University Press, 2000), 67–87; Lisa Cardyn, "Sexualized Racism/Gendered Violence: Outraging the Body Politic in the Reconstruction South," *Michigan Law Review* 100 (February 2002): 813–35; Lisa Cardyn, "Sexual Terror in the Reconstruction South," in *Battle Scars: Gender and Sexuality in the American Civil War,* ed. Catherine Clinton and Nina Silber (New York: Oxford University Press, 2006), 140–67; Steven Hahn, *A Nation under Our Feet: Black Political Struggles in the Rural South from Slavery to the Great Migration* (Cambridge, Mass.: Harvard University Press, 2003); Elaine Franz Parsons, "Midnight Rangers: Costume and Performance in the Reconstruction-Era Ku Klux Klan," *Journal of American History* 92, no. 3 (2005): 811–36; Elaine Franz Parsons, *Ku Klux: The Birth of the Klan during Reconstruction* (Chapel Hill: University of North Carolina Press, 2016); Kidada E. Williams, *They Left Great Marks on Me: African American Testimonies of Racial Violence from Emancipation to World War I* (New York: New York University Press, 2012); Carole Emberton, *Beyond Redemption: Race, Violence, and the American South after the Civil War* (Chicago: University of Chicago Press, 2013); Kate Côté Gillin, *Shrill Hurrahs: Women, Gender, and Racial Violence in South Carolina, 1865–1900* (Columbia: University of South Carolina Press, 2013).

2. For works that analyze specific forms taken by racial violence, see, for example, Clinton, "Bloody Terrain" and "Reconstructing Freedwomen"; Hodes, *White Women, Black Men* and "Sexualization of Reconstruction Politics"; Nelson, "Livestock, Boundaries, and Public Space in Spartanburg" and *Iron Confederacies,* esp. chap. 5 and 6; Cardyn, "Sexualized Racism/Gendered Violence" and "Sexual Terror"; and especially Parsons, "Midnight Rangers" and *Ku Klux.* Parsons analyzes the ways various popular cultural practices from the nineteenth-century

urban North shaped acts of violence by the Ku Klux Klan during Reconstruction. See also Hahn, *Nation under Our Feet*, 265–88.

3. Saidiya Hartman, *Scenes of Subjection: Terror, Slavery, and Self-Making in Nineteenth-Century America* (New York: Oxford University Press, 1997), 4.

4. The incidents and analysis considered here are drawn from Hannah Rosen, *Terror in the Heart of Freedom: Citizenship, Sexual Violence, and the Meaning of Race in the Postemancipation South* (Chapel Hill: University of North Carolina Press, 2009), chap. 5.

5. Feminist scholars have also argued that white-on-black rape during Reconstruction was a continuation of the prevalent sexual abuse of enslaved women in the antebellum southern society as well as evidence of the magnitude of the rage white southern men felt about the loss of power represented by emancipation and establishment of formal political equality across race. See, for example, Cardyn, "Sexual Terror" and "Sexualized Racism/Gendered Violence," esp. 679, 827–29; Clinton, "Bloody Terrain" and "Reconstructing Freedwomen."

6. See the following from Joan Wallach Scott: *Gender and the Politics of History* (New York: Columbia University Press, 1988); "On Language, Gender, and Working-Class History," *International Labor and Working-Class History* 31 (Spring 1987): 1–13; review of *Heroes of Their Own Lives: The Politics and History of Family Violence* by Linda Gordon, and "Response to Linda Gordon," *Signs* 15 (Summer 1990): 848–51, 859–60; "'The Tip of the Volcano,'" *Comparative Studies in Society and History* 35 (April 1993): 438–43; "The Evidence of Experience," in *Questions of Evidence: Proof, Practice, and Persuasion across the Disciplines*, ed. James Chandler, Arnold I. Davidson, and Harry Harootunian (Chicago: University of Chicago Press, 1994), 363–87, and a shorter version of the same essay, titled "Experience," in *Feminists Theorize the Political*, ed. Judith Butler and Joan Wallach Scott (New York: Routledge, 1992), 22–40. For historians who are implicitly in sympathy with Scott's approach, see Elsa Barkley Brown, "'What Has Happened Here': The Politics of Difference in Women's History and Feminist Politics," *Feminist Studies* 18 (Summer 1992): 295–312; Nancy A. Hewitt, "Compounding Differences," *Feminist Studies* 18 (Summer 1992): 313–26. See also Judith Butler, "Contingent Foundations: Feminism and the Question of 'Postmodernism,'" in Butler and Scott, *Feminists Theorize the Political*, 3–21. For critiques of Scott, see Laura Lee Downs, "If 'Woman' Is Just an Empty Category, Then Why Am I Afraid to Walk Alone at Night? Identity Politics Meets the Postmodern Subject," and "Reply to Joan Scott," both in *Comparative Studies in Society and History* 35 (April 1993): 414–37, 444–51; Linda Gordon, review of Joan Wallach Scott's *Gender and the Politics of History* and "Response to Joan Scott," in *Signs* 15 (1990): 853–59, 852–53. Christine Stansell also expressed concerns about Scott's approach to history in "A Response to Joan Scott," *International Labor and Working-Class History* 31 (Spring 1987): 24–29. For works that invoked sexual violence as a caution against employing poststructuralist analysis for feminist concerns, see Downs,

"If 'Woman' Is Just an Empty Category," 414; Mary E. Hawkesworth, "Knowers, Knowing, Known: Feminist Theory and Claims of Truth," *Signs* 14 (Spring 1989): 533–57; Gordon, "Response to Scott," 853.

7. Gladys-Marie Fry, *Night Riders in Black Folk History* (Athens, Ga.: Brown Thrasher Books, University of Georgia Press, 1991 [1975]), 154–60.

8. Based on information in affidavits of Henry Willis, Stanford Willis, and Amanda Willis, in Records of the Assistant Commissioner for the State of Tennessee, microfilm 999, Bureau of Refugees, Freedmen, and Abandoned Lands, RG 105, National Archives and Records Administration, Washington, D.C. (hereafter BRFAL), microfilm roll 34, "Affidavits Relating to Outrages." For more on the attack on the Willis family home, see Rosen, *Terror in the Heart of Freedom*, 203–7. The Willises' experience is also discussed in Cardyn, "Sexual Terror" and "Sexualized Racism/Gendered Violence," 729–30.

9. Affidavit of George Moore and letter from John Hamilton to Lieut. James Miller, August 29, 1869, appended to Testimony of General Samuel W. Crawford, in U.S. Congress, Joint Select Committee to Inquire into the Condition of Affairs in the Late Insurrectionary States, *Testimony Taken by the Joint Select Committee to Inquire into the Condition of Affairs in the Late Insurrectionary States* (hereafter *KKK Testimony*), 9:1188, 1189–90.

10. Recounted in Trelease, *White Terror*, 195, citing Thomas A. Ragland et al. to Justice Thomas Settle, Wentworth, July 13, 1869, and Settle to Gov. Holden, Wentworth, July 28, 1869, W. W. Holden Papers, Duke University. See also Cardyn, "Sexual Terror," 144.

11. See Thomas Holt's discussion of W. E. B. Du Bois being stopped in his tracks both literally and figuratively by "the sheer incomprehensibility of racist phenomena" in "Marking: Race, Race-Making, and the Writing of History," *American Historical Review* 100 (February 1995): 3–5.

12. See Rosen, *Terror in the Heart of Freedom*, 1–4, 77–80, and chap. 6; Williams, *They Left Great Marks on Me*. For a groundbreaking, thoughtful exploration of the difficulties of speaking publicly about rape for African American women in the nineteenth and early twentieth centuries, see Darlene Clark Hine, "Rape and the Inner Lives of Black Women in the Middle West: Preliminary Thoughts on the Culture of Dissemblance," *Signs* 14 (1989): 912–20.

13. Holt, "Marking," 5.

14. "I Am Committee," enclosed in Lt. Chas B. Brady to Bvt. Lt. Col. A. L. Hough, January 29, 1867, Letters Received, series 4720, Dept. of the Tennessee, U.S. Army Continental Commands, reproduced in *Families and Freedom: A Documentary History of African American Kinship in the Civil War Era*, ed. Ira Berlin and Leslie Rowland (New York: New Press, 1997), 189. For more on Harper's gang and the I Am Committee document, see Rosen, *Terror in the Heart of Freedom*, 184–87.

15. This claim was most likely false. See Affidavits of Henry Willis and Stanford

Willis, BRFAL), microfilm roll 34, "Affidavits Relating to Outrages," and Rosen, *Terror in the Heart of Freedom*, 203–4.

16. See especially Stephanie McCurry, "The Politics of Yeoman Households in South Carolina," in Clinton and Silber, *Divided Houses*, 22–38; Stephanie Mc-Curry, *Masters of Small Worlds: Yeoman Households, Gender Relations, and the Political Culture of the Antebellum South Carolina Low Country* (New York: Oxford University Press, 1995).

17. Events described in Affidavits of George Moore, Cynthia Bryant, and Rina Barry, and letter from John Hamilton to Lieut. James Miller, August 29, 1869, all appended to Testimony of General Samuel W. Crawford, *KKK Testimony*, 9:1187–90.

18. Testimony of William Hampton Mitchell, *KKK Testimony*, 7:642.

19. See esp. Laura F. Edwards, *Gendered Strife and Confusion: The Political Culture of Reconstruction* (Chicago: University of Illinois Press, 1997), and McCurry, *Masters of Small Worlds* and "The Politics of Yeoman Households."

20. Hamilton letter, August 29, 1869, *KKK Testimony*, 9:1189.

21. Ibid. Rina Barry told her story to her neighbor, John Hamilton, three days after the attack. Both Cynthia Bryant and Rina Barry subsequently left affidavits themselves with a local justice of the peace almost a month later. In those affidavits, both women mentioned that intruders came into the house, took George outside and beat him, and then one of the men spoke to them while they lay in bed. They did not mention, though, that Cynthia Bryant was raped, each repeating instead, "We were not troubled any more." Affidavits of Cynthia Bryant and Rina Barry, appended to Testimony of General Samuel W. Crawford, in *KKK Testimony*, 9:1188–89. What to make of this? Would John Hamilton and George Moore have made up the story of rape? That seems improbable, especially as Hamilton's account contains details he would have been unlikely to invent. Hamilton himself explained in his letter to James Miller that the omission was due to his warnings to the Barry-Moore household that speaking about the attack placed them in danger. He wrote, "When I saw [Rina] and George, and some other colored folks, I told them not to tell anything unless it was to some one of the republican party, and they told me they would not. I told them if they told what had taken place, they might kill some of them. . . . If they have not stated to you just as I have, I have no doubt but what it is from the caution I gave them as a friend." The women's affidavits were copied by Miller but sworn before the justice of the peace; George Moore's affidavit does not indicate that it was similarly made before the local official. Hamilton also feared retribution from the vigilantes for telling his story. He explained to Miller, "I would have come to see you before now, but I would be in danger of my life if it was known." Hamilton letter, August 29, 1869, *KKK Testimony*, 9:1190. The fact that there was so much risk involved in recounting incidents of rape and yet freedpeople did so nonetheless further highlights the importance to them of protesting this form of violence.

22. Affidavit of Amanda Willis, BRFAL, microfilm roll 34, "Affidavits Relating to Outrages." For more on Amanda Willis's affidavit, see Rosen, *Terror in the Heart of Freedom*, 205–6.

23. Rosen, *Terror in the Heart of Freedom*; on particular gender and racial "scripts" leading to rape, see also Sharon Marcus, "Fighting Bodies, Fighting Words: A Theory and Politics of Rape Prevention," in Butler and Scott, *Feminists Theorize the Political*, 385–403.

Emancipating the Evidence

The Ontology of the Freedmen's Bureau Records

JIM DOWNS

The history of emancipation would not be possible without the Bureau of Refugees, Freedmen, and Abandoned Lands records, commonly referred to as the Freedmen's Bureau records, housed at the National Archives. While scores of historians have drawn on these records to inform their studies, few have paused to consider the unintended consequences, political implications, and alternative meanings of these documents.

When historians, who were part of the Dunning school, first began to chronicle emancipation in the early part of the twentieth century, they portrayed formerly enslaved people as indolent and feckless. Their interpretation of black people as inferior was not just a matter of interpretation; it became the artifice for policy decisions at the time and substantiated segregation.[1] Black intellectuals, particularly women, who studied at Howard University and other institutions began to refute these interpretations in their master's essays on black suffrage, education, and culture. They uncovered evidence that revealed how freedpeople built schools and churches and waged political campaigns for equality.[2] At the center of this crusade stood W. E. B. Du Bois, who wrote the leading study of the postwar period, *Black Reconstruction: An Essay toward a History of the Part Which Black Folk Played in the Attempt to Reconstruct Democracy in America, 1860–1880*, which powerfully illustrated the central role that black people played in the rebuilding of the nation after the Civil War.[3] Despite being the most recognized black intellectual of the early twentieth century, Du Bois was not the only one. A. A. Taylor published an essay that refuted the Dunning school as well and, most of all, criticized their neglect of evidence that revealed black agency.[4]

Taylor, Du Bois, and other black scholars in the first half of the twentieth century mined impressive evidence that underscored the ways in which freedpeople were central actors in the Reconstruction South, but racism prevented their studies from becoming part of both the academic and popular understanding of the period. White supremacy prevailed and continued to dictate for decades the interpretation of black people as hapless bystanders who got in the way of white people's plans and promises for the postwar period. Not until the start of the black civil rights movement did a cadre of historians committed to social justice, who took their cue from Du Bois and black scholars from earlier in the century, shatter the dominant, racist view of the period.

These historians defeated a racist interpretation of the past not only because they were supported by the political fervor of the civil rights movement but because they, taking their cue from Du Bois, found convincing evidence in the National Archives among the Bureau of Refugees, Freedmen, and Abandoned Lands records that demonstrated freedpeople's political will and might after the Civil War. Labor records attested to freedpeople negotiating the terms of their contracts. Educational reports illustrated the passionate claims of black children and adults to attend school to learn how to read, often pleading for classes at night so that working adults could attend where white women from the North would teach them. Correspondence drafted by military officials and field agents depicted efforts of black people gathering in churches and at outdoor meetings to advance the cause of suffrage. Monthly summaries written by military and government officials offer insight into the religious, medical, and social life of the postwar period.

Drawing on these records, a cohort of historians founded the Freedmen and Southern Society Project at the University of Maryland in 1976 in order to anthologize them into published volumes that could be widely circulated to scholars, students, and librarians. The historians at the Freedmen and Southern Society Project examined tens of thousands of documents, long reports handwritten in nineteenth-century prose by assistant commissioners, who reported on the postwar conditions of a particular state under their charge—noting the labor potential of formerly enslaved people, the climate and crops, the health of the population and the distribution of rations, the status of the schools, the registration of marriages, the drafting of labor contracts, the disputes between white southern denizens and the northern military that attempted to discipline them. These historians uncovered evidence of formerly enslaved people agreeing to the terms of a labor contract or a court decision by honing in on the faint marking of an "x" that translated to the signature of a former bondsperson who could not sign his or her name. These historians also unfurled crumbling envelopes and carefully lifted the painted seal to retrieve delicate notes that often provided no more than confirmation of a receipt of a letter from the previous month. They pieced together correspondences, matching an archival trail of "letters received" to "letters sent" in order to reconstruct forgotten episodes in the nation's history of the transition from slavery to freedom. These records—ranging from scant insights to full-blown narratives—became the basis for historians to shatter racist interpretations of the South and to offer cogent evidence of how formerly enslaved people were chief agents in the social, political, and economic reconstruction of the nation.[5]

The wealth of records, which includes 6,468 containers that span more than a quarter mile in the National Archives, continues to offer contemporary historians the raw data to study slavery and its aftermath. Yet few if any scholars have paused to interrogate the epistemological and symbolic significance of the voluminous records in the National Archives in Washington, D.C. Instead, recent generations of scholars have rushed headlong into the archives in order to pull out evidence of the freedpeople's experience to support their theses. The studies have ranged from those who were hell-bent on proving Dunning wrong and W. E. B. Du Bois right to more recent scholars who have offered a much-needed gender analysis of the period.[6]

What, though, do the records actually reveal? How do the copious, almost incalculable number of reports that emerged from the postwar South suggest that the chaos of the postwar period could possibly be narrated, summarized, and even quantified in charts and tables? How did the mere production of a single document or an isolated report assign a particular logic and coherence to the postwar South? How have the records established the geographic parameters of Reconstruction? How did the preservation of the records attempt to demonstrate a sense of federal control over an unknown region—a region that before the war was referred to as "peculiar" and "backwards"? How did the records only illustrate what the bureau agents wanted to hear and know?

The Freedmen's Bureau records have been so appealing to generations of scholars because they offer historians the opportunity to excavate freedpeople's "voices" from affidavits, court cases, labor disputes, employment contracts, and even from federal correspondence in which freedpeople were informally and indirectly quoted. The recovery of these first-person "voices" has provided a much-needed intervention into a field that had been dominated by institutional and political history. But what were the political, social, and economic forces that enabled black people's voices to enter the record at a particular time and place? Many scholars have been so preoccupied with the mere discovery of "the voice" that we, as a field, have failed to ask how the testimony got there in the first place.

To be sure, freedpeople's voices only appear in some of the Freedmen's Bureau records, and not as part of a systematic effort to catalog their experience after slavery. Court records and legal disputes, for example, captured freedpeople's voices because these interactions required their testimony. In the education records, northern benevolent reformers, who became the chief allies and the unofficial representatives of formerly enslaved people, included quotations and statements made by freed slaves in their reports to their sponsoring northern organizations to demonstrate the continued need for schools in the South. Yet in medical records, freedpeople's voices rarely appear, because it was not necessary to include their testimony to facilitate the operation of Freedmen's hospitals or to assess the health conditions of the region. According to federal mandates, physicians needed only to tally the number of sick or to describe the necessity for a hospital to continue its operation.[7]

Given these distinctions, we, as historians, need to more carefully investigate when, where, and how freedpeople's voices entered the record, and, more importantly, we need to consider the forces that prevented them from entering the archive. Due to the large number of records dealing with labor conflicts in the South, for example, many scholars have assumed that freedpeople's voices run rampant throughout the bureau records, instead of realizing that the bureau's concern with labor in the Reconstruction South produced this archive. Similarly, religion, faith, and spirituality, all of which mattered to many formerly enslaved people, mattered little to the federal government, and thereby freedpeople's voices are not as loquacious on this topic.[8]

The danger arises when we assume that silence in the Freedmen's Bureau archive is silence in fact. Just because an agent did not write about a subject does not mean that it did not happen, or that it did not matter if it *did* happen. Furthermore, bureau officials often recorded freedpeople's statements within the context of their own vexed experience in the South, not with the intent of documenting black life in the aftermath of the war. The majority of bureau officials desired to vacate their positions as soon as possible; many had served in the military during the war and resented having to work in the postwar South. Many were tired, and some were even injured during the war; due to their disability, some were assigned to work in the South as record keepers. Their correspondence is rife with statements about how their temporary role in facilitating arrangements between freedpeople and white planters was no longer necessary. They revealed, for example, how the bureau no longer needed to provide medical care; they showed how state governments took control of freedpeople's health.[9] Bureau agents also described former slaves' earnest desire to build their own schools in an effort to show how freedpeople no longer required federal support, and they also empowered northern benevolent agencies to take ownership of the educational system in the South, further relieving the bureau of any responsibility. Bureau agents often downplayed the violence and conflict that erupted throughout the region.[10]

Therefore, when they included quotations in their reports, they often featured freedpeople who articulated claims that buttressed their view of Reconstruction's progress. Freedpeople's voices need to be interrogated within this context, not as part of an endless arsenal of first-person narratives about emancipation. Additionally, historians have no way of knowing what bureau agents shortened, paraphrased, and possibly fabricated when they recorded freedpeople's testimony.

Yet so much of the hype surrounding the value of the records lies in the notion that they reflect the unalloyed voices of former slaves. Few black voices made it into the National Archives without a white pen. White people consistently ventriloquized, paraphrased, or at best summarized what freedpeople said in order to bolster the logic of their report. While scholars have smartly questioned the authenticity of black people's voices in nineteenth-century slave narratives and the Works Progress Administration's collection of enslaved people's interviews, the Freedmen's Bureau records have not been subjected to similar scrutiny.[11] Instead, the bureau records have been heralded as an unproblematic treasure trove, in part due to the herculean excavations conducted by the historians at the Freedmen and Southern Society Project to overturn the then dominant white supremacist interpretations of the period.[12]

The Labor Records

Much of the post-1980 historiography would not be possible without the Freedmen and Southern Society Project (FSSP). But how has the FSSP reinforced the bureau's portrait of the South? So many historians study labor because labor dominates the record. The bureau's focus on the legal and employment disputes between formerly enslaved people and former slaveholders certainly reflects actual, often chronic problems of unpaid wages, unfair contractual terms, and other employment disputes, but how did the proliferation of these documents help establish a framework that posited class conflict in the postwar South as one of the major themes of Reconstruction? In other words, was class conflict central because it was, in fact, central, or was it central because the Freedmen's Bureau made it central? What is at stake when economic conflict becomes the operating rhetorical discourse that defines freedpeople's experiences? One possibility is to hold class conflict apart enough to at least allow recognition of other aspects of the freedpeople's experience. We need to stop long enough to listen to the freedpeople and let them tell us how central labor was to their postemancipation experience. It was big, but was it that big?

Certainly the Freedmen's Bureau originated to facilitate the creation of a new free labor economy and to ease the tensions that developed as former slaves and slaveholders transitioned to employee and employer. While myriad boxes of documents in the National Archives reveal disagreements and problems that erupted during this transition, were these the major conflicts that freedpeople faced after slavery? Were former slaveholders their main economic adversaries? On one level, the answer is clearly yes. Yet on another level the archive has framed postwar economic conflict in the South almost exclusively in terms of black and white struggle. Is there evidence in the complaint of registers or other state and local archives that captured conflict within and among black people, for example?[13]

There is also a question of representation: how many freed slaves had direct contact with white people after the war? For one, white planters preferred making contracts only with black men who served as head of the household, who then doled out work assignments to his family members, which suggests that a great majority of freedpeople dealt directly with black, not white men.[14] Moreover, the designated head of the household not only represented blood relatives but also members of extended kin networks, which further lessened the amount of direct contact that many freedpeople had with white employers.[15] Given this hierarchy, what struggles existed among freedpeople themselves during this period? With the exception of Susan Eva O'Donovan's book on the transition from slavery to freedom in Georgia, few historians have considered the question of whether black men in charge fairly doled out responsibilities and evenly split the profits. Did they assign tasks equitably to members of their families and kin networks?[16]

While some Reconstruction scholars certainly recognize that the Freedmen's Bureau sources do not capture the entire economic and labor system in the South, the voluminous number of records as well as the nature of the records tends to implicitly suggest that black and white conflict defined the southern postwar economy. Additionally, the sheer volume of the records seems to cast a shadow over other archival sources, and the labor records become the default archive.

The bureau records also suggest that conflict was rather a new phenomenon for formerly enslaved people and white planters. Historians write about how freedom portended a moment when black and white people met on common ground, facing each other eye to eye—you can almost hear the thundering soundtrack of drums playing in the background as historians write about this new moment. But how new was it? If we accept the institution of slavery as a static institution, then freedom does present a radically new moment. But if we understand that enslaved people constantly negotiated with their owners, that confrontations and face-offs defined how black and white people interacted during slavery, what new labor challenges did freedom present?

Indeed, freedom promised enslaved people wages and ushered in new dynamics that produced more opportunity for formerly enslaved people. But how did their experience as laborers during enslavement shape their experience during freedom?[17] In other words, did their dealings with greedy and prejudicial planters surprise them? So much of the historiography emphasizes the novelty of emancipation and does not adequately see how it evoked familiar themes or drew on past experiences. The Freedmen's Bureau records encourage this sort of interpretation because white northern officials who are witnessing life in the South for the first time are writing the records. Yet historians have overlooked this crucial factor and have overemphasized how the documents offer examples of freedpeople's voice and agency. The bureau papers are a magnificent bureaucratic gift, but we have to fight the urge to let them dictate our reasoning.

This is not to suggest that emancipation did not create a new economic order, or that it was not revolutionary, but that it was part of a chronology that grew out of master/slave relations. Reconstruction triangulates the master/slave dynamic by adding a third party, the white northern bureau official, who witnessed the tumultuousness of the South firsthand for the first time and then processed complaints, disputes, and economic problems between white and black people through this register.[18]

For freedpeople, however, slavery was tumultuous. One aspect of slavery that continued to upset, transform, and redefine the relationship between enslaved people and slaveholders before the war was the prevalence of the domestic slave trade, which dramatically shifted the population from the Upper South to the Mississippi Valley and parts of the Low Country.[19] The domestic slave trade forced enslaved people into new environments where they came into face-to-face contact with new owners, overseers, and others with power over them. Bondspeople learned how to adjust to these scenarios. Although freedom led to payment for their labor and offered them the ability to quit their jobs, what did their experience in the domestic slave trade teach them about how to deal with radical and tumultuous changes during freedom?

According to the Freedmen's Bureau records, conflict and consternation rank as major themes that defined this economic transition. But the archive only provides a snapshot of a particular postwar episode and does not contextualize how the experience of enslavement shaped conflict during Reconstruction. Throughout slavery, bondspeople lived in a state of uncertainty and transition, which often led to deep conflict with their masters. As Harriet Tubman once powerfully stated, "slavery is war."[20]

In keeping with Tubman's assertion, when conflict surfaced among freedpeople and former masters, it likely seemed less of an aberration to freedpeople and planters and more of a shock to the record keeper, the northern bureau agent, who for the first time observed these showdowns. Slavery had taught many former bondspeople that masters did not keep their word and did not care about former enslaved people's well-being. When these problems continued after the war ended, freedpeople were likely more frustrated than they were during slavery and they now possessed the opportunity to legally retaliate. But did their conflict with white owners become the defining way of understanding emancipation—or did it become the way in which the bureau articulated the meaning of conflict during Reconstruction?

The bureau's presence in the South also reinforced a kind of paternalism, as many scholars have noted. The bureau implicitly assumed that freedpeople needed the help of white northerners to find work. While some historians have touched on the paternalistic nature of the bureau, my point here is less to impugn the bureau than to shift historians' attention to bureau officials as record keepers who produced documents that reveal more about northern assumptions than southern realities; more about what northerners valued than what white and black southerners recognized as the chief issues of the postwar South. For example, the bureau records reveal less about freedpeople's economic interests or labor power and more about the federal government's desire to return formerly enslaved people to southern plantations as agricultural workers. While many historians might agree with this assertion, it has not been analyzed as a central factor in shaping the content, biases, and implications of the documents. Some of the bureau agents, for example, were not northerners but white southerners, former Confederates and slaveholders. Yet that distinction has been blurred in many historians' portraits of the bureau as a unified coalition with a similar ideological vision for the Reconstruction of the South.

One issue that many bureau officials seldom documented but remained of paramount concern among both black and white southerners was the question of the fertility of the land, the environmental capability to sustain an agricultural economy. In *DeBow's Review*, southern planters continually lament northern ignorance about crop production, the arability of the land, and the uniqueness of the southern climate. Meanwhile, as skilled agricultural workers, freedpeople knew when, where, and how to plant cotton and other crops, but their concerns about the land often receded in the historiography before the overarching theme of black and white labor and economic conflicts.[21] For example, in 1866 a massive drought swept over the South, leading to high rates of starvation and even death; indeed, the drought and an ensuing famine registered as critical problems for freedpeople. A New York–based group of reformers organized a commission that collected data about the famine, published reports about it, and then sent resources to the South. The records of these relief efforts provide the most detailed account of the drought and famine.[22] Although unpaid wages and broken contracts exacerbated the famine, the drought and other environmental and agricultural problems barely make a cameo appearance in the bureau records. Presumably, the famine, the quality of the land, the effectiveness of the tools, the health of the animals, the proximity to water, and the fecundity of the soil mattered more to freedpeople than just the actions of rapacious evil white planters, who they knew since slavery were inept and unfair.

Education Records

In a truly unprecedented move, the federal government established schools throughout the South for freedpeople. At the time, public education barely existed in the rest of the United States. In late-eighteenth-century Virginia, Thomas Jefferson had proposed a plan for public education for male students in *Notes on the State of Virginia*. Meanwhile, in the 1830s Horace Mann became a fierce advocate for "common schools" in Massachusetts, which were free and open to the public. In general, the notion of public education or schools for all young citizens was a fairly new concept on the eve of the American Civil War. Therefore, the federal government's decision to build schools, roughly a thousand by some estimates, suggests a truly revolutionary turning point in the history of the United States.[23] While some historians have certainly celebrated the creation of schools as institutions founded for mostly black children as a sign of progress that overturned antebellum restrictions against literacy, others have questioned how the establishment of schools facilitated the federal government's efforts to turn young black children and even black adults into an educated labor force and in so doing advance the goals of capitalism.[24]

The bureau schools provided freedpeople the opportunity to learn to read and write, to solve basic math equations, to gain moral and religious instruction, and to even be trained in northern Victorian etiquette, which turned out to be polemical. Some of the teachers were middle- and upper-class women from the North who believed that part of their social mission was to teach religion, manners, and how to speak without a plantation accent. While these efforts were certainly problematic, not all teachers understood these latter issues as part of their pedagogical agenda. The curricula of the schools varied, and one instructor often taught students of all ages in a single classroom. Although there were many white northern women teachers, scores of black women founded schools in their homes, in churches, in former hospitals, and in many other spaces that could be easily converted into classrooms.[25]

Since the bureau understood its mission mostly as an agency devoted to economic and labor issues, it quickly handed over the formal responsibility of building schools, hiring teachers, and establishing a curriculum to northern benevolent associations. The educational records of the Freedmen's Bureau in the National Archives thus only represent a tiny fraction of the life of Freedmen's Bureau schools. Records held by northern benevolent associations, such as the New England Freedmen's Aid Society, which are housed at the Massachusetts Historical Society in Boston, and the American Missionary Association records, which are held at Amistad Research Center at Tulane University, provide a more comprehensive account of education in the postwar South. Additionally, Quaker organizations from Boston, New York, Philadelphia, and other northeastern locations wrote copiously about freedpeople's education. Their impressions can be found in diaries, correspondences, newspapers, manuscript collections, and other ephemera in local archives throughout the country.

The records of the Education Division of the Freedmen's Bureau, nevertheless, contain important insights about freedpeople's education and the federal government's unprecedented efforts to establish schools in the Reconstruction South. But the records also offer a unique insight into life in the South that extends beyond questions of education and can be mined by cultural, legal, social, gender, and even environmental historians. As newcomers to the South, northern teachers were prolific recorders of the world they lived in, for better or worse, and their comprehensive notes can illuminate many other details about the postwar South. Beyond the effort to describe freedpeople's education, these records uncover important data about the geographic parameters and even limits of federal authority. For instance, famed abolitionist author Harriet Jacobs served in the South with her daughter, Louisa, and her friend Julia Wilbur, who was part of abolitionist circles in Rochester; they criticized how the bureau handled freed slaves' living conditions. Their criticism highlighted the environmental conditions of the postwar South—the inhabitable climate, the rain and cold, and the mud and trash that threatened the health of the people as well as the poor quality of the housing structures and the lack of food. Their letters also exposed the fractures in federal policy and powerfully indicated how three women—two black, one white—waged a campaign that reached the White House. Within the broader narrative of Reconstruction, historians, often for good reason, explain how northern reformers worked alongside bureau officials, but Jacobs's and Wilbur's letters reveal how federal policy fell apart on the ground and how civilian women became fierce advocates for the improvement of freedpeople's lives. Their letters offer brilliant insight, beyond the history of Reconstruction, about the history of women in the nineteenth century, illustrating female agency and the politics of intersectionality at work among nineteenth-century women actors.[26]

Moreover, the education documents produced a system of order that conformed to nineteenth-century notions of rationality.[27] Lists indicated order and control, perpetuating the logic that people could be reduced to a number, a name, a place on the ledger—to be counted, defined, and, most of all, understood. The records of the Education Division include long lists of students' names and locations of schools. The government likely continued to maintain these records in an effort to demonstrate the ongoing success of Reconstruction. In fact, throughout the historical record and historiography, education continually becomes defined as the solution, but the problem remains unclear. Was it simply illiteracy? If we suspend our twenty-first-century notions of the value of education, what did education mean for people liberated from slavery in 1865? Certainly for some former bondspeople, it represented literacy. Living in the antebellum South, some former enslaved people would have seen the value in learning how to read and write, but beyond that point, what do the records reveal? Were freed slaves ever suspicious of education efforts? Like most nineteenth-century Americans, they would have been unfamiliar with formal education. Yet many historians have shied away from questioning the purpose of education. The history of freedpeople's education seems to oscillate between the preoccupation of twentieth-century historians who have projected backward the efforts to see a long history of black people desiring schooling as a means to upward mobility, and the bureau's efforts to create order.

If we flip the script and ponder the tumultuous postwar years, schools then represent places to hold, restrict, and, most of all, define freedom. The proliferation of the education documents has produced a narrative about the virtuous freed person who nobly and obediently wanted to learn to read and write. But this was a narrative that bureau and northern reformers created and one that became substantiated by the records. Education began as a federal concern, an endeavor to document and to promulgate to suspicious northerners about the progress of Reconstruction.[28] As O. O. Howard, the leader of the Freedmen's Bureau, explained, "the most urgent want of the freedmen was a practical education; and from the first I have devoted more attention to this than any other branch of work."[29]

Given that the Civil War produced the largest biological crisis of the nineteenth century and more soldiers died of disease than in battle, it seems odd that freedpeople's most urgent need was "a practical education" and not food, shelter, and clothing. Furthermore, it seems that more freedpeople would have wanted to build a home or church rather than a school. Education dominates the bureau records more than religion and spirituality, which also seems odd given the broader religious tradition that defined the lives of many black people in the nineteenth century and later. As Albert J. Raboteau argued, religion has been "the invisible institution," and that invisibility has only been further perpetrated by the bureau's emphasis on education and even labor in the content of the majority of the documents.[30]

Given this context, O. O. Howard's assertion that education represented "the most urgent need" for four million people seems more like propaganda than freedpeople's testimony. The education records reveal how the government could not collectively capture the entire experience of millions of people and render their needs into a simple declarative sentence. Instead, the records suggest how bureau agents created categories that shoehorned freedpeople's aspirations into recognizable maxims. The sources also represent the federal government's anxieties about the moment of freedom. The production of reports, names, and the progress of the school systems suggest that the hundreds of thousands of freed children and adults in various parts of the South had been contained. The records provide geographic coordinates where schools were built and where the anxiety surrounding emancipation loomed largest. While the land and labor records documented the so-called leading conflicts that freedpeople encountered, the education records raise questions about freedpeople's aspirations and desires.

Medical Records

In addition to establishing schools throughout the South, the bureau also established more than forty hospitals, employed 120 physicians, and provided medical treatment and relief to more than a million newly freed slaves. The bureau created a medical division in response to the health crises that developed during the war and emancipation. Given that more soldiers died from camp diseases—infectious disease, yellow fever, pneumonia—than battle, newly freed slaves entered a world plagued by illness and suffering. Compounding matters, once liberated from plantation slavery, former bondspeople had nowhere to live, with no direct access to food, clean clothing, or medical care. The bureau thus established the first ever system of national health care in the postwar South in order to provide freed slaves with basic necessities to survive.[31]

The bureau, in turn, collected extensive health and medical records. Unfortunately, these documents provide less detail about health conditions and more about the federal government's anxieties about creating a labor force. The records provide scant evidence about the actual health conditions of freedpeople and instead tabulate the number of freedpeople who could work. Most of these documents provide statistical estimates on the number of people who were admitted, discharged, and died in freedmen's hospitals—all with an eye toward creating a labor force.[32]

Throughout the records, bureau doctors and officials consistently use the terms "destitute" and "dependent" interchangeably, both of which had economic connotations. The federal government employed the term "dependent" to refer to those whom the government feared would rely on federal or charitable relief for their livelihood. According to bureau agents, "destitute" often became the label for freedpeople who were un-employed. Bureau officials, stationed throughout the Reconstruction South, calculated the number of sick and healthy freedpeople based on this lexicon. They then sent these reports to an assistant commissioner, who oversaw the operations of the bureau in a given state. The assistant commissioner summarized these reports and sent them to Washington, D.C., where federal officials collated the various state reports and pub-lished excerpts as *Laws in Relation to Freedmen*, which became the official record of the bureau's work to be read by Congress.[33]

Crucial details about freedpeople's health went undocumented and often slipped off the page in the various summaries that took place along the paper trail; the records invariably erased the sobering, painful, and often heartbreaking moments that transpired within the walls of freed-men's hospitals. The reports reduced black patients to a number—a statistic that simply evaluated whether they could work. The reports also rendered the problems that physicians reported—from lack of manpower and resources to the inability to stop the arresting spread of epidemics—to a simplified phrase such as "health conditions are wors-ening" or "improving."[34]

Similar to the education records, the medical reports obfuscated the chaos that the freedmen's hospitals endured and instead suggested order and control. As anthropologist Ann Stoler argues, "what was often left as 'unwritten' in the archive resulted from 'what could go without saying' and 'everyone knew it,' what was unwritten because it could not yet be articulated, and what was unwritten because it could not be said."[35] What could not be said, what could not be articulated was that the triumphant destruction of slavery also led to disease and death for many freedpeople.

Conclusion

The Freedmen's Bureau records in the National Archives came into exis-tence because the North won the Civil War, thereby beginning a massive literary project of collecting records. On the surface, these records serve many bureaucratic functions and reveal the administrative operations of the federal government, but on a deeper, theoretical level, the collection of this material mimics the process of orientalism described by theorist Edward Said in his study of British and French authorities who collected copious information about the Middle East as part of their imperialist project and then catalogued it encyclopedically.[36] The Civil War enlarged the powers of the federal government by placing, as many historians have noted, federal officials in face-to-face contact with ordinary citizens, but it also institutionalized the portrayal of the South as a backward, defeated place in need of reconstruction. The documentation, organization, and collection of records that detail the interplay between federal officials and southern citizens seals this interpretation into the National Archives and sears it into historical imagination.

Describing the South continually and repeatedly as defeated or in need of reconstruction became a way of explaining it. The trope of the South as defeated becomes an easy way to categorize a region that cannot be easily explained or solely represented.[37] Indeed, the archival collection of the bureau documents and the discourse of reconstruction, while attending to a number of historiographical questions and scholarly debates, nevertheless unwittingly contributes to a broader popular discourse about the South that began in the nineteenth century and continues today. Just as French and British authors engaged in the process of orientalism, well-intentioned bureau agents often unwittingly engaged in a political project that has fueled an ideological construction of the South as backward without fully recognizing it. Said warns against "the assumption that the Orient is not an inert fact of nature. It is not merely there, just as the Occident is not just there." The mere construction of the South as site of war and reconstruction only further advanced this notion of the South as inert. Through the vantage point of the bureau records, we only see the South as inert—still and passive. Applying Said's analysis, we can start asking more questions. Is there another way to see the South—not from the vantage point of war and reconstruction? How has our analysis of the documents continued to emphasize the South as inert? In fact, reading the records almost requires an interpretation of the South as lacking the ability to move.[38]

Similar to the process of orientalism, a particular pattern of representation of freedpeople emerges throughout the records. What has often been described as uncovering the authentic representation of freed slaves' autonomy and indefatigable agency follows similar rhetorical patterns found in the colonial archives on the Middle East and throughout the British empire. Just as the reports produced about the colonized people in the British empire tell us more about British colonial officials than about the people living in those places, the voices of freedpeople as independent and fit for freedom reveal a trope that tells us more about the bureau official than the formerly enslaved. Like colonial documents, the bureau records assign a particular narrative logic to a process that lacks order and efficiency.[39] In short, the bureau records have produced very specific knowledge about the South.[40]

Finally, the bureau records—from the labor division to the educational records to the medical reports—do not function like an open net that simply captured the diverse feelings and comprehensive experiences that accompanied the aftermath of slavery. Instead, the bureau invented ways of viewing this period and developed categories—labor, education, and medicine—in which to insert freedpeople's experiences. Education records, employment contracts, legal battles, land disputes, and medical statements became silos that eventually morphed into archives that defined emancipation. These archives have evolved a step further over the past century into political arsenals that defeated the racist arguments put forth by Dunning, and in the process they have gone largely uninterrogated in their own right. The Freedmen's Bureau archives have produced very specific knowledge about the South, and we have often inherited that knowledge without recognizing that it is a creation of the archive and not of the freedpeople. What freedom meant to freedpeople has only been partially told.[41]

NOTES

1. William Archibald Dunning, *Reconstruction, Political and Economic* (New York: Harper, 1935), 31–34.

2. On studies conducted by black scholars, see Thelma Bates, "The Legal Status of the Negro in Florida," *Florida Historical Society Quarterly* 6, no. 3 (1928): 159–81; Howard University and Dorothy Porter Wesley, Howard University Masters' Theses Submitted in Partial Fulfillment of the Requirements for the Master's Degree at Howard University, 1918–1945. See also Jacqueline Goggin, *Carter G. Wilson: A Life in Black History* (Baton Rouge: Louisiana State University Press, 1997), 68; Bruce E. Baker, *What Reconstruction Meant: Historical Memory in the American South* (Charlottesville: University of Virginia Press, 2009), 115–16.

3. W. E. B. Du Bois, *Black Reconstruction in America: An Essay toward a History of the Part Which Black Folk Played in the Attempt to Reconstruct Democracy in America, 1860–1880* (New York: Harcourt, Brace, 1935).

4. A. A. Taylor, "The Negro in South Carolina during the Reconstruction (Concluded). Corruption Exposed to Justify Intimidation," *Journal of Negro History* 9, no. 1 (1924): 532.

5. The success of the Freedpeople and Southern Society Project led to the publication of many crucial volumes in the study of labor, politics, military, law, and culture during Reconstruction.

6. Susan E. O'Donovan, *Becoming Free in the Cotton South* (Cambridge, Mass.: Harvard University Press, 2009); Thavolia Glymph, *Out of the House of Bondage: The Transformation of the Plantation Household* (Cambridge: Cambridge University Press, 2008); Hannah Rosen, *Terror in the Heart of Freedom: Citizenship, Sexual Violence, and the Meaning of Race in the Postemancipation South* (Chapel Hill: University of North Carolina Press, 2008); Mary Farmer-Kaiser, *Freedwomen and the Freedmen's Bureau: Race, Gender, and Public Policy in the Age of Emancipation* (New York: New York University Press, 2010); Kidada Williams, *They Left Great Marks on Me: African American Testimonies of Racial Violence from Emancipation to World War* (New York: New York University Press, 2012).

7. For more on the medical division's record keeping, see Jim Downs, "#Black-LivesMatter: Toward an Algorithm of Black Suffering during the Civil War and Reconstruction," *J19: The Journal of Nineteenth-Century Americanists* 4 (Spring 2016): 198–205. See also Downs, *Sick from Freedom: African-American Illness and Suffering during the Civil War and Reconstruction* (New York: Oxford University Press, 2012).

8. Historian Abigail Cooper is currently revising for publication her dissertation, which investigates spirituality and religion during the Civil War and Reconstruction. Abigail Cooper, "'Lord, Until I Reach My Home': Inside the Refugee Camps of the American Civil War," PhD diss., University of Pennsylvania, 2015.

9. Downs, *Sick from Freedom*, 146–61.

10. For a general overview of the bureau's impressions and attitudes toward their work in the Reconstruction South, see, for example, U.S. War Dept., Bureau of Refugees, Freedmen and Abandoned Lands Record Group 105, National Archives and *Laws in Relation to Freedmen*, 39th Cong., 2nd sess., Senate Executive Document, no. 6, 1866–67. For arresting scholarly accounts of violence after the Civil War, see Carole Emberton, *Beyond Redemption: Race, Violence, and the American South after the Civil War* (Chicago: University of Chicago Press, 2013); Rosen, *Terror in the Heart of Freedom*. On violence, see Freedmen's Bureau Report of Outrages in North Carolina, June 1866–January 1867, transcribed from National Archives Publication M843, Records of the Assistant Commissioner for the State of North Carolina, Bureau of Refugees, Freedmen and Abandoned Lands, M843, Roll 33, "Reports of Outrages."

11. I make a similar argument in Downs, "The Future of Civil War Studies: Race," *Journal of the Civil War Era*, March 2012, http://journalofthecivilwarera .org/forum-the-future-of-civil-war-era-studies/the-future-of-civil-war-era-studies -race/.

12. On the WPA records, see Edward E. Baptist, "'Stol' and Fetched Here': Enslaved Migration, Ex-Slaves Narratives and Vernacular History," in *New Studies in the History of Slavery*, eds. Edward Baptist and Stephanie Camp (Athens: University

of Georgia Press, 2005); Stephanie J. Shaw, "Using the WPA Ex-Slave Narratives to Study the Impact of the Great Depression," *Journal of Southern History* 69, no. 3 (August 2003): 623–58; Sharon Ann Musher, "Contesting 'the Way the Almighty Wants It': Crafting Memories of Ex-Slaves in the Slave Narrative Collection," *American Quarterly* 53, no. 1 (March 2001): 1–31; Donna J. Spindel, "Assessing Memory: Twentieth-Century Slave Narratives Reconsidered," *Journal of Interdisciplinary History* 27, no. 2 (Autumn 1996): 247–61; John Blassingame, "Using the Testimony of Ex-Slaves: Approaches and Problems," *Journal of Southern History* 41, no. 4 (November 1975): 473–92. On slave narratives, see Henry Louis Gates Jr., *In Search of Hannah Crafts: Critical Essays on the Bondwoman's Narrative* (New York: Civitas, 2004); Jean Fagan Yellin, *Harriet Jacobs: A Life* (New York: Civitas, 2005).

13. In an arresting account on antebellum slavery, historian Jeff Forret challenges the notion of the antebellum slave community as harmonious and unified, citing legal cases, laws, and other sources that illustrate the conflict that tore through the slave community. See Forret, *Slave against Slave: Plantation Violence in the Old South* (Baton Rouge: Louisiana State University Press, 2015).

14. Downs, *Sick from Freedom,* 129–33.

15. On kin networks, see Dylan C. Penningroth, *The Claims of Kinfolk: African-American Property and Community in the Nineteenth-Century South* (Chapel Hill: University of North Carolina Press, 2003); Elsa Barkley Brown, "To Catch a Vision of Freedom: Reconstructing Southern Black Women's Political History, 1865–1880," in *Unequal Sisters: A Multicultural Reader in U.S. Women's History,* ed. Ellen DuBois and Vicki Ruiz, 3rd ed. (New York: Routledge, 2000), 124–46; Barkley Brown, "Womanist Consciousness: Maggie Lena Walker and the Independent Order of Saint Luke," *Signs: Journal of Women in Culture and Society* 14, no. 3 (Spring 1989): 610–33; Steven Hahn, *A Nation under Our Feet: Black Political Struggles in the Rural South from Slavery to the Great Migration* (Cambridge, Mass.: Harvard University Press, 2005). On the bureau's encouragement of the family unit, see "Addresses and ceremonies at the New Year's festival to the freedmen, on Arlington Heights and statistics and statements of the educational condition of the colored people in the southern states, and other facts," 10–17, pamphlets from the Daniel A. P. Murray Collection, 1818–1907, Library of Congress; John Eaton, *Grant, Lincoln, and the Freedmen: Reminiscences of the Civil War* (New York: Longman, Green, 1907), 34–36; Jacqueline Jones, *Labor of Love, Labor of Sorrow: Black Women, Work, and the Family from Slavery to the Present* (New York: Vintage, 1985), 62.

16. Susan Eva O'Donovan, *Becoming Free in the Cotton South* (Cambridge, Mass.: Harvard University Press, 2007). In her classic study of black women's labor, Jacqueline Jones revealed how many black women fought against the gang labor system in favor of sharecropping because such arrangements enabled freedwomen to cultivate their domestic roles as mothers within the household. On the surface, this example suggests that for black women dealing with black men proved to be a threat to their economic independence. Yet on closer inspection, the agent

whom Jones cites was a former Confederate, which then raises a whole set of other questions about the veracity and implications of the source. See Jones, *Labor of Love*, 61–63.

17. Susan O'Donovan and Thavolia Glymph are among a few of a handful of historians who track the transition to freedom by closely following how slavery shaped emancipation. See O'Donovan, *Becoming Free in the Cotton South*, and Glymph, *Out of the House of Bondage*. See also Leon Litwack, *Been in the Storm So Long: The Aftermath of Slavery* (New York: Vintage, 1980).

18. Historian Willie Lee Rose was one of the first chroniclers of Reconstruction to capture this relationship, but historians of late have not been as attentive to the dynamics that Rose put forward. Rose, *Rehearsal for Reconstruction: The Port Royal Experiment* (Indianapolis: Bobbs-Merrill, 1964).

19. Walter Johnson, *Soul by Soul: Life inside the Antebellum Slave Market* (Cambridge, Mass.: Harvard University Press, 1999).

20. Catherine Clinton, "'Slavery Is War': Harriet Tubman and the Underground Railroad," in David W. Blight, ed., *Passages to Freedom* (Washington, D.C.: Smithsonian Books, 2004).

21. Julia Floyd Smith, *Slavery and Rice Culture in Low Country Georgia, 1750–1860* (Knoxville: University of Tennessee Press, 1985).

22. Southern Famine Relief Commission Papers, New York Historical Society, MS 2430.

23. Annual Report of the Secretary of War. Report of the Commissioner of the Bureau of Refugees, Freedmen and Abandoned Lands, 39th Cong., 2d sess., 1866, H. Ex. Doc. 1, pt. 3, serial 1285; George R. Bentley, *A History of the Freedmen's Bureau* (New York: Octagon, 1970), 180–82; Paul Skeels Peirce, *The Freedmen's Bureau: A Chapter in the History of Reconstruction* (Iowa City, Iowa: The University Press, 1904), 82.

24. For the best overviews on education during Reconstruction, see James D. Anderson, *The Education of Blacks in the South, 1860–1935* (Chapel Hill: University of North Carolina Press, 1988); Heather Andrea Williams, *Self-Taught African American Education in Slavery and Freedom* (Chapel Hill: University of North Carolina Press, 2005); Ronald E. Butchart, *Schooling the Freed People: Teaching, Learning, and the Struggle for Black Freedom, 1861–1876* (Chapel Hill: University of North Carolina Press, 2010); James M. McPherson, *Ordeal by Fire: The Civil War and Reconstruction* (New York: Knopf, 1982), 17–19.

25. On black women's efforts to construct their own schools, see Jim Downs, "Uplift, Violence, and Service: Black Women Educators in the Reconstruction South," *Southern Historian* 24 (Spring 2003): 29–39. See also Heather Andrea Williams, *Self-Taught African American Education*.

26. On Wilbur and Jacobs, see Ira Berlin, *The Wartime Genesis of Free Labor: The Upper South* (Cambridge: Cambridge University Press, 1993), 250–51; Yellin, *Harriet Jacobs*; Harriet A. Jacobs, John S. Jacobs, Louisa Matilda Jacobs, and Jean

Fagan Yellin, *The Harriet Jacobs Family Papers* (Chapel Hill: University of North Carolina Press, 2008).

27. For an excellent analysis on governmental use of statistical reports and pamphlets to create social order, which led to various formulations of rationality, see Gyan Prakash, *Another Reason: Science and the Imagination of Modern India* (Princeton, N.J.: Princeton University Press, 1999).

28. I am building here on Heather Cox Richardson's argument about how the North eventually withdrew support for Reconstruction because they no longer believed in the efficacy of the federal government's role in the South. Heather Cox Richardson, *The Death of Reconstruction: Race, Labor, and Politics in the Post-Civil War North, 1861–1901* (Cambridge, Mass.: Harvard University Press, 2004).

29. Oliver Otis Howard, *Autobiography of Oliver Otis Howard* (New York: Baker & Taylor, 1907), 2:368.

30. Albert J. Raboteau, *Slave Religion: The "Invisible Institution" in the Antebellum South* (New York: Oxford University Press, 1978). On the importance of religion and spirituality among black people in the mid-nineteenth century, see Clarence E. Walker, *A Rock in a Weary Land: The African Methodist Episcopal Church during the Civil War and Reconstruction* (Baton Rouge: Louisiana State University Press, 1982); Margaret Washington, *A Peculiar People: Slave Religion and Community-Culture among the Gullahs* (New York: New York University Press, 1988); Neil Painter, *Sojourner Truth: A Life, a Symbol* (New York: Norton, 1996).

31. For more on the creation of the bureau's Medical Division and the health conditions in the postwar South, see Downs, *Sick from Freedom.*

32. Ibid., 42–64, 120–45. For more on the problematical statistical nature of the records, see Downs, "#BlackLivesMatter."

33. U.S. War Dept., Bureau of Refugees, Freedmen and Abandoned Lands, *Laws in Relation to Freedmen*, 39th Cong., 2nd sess., 1866–67.

34. Downs, *Sick from Freedom.*

35. Ann Laura Stoler, *Along the Archival Grain: Epistemic Anxieties and Colonial Common Sense* (Princeton, N.J.: Princeton University Press, 2009), 3.

36. Edward Said, *Orientalism* (New York: Vintage, 1979). Building on Natalie Ring's scholarship on the late nineteenth and early twentieth centuries, which examines how federal officials followed transnational practices in their interactions with the South, I view the organization of the archive in the late 1860s and early 1870s as part of a broader transnational practice of knowledge production. Natalie J. Ring, *The Problem South: Region, Empire, and the New Liberal State, 1880–1930* (Athens: University of Georgia Press, 2012).

37. More to the point, the constant representation of the Reconstruction South and the hefty archival evidence that buttressed these claims cannot be divorced from the historical process of industrial migration out of the South—the demise of southern agriculture and then later the refusal of major American companies to invest in the South. On transitions of Southern economy, see

Adrienne Monteith Petty, *Standing Their Ground: Small Farmers in North Carolina since the Civil War* (New York: Oxford University Press, 2013); Tami J. Friedman, "Exploiting the North-South Differential: Corporate Power, Southern Politics, and the Decline of Organized Labor after World War II," *Journal of American History* 95 (September 2008): 323–48.

38. Said, *Orientalism*, 4.

39. On the postcolonial representation of voice, I am thinking here of Gayatri Chakravoty Spivak, "Can the Subaltern Speak?" in *Marxism and the Interpretation of Culture,* ed. Cary Nelson and Lawrence Grossberg (Urbana: University of Illinois Press, 1988), 271–313.

40. In general, I am arguing that this is an example of knowledge production. While this theory does not relate to the postwar South, literary critic Lisa Lowe describes this theoretical move in her book *The Intimacies of Four Continents* (Durham, N.C.: Duke University Press, 2015).

41. See also Downs, "Future of Civil War Studies."

Contributors

JUSTIN BEHREND is an associate professor of history at SUNY Geneseo. His book *Reconstructing Democracy: Black Grassroots Politics in the Deep South after the Civil War* (University of Georgia Press, 2015) won the 2016 McLemore Prize from the Mississippi Historical Society. He has published on slave rebellions, urban history, and the memory of Reconstruction.

DAVID W. BLIGHT is Class of 1954 Professor of American History at Yale University and the director of the Gilder Lehrman Center for the Study of Slavery, Resistance, and Abolition at Yale. Blight is also the author of *Race and Reunion: The Civil War in American Memory* (Harvard University Press, 2001), which received the Bancroft Prize, the Abraham Lincoln Prize, and the Frederick Douglass Prize as well as four awards from the Organization of American Historians, including the Merle Curti prizes for both intellectual and social history. Other published works include a book of essays, *Beyond the Battlefield: Race, Memory, and the American Civil War* (University of Massachusetts Press, 2002), and *Frederick Douglass's Civil War: Keeping Faith in Jubilee* (Louisiana State University Press, 1989).

GREGORY P. DOWNS is associate professor of history at University of California, Davis. He is the author of *After Appomattox: Military Occupation and the Ends of War* (Harvard University Press, 2015) and *Declarations of Dependence: The Long Reconstruction of Popular Politics in the South, 1861–1908* (University of North Carolina Press, 2011), coauthor (with Kate Masur) of the first National Park Service National Historic Landmark Theme Study on Reconstruction, and coeditor (with Kate Masur) of *The World the Civil War Made* (University of North Carolina Press, 2015).

JIM DOWNS is associate professor of history at Connecticut College. He is the author of *Sick from Freedom: African American Illness and Suffering during the Civil War and Reconstruction* (Oxford University Press, 2012).

CAROLE EMBERTON is associate professor of history at the University at Buffalo. She is currently working on a study of the Federal Writers' Project Ex-Slave Narratives. Her first book, *Beyond Redemption: Race, Violence, and the American South after the Civil War* (University of Chicago Press, 2013), won the Willie Lee Rose Prize for best book on southern history from the Southern Association for Women Historians.

ERIC FONER, DeWitt Clinton Professor of History at Columbia University, is the author or editor of more than twenty books, most recently *Gateway to Freedom: The Hidden History of the Underground Railroad* (W. W. Norton, 2015).

THAVOLIA GLYMPH is professor of history at Duke University and an Organization of American Historians Distinguished Lecturer. Glymph is the author of *Out of the House of Bondage: The Transformation of the Plantation Household* (Cambridge University Press, 2008) and *Women at War: Race, Gender, and Power in the American Civil War* (forthcoming, University of North Carolina Press).

CHANDRA MANNING is professor of history at Georgetown University. She has also taught at Pacific Lutheran University in Tacoma, Washington, and served as special advisor to the dean of the Radcliffe Institute at Harvard University. Her most recent book, *Troubled Refuge: Struggling for Freedom in the Civil War* (Knopf, 2016), is about Civil War contraband camps and the lived experience—as well as the legal, military, and political processes—of emancipation.

KATE MASUR is an associate professor of history at Northwestern University and author of *An Example for All the Land: Emancipation and the Struggle over Equality in Washington, D.C.* (University of North Carolina Press, 2010). She has written numerous essays on emancipation, race, and politics during the Civil War and is coeditor, with Gregory P. Downs, of *The World the Civil War Made* (University of North Carolina Press, 2015). She and Downs are also coauthors of the National Park Service's National Historic Landmark Theme Study on Reconstruction. She is currently working on a book about personal liberty, policing, and constitutional change from the early nineteenth century through Reconstruction.

RICHARD NEWMAN is a professor of history at Rochester Institute of Technology and the coeditor of the "Race in the Atlantic World Series" with the University of Georgia Press. He is the author and/or coeditor of six books on abolitionism and American reform movements, including *Freedom's Prophet: Bishop Richard Allen, the Black Founding Fathers, and the AME Church* (New York University Press, 2009). His forthcoming book *American Emancipations: The Making and Unmaking of Black Freedom* will be published by Cambridge University Press.

JAMES OAKES is Distinguished Professor of History and Graduate School Humanities Professor at the Graduate Center of the City University of New York. He earned his PhD at Berkeley in 1981 and previously taught at Princeton and Northwestern University. He is the author of several books and articles on the subject of slavery, antislavery, and emancipation, including *The Ruling Race: A History of American Slaveholders* (Knopf, 1982); *Slavery and Freedom: An Interpretation of the Old South* (W. W. Norton, 1990); *The Radical and the Republican: Frederick Douglass, Abraham Lincoln, and the Triumph of Antislavery Politics* (W. W. Norton,

2007); *Freedom National: The Destruction of Slavery in the United States* (W. W. Norton, 2012); and *The Scorpion's Sting: Antislavery and the Coming of the Civil War* (W. W. Norton, 2014). He is currently editing a multi-authored collection of essays on the history of antislavery politics as well as a documentary history of emancipation. His next book, should he live that long, will be a new general history of the American Civil War.

SUSAN O'DONOVAN is associate professor of history at the University of Memphis. She is a former editor with the Freedmen and Southern Society Project, the coeditor of two volumes of *Freedom: A Documentary History of Emancipation, 1861–1867* (University of North Carolina Press, 2008 and 2013), and author of *Becoming Free in the Cotton South* (Harvard University Press, 2007). An OAH Distinguished Lecturer, she has been the recipient of several awards, including fellowships at the Newberry Library and the Gilder Lehrman Center for the Study of Slavery, Resistance, and Abolition. She is completing a political history of slaves.

HANNAH ROSEN, associate professor of history and American studies at William and Mary, received her PhD from the University of Chicago. She is the author of *Terror in the Heart of Freedom: Citizenship, Sexual Violence, and the Meaning of Race in the Postemancipation South* (University of North Carolina Press, 2009), recipient of the Berkshire Conference of Women Historians First Book Prize, the Avery O. Craven Award from the Organization of American Historians, and the Willie Lee Rose Prize from the Southern Association for Women Historians. Her current research treats African American experiences surrounding death and mourning in the nineteenth-century South and the increasing segregation of southern cemeteries in the postemancipation period. She is also codirector, along with Professor Martha Jones, of The Celia Project: The History and Memory of Slavery and Sexual Violence, a collaborative, interdisciplinary research endeavor.

BRENDA E. STEVENSON is professor and Nickoll Family Endowed Chair in History as well as professor of African American Studies at UCLA. Her work centers on race, racial violence, gender, family, and slavery in the Atlantic world and the U.S. South. Her previous publications include *The Journals of Charlotte Forten Grimké* (Oxford University Press, 1988); *Life in Black and White: Family and Community in the Slave South* (Oxford University Press, 1996); *The Contested Murder of Latasha Harlins: Justice, Gender and the Origins of the L.A. Riots* (Oxford University Press, 2013); and *What Is Slavery?* (Polity Press, 2015).

Index

UnCivil Wars

CPSIA information can be obtained
at www.ICGtesting.com
Printed in the USA
LVOW03s1759171017
552756LV00002B/337/P